DANNY BUDERUS is a not just a rec⟨ rugby league competition in the world – ͻtate oι Uιιgιιι – but a footballer respected Australia-wide and internationally, not just for the way he passionately plays the game but also for taking seriously his responsibility as a role model.

The New South Wales captain in every match from 2004–2008, Buderus holds the record for most successive appearances (21) of any NSW Origin player as well as the most as captain (15). He was unchallenged as Australia's hooker from 2001–2006 before he decided to stand down to witness the birth of his first baby with wife Kris.

The 2005 Dally M Medal winner (best player in the National Rugby League) competed in 220 first grade games for the Newcastle Knights over 11 seasons from 1997–2008, and now plays for the Leeds Rhinos in the British Super League.

NEIL CADIGAN, an Australian Sports Writer of the Year, has had seven books published in the past three years since co-writing the bestselling Andrew Johns autobiography *The Two of Me*, which was nominated for the 2007 Australian biography of the year. He has also recently written the autobiography of iconic Queensland rugby league figure Wally Lewis (*Out of the Shadows*), compiled *Rugby League Yarns*, a collection of humorous and amazing stories from rugby league's century-old history, and previously co-wrote the life stories of footy legends Ray Price and Brett Kenny.

Outside of rugby league, he has written the story of pioneering Australian aviator Lester Brain (*Man Among Mavericks*), co-written *When Silver Is Gold*, the autobiography of Olympic swimmer Brooke Hanson, and written the incredible life story of tsunami hero Donny Paterson (*No Ordinary Bloke*), just released.

TALENT IS NOT ENOUGH

DANNY BUDERUS

AND NEIL CADIGAN

EBURY
PRESS

An Ebury Press book
Published by Random House Australia Pty Ltd
Level 3, 100 Pacific Highway, North Sydney NSW 2060
www.randomhouse.com.au

First published by Ebury Press in 2009

Addresses for companies within the Random House Group can be found at
www.randomhouse.com.au/offices.

National Library of Australia Cataloguing-in-Publication entry

Cadigan, Neil.
Danny Buderus: talent is not enough.

ISBN 978 1 74166 884 1 (pbk).

Buderus, Danny.
Rugby football players – Australia – Biography.
Rugby league football – Australia – Biography.

Other authors/contributors: Buderus, Danny.

796.3338092

Cover design by Luke Causby/Blue Cork
Internal design by Midland Typesetters, Australia
Typeset in 13/17 pt Adobe Garamond by Midland Typesetters, Australia
Printed and bound by Griffin Press, South Australia

Random House Australia uses papers that are natural, renewable and recyclable products and made from wood grown in sustainable forests. The logging and manufacturing processes are expected to conform to the environmental regulations of the country of origin.

10 9 8 7 6 5 4 3 2 1

To every young footballer who is prepared to work hard to play professional rugby league. Chase your dream.

CONTENTS

CONTENTS

FOREWORD

BY ANDREW JOHNS,
AUSTRALIAN HALFBACK OF THE CENTURY

I STILL vividly remember when I first met Danny Buderus; it was 1995 and he'd been selected in the Australian Schoolboys side and had a fund-raiser in his home town of Taree. I was injured at the time and agreed to attend to help him out; he picked me up for the two-hour drive from Newcastle to Taree and we spoke mostly about football all the way up.

The thing that struck me then was what a genuine, well-mannered young man he was; the type a mother would like to marry her daughter. That day I met his family and realised where those values came from.

I can honestly put my hand on my heart and say the young man I met that day hasn't changed a bit – except for some grey flecks in his hair. Ask anyone who has played with or against Danny Buderus and he would not have a bad word to say against him; he is that popular.

The Newcastle Knights' motto is 'Courage, unity and pride'. No one epitomises this more than Danny Buderus. Images of him playing with his jumper torn to shreds and hanging off him, or playing with injury yet still unselfishly throwing his body into his task in every set of six tackles, will remain forever in my mind. The Knights' creed is to be the player every other player wishes to play with; this looks like it was written for Danny Buderus.

Rooming with him, I have seen him at closer quarters than others – including his strange, quirky cleanliness and his mispronunciation of his last name; but also the mental and physical torture he put himself through to play with injury.

One game stands out; it was against Penrith in 2003. 'Beds' woke up with back spasms and couldn't get out of a walk. I took him to osteopath Kay MacPherson for a two-hour torture session and somehow he played that night and won the Channel 9 man of the match award . . . incredible toughness and strong will.

His record in State of Origin backs his ironman status. Playing a record 21 consecutive games, plus backing up for the Knights after most of them, is an outstanding feat. When you saw him play at this level, throwing his body around with no room for self-regard, it was truly amazing; legendary in the eyes of his team-mates.

The culture he inspired at club and rep level will never be forgotten by those who played with him, nor will it be lost on those who succeed him at Newcastle. His tenacity and dedication at training was infectious. The sacrifices he made to play at his highest standards, his manner that made everybody feel comfortable being around him and the will to win that would see him push himself to the point of exhaustion all combined to make him the most inspirational team-mate I had.

No image better epitomises Danny Buderus than State of Origin 2003, game one – the re-opening of Suncorp Stadium in Brisbane. 'Bedsy' sprints downfield to chase the opening kick-off, leads the Blues defence and absolutely smashes Queensland front-rower Shane Webcke. This single effort set the tone for the rest of the game – and the series, which we won.

Another record Danny Buderus holds is the most capped New South Wales Origin captain, with 15 matches. What an honour and proof of what an inspirational performer he has been at Origin level, which is the greatest individual test a player can face. He also captained Australia four times in 2004–05.

People often ask me who was the best player I played with at club level; without hesitation I say Matt Johns . . . sorry, brother; no, it's Danny Buderus. It wasn't until I was injured that he received the acknowledgement he deserved (sorry 'Blubs').

One thing about him that stands out is that no one has played the game tougher. He has still enjoyed himself off the field, yet there has never been any scandal, except when on a plane going home from Townsville in 2001 and that was only because of a case of mistaken identity; it was me that tripped getting on the plane and attracted the attention of cabin crew, but unfortunately they blamed you, 'Beds'. A lot of young players could learn from Danny's standards and the way he holds himself in public.

Danny, I feel honoured to write the foreword for this book, which I recommend to any young footballer wishing to learn about the dedication, passion, toughness and sacrifices required to make it in the game these days.

I feel lucky to have played most of my career with you and to have enjoyed so many good times in your company. I feel very privileged to call you a mate. Congratulations on a great career and for being a special human being. I wish you, Kris ('Darwin') and your beautiful daughter Ella much happiness and good health in the future – you deserve every success in life that comes your way.

1

TALENT IS NOT ENOUGH

I HAVE decided to start this book with this statement because it best sums up my attitude to sport and life in general, and also sets the platform for the journey I'll take you through – of a pretty shy country kid who had above average ability but wasn't any special talent; just someone with a very big desire to be successful as a footballer.

It was an afternoon in 2002. Mark Hughes and I had been asked by assistant coach Phil Williams to speak to the Knights SG Ball (under 18s) team at training as he thought a few of the players were a bit out of control and thought they'd 'made it' as talented young footballers. I was 24 and had established myself in the Newcastle Knights first grade team and had played for Australia, and 'Boozy' had played in two Knights premiership-winning sides and for New South Wales in State of Origin.

Most of the players looked up with faces that seemed to be taking in everything Mark and I said and it brought back memories of when I was in the Knights SG Ball team (then under 17s); a few others were attentive but their thoughts obviously drifted away a bit as if they'd heard it all before.

I remember telling them that the law of averages, proved over a lot of seasons, was that three or maybe four of them would go on to have extended first grade careers, and the rest would fall by the wayside. What was going to determine who would be in that elite group, I told them, would not be talent but how hard they worked and how focused they were. And I firmly believe that; because I reckon I'm a fair example.

From that side, who are 23 or 24 years old now, only Riley Brown and Dane Tilse have gone on to play more than 50 first grade games. No one remembers who the great SG Ball or Jersey Flegg (under 20s) players were because the game is full of talented teenagers, many of them more talented than I ever was, and not a lot go on to become household names. Because talent is not enough.

Don't get me wrong – you can't get by on fitness and hard work only, either; you have to have a fair degree of natural athleticism or skill. And I've seen a lot of unbelievably gifted young players whose talent took them a long way. But eventually you will get found out unless you have a professional attitude to go with it.

One boy genius I mention for the sake of this story is Owen Craigie, who was the most freakish talent I came across in my junior days. 'Owie' played for the Australian Schoolboys three years running, from when he was 16 in 1994 to 1996, and is still the only player in history to have done that.

Owen was scouted by the Knights from Inverell in 1994 and played in the SG Ball (under 17s) when he was only 16. He scored 19 tries in 12 matches for Newcastle (with another pretty fair player, Matthew Gidley, scoring 10 tries). Incredibly, after going through undefeated, the team was beaten 22–20 by Souths in the grand final. Just to prove my point about the ratio of 'whiz kids' who go on to 'make it', Owen and Matt

Gidley were the only players from both teams in that grand final who went on to successful first grade careers.

The next year I joined Owen in the SG Ball team and 'Gids' (Matt), Owie and I went on the 1995 Australian Schoolboys tour to England and France (with three other players from the Hunter – Leigh McWilliams, Daniel Quinn and Jarrod O'Doherty) – after I'd come down from Taree to join the Knights' development system. Owen and I started the season in the SG Ball squad and I thought it was a real honour to be called up at the end of that competition to play in the President's Cup side (under 21s). But Owen was regarded as being so good, and big enough at that stage too, that he went into the reserve grade where he played in a winning grand final and also played four games in first grade – and he was only 17! He could break tackles with his strength, step or speed; he could kick and regather like no player I've ever seen; his overall skills package was extraordinary.

In 1997 he was in the Knights' first-ever first grade premiership side and everyone was tipping he'd play for Australia. I remember Owie, from age 16 to 19, had so much success that people were constantly patting him on the back and telling him how good he was going to be. I was in awe of him, and loved being around him; he's such an easygoing person and was certainly not big-headed at all. But his physique was always going to be something he had to battle against as he got older and I just think such naturally gifted players as he was don't always come to grips with how hard they still have to work to maintain that boom-boom-boy tag.

In late 1997 we moved into a house together at New Lambton and were there for two years. I was two months older than him and, at 19, I thought how great it was to surpass my expectations and play the whole season in reserve grade, plus make my first grade debut off the bench. By the end of that season Owie had played 38 first grade games and had won two premierships (reserves 1995, firsts 1997); while Matt Gidley, born the year before us, was also a regular first grader and had represented Country Origin.

Owen started to put on weight; he started to realise he had to train harder and his diet wasn't the best as we were eating out a bit after training hard. About then our careers went in different directions. I was just starting to make my way, developing physically to be able to handle playing against more powerful blokes in first grade and coming out of my shell as a person, while he was established in first grade and had the world at his feet – if he wanted it enough.

He'd succeeded early in his career with his phenomenal talent that was miles in front of mine; I was starting to realise I didn't have the natural skills to be a five-eighth or halfback in first grade – especially with Matthew and Andrew Johns and Craig and Brett Kimmorley in front of me. But I knew what I wanted to be and I developed a work ethic that I hoped just might get me there. I was working at Boots Plumbing, a plumbing supply business, and had to squeeze in training before and after work (luckily reserve grade coach Steve Linnane also worked at Boots, which was great for me), while Owie worked a few hours a day with the Knights' development office. I didn't want to fall away with my diet and training and had to get disciplined with time management and organisation. Owen was then going out with Kristie Newton, daughter of famous golfer Jack and brother of future Knights player Clint, so he ate at their place a lot while I cooked for myself at home.

Anyway, by the time I played in the first grade grand final in 2001, Owen Craigie had gone to the Wests Tigers and was struggling with fitness and inconsistent form. He then spent three seasons at Souths and only occasionally showed his amazing talent. I wish he had never left the Knights because I don't think he was ever happy anywhere else. I knew how good Newcastle was for him and I learned from that too; I never wanted to be in a situation where I had to leave, or if it had to happen late in my career it would be on my terms. Malcolm Reilly got the best out of Owie by 'cuddling' him a bit, where Warren Ryan (who took over from Malcolm in 1999) was more a hard-line coach and Owen didn't respond greatly to that attitude. He probably needed a bit of a kick but different people respond to different ways and maybe no one found the right way to get the best out of him.

Owen finished with the NRL after the 2004 season when he was just 26 and had less than half a season with Widnes in England the next year before he was released to go back to Australia because he never adapted to the scene over there. His top grade career was over at age 27. I regard it as a great tragedy that such a brilliant player and great person didn't play major representative football, not even for New South Wales Country Origin, and that he probably had only two seasons (1997 and 1998) where people regularly saw how good he was. He was the only member of the Knights backline in the 1997 grand final not to play State of Origin and the only one of the run-on 13 not to play City–Country or Origin. Yet he was the most naturally gifted of them all, other than maybe Andrew Johns. Owen did play 153 first grade games, scored 50 tries and won a premiership, so he still had a career to be proud of.

I want to stress I'm only using Owie as a prime example of the principle I'm trying to get across, because I've seen plenty of players over the years promise the world and not deliver. It's just that Owie was the best young talent I ever came across when I was making my way. You see a lot of whiz kids who don't have to work for the tag; but when they reach first grade, or even the lower grades, they need to work a lot harder and develop the aspects of their game that don't come to them so naturally. All the natural gifts that got them so far on the way up don't count for much then, because every second player they play with or against isn't far behind or ahead of them in the talent department. It's like starting all over again, in many ways.

I think that, because so many teenagers are given good contracts straight out of school and introduced to first grade at 18 or 19, they don't get a full appreciation that life, not just football, doesn't always come that easily. They get in a full-on football environment, mixing with their heroes, getting plenty of adulation and money and get cut off from the real world outside to a degree. I think a lot of players don't kick on because they didn't do a real apprenticeship; others just mightn't have the luck, or they encounter injury problems, or don't develop physically. I certainly had a lot of luck; but I'd like to think my determination and ability to listen and respect my place among other footballers, and the fact I did a 'real' apprenticeship, held me in good stead.

I recently found a letter from Peter Robinson, my first coach at the Newcastle Knights (SG Ball in 1995), in the many, many scrapbooks my mum has kept during my career. ('You'll thank me one day,' she used to say when I questioned why she so meticulously compiled the books; well, I thank you now, Mum.) It was dated 1 September 1998, just before I played my first semi-final in first grade (and my fifth game as a run-on player) after filling in at centre, fullback and hooker during the season. It says a lot about what this chapter is about, and what my values as a footballer and in life generally are about. It is a note that really inspired me as a rookie first grader.

Dear Danny

What an exciting time for you.

It is great to see all your hard work paying off. One of the great joys of coaching is to watch young, talented athletes with courage and dedication set out after the things they want in life. Many, many young players think that talent is all they will ever need. In actual fact, talent only gets them looked at. The local Newcastle comp is chock-a-block full of such 'talented' people. Only those who wish to do something with that talent go further.

One of the qualities that untrained eyes can't see is the quality of a lad that wants to make it so badly, he will do anything to get it and let nothing and no man stand in his way. The enthusiasm you have displayed in your first grade games so far suggests such quality.

Your form has demanded that the coach find a place for you in the football team. It is just as obvious that the team members have accepted you readily and enjoy playing with you. I know success will follow you and I am doubly sure you have earned it.

Good luck to you, Dan. You are a credit to yourself and your wonderful family.

I am a firm believer that good things do not come to those who wait. Good things come to those with the courage and convictions to go get them.

Go and chase the things that you seek. And don't let anyone steal your dreams.

Regards

Robo

2

HUMBLE BEGINNINGS

I WAS only four when I started playing footy, in my older brother Broc's team (he's 22 months older than me) at the Chatham Cundle club at Taree where I grew up. I wasn't a lot older when I made up my mind that I wanted to be a footballer.

My break came in 1994 when my schoolteacher and my school's team coach, Peter Killen, received an invitation for me to trial at Newcastle. The Knights used to send out nomination forms to country schools and clubs in their region and they would check out the applications and invite those they thought had potential to open trial days. Around the same time – I was 16 and in Year 11 at school – I also attended an open trial at St George. I had an aunty and uncle, Roy and Maree Langham, who lived at Kogarah. I used to stay with them during Christmas holidays and I always wanted to go down there and live with them, because I loved the Dragons and wanted to play for them.

I went down for the weekend and attended trials for SG Ball (under 17s) at Kogarah Oval but I wasn't on the field for any more than 10 minutes; so it was pretty much a waste of time. All these kids turned up with their St George socks and kit bags showing they'd obviously already played junior representative football for them and that was pretty intimidating.

A week later, in late September, I went down to Newcastle and it was a completely different story. I was on and off the field at Lyle Peacock Oval constantly from 8 am to 5 pm; I played in eight games, which showed what a good system the Knights had. That night I met Keith Onslow, who was the Knights development manager, and he eventually invited me down on a scholarship, which involved me staying with a family in a 'guardian house' and attending St Francis Xavier College. This was a bit of an elite football school in the district and had Mark Wright, the Knights first grade trainer, on the PE staff. I still have a copy of my first contract: $500 for 1995 and $750 for 1996, plus $1500 to go towards schooling costs and $100 a week living away from home allowance which went to my guardians for their costs of housing me. I was also offered a bonus of $1000 if I made the Australian Schoolboys side.

John Jones was also picked up from Taree and we came down every Sunday for three months to train with the Knights SG Ball train-on squad before we moved in with families in January and started school. My hosts were Warren and Libby Sowter, wonderful people who lived in Belmont North, with their two daughters, Renee and Michelle. They weren't into footy at all really until they started watching me, but they made me feel at home, although it was a pretty tough transition being away from my family in Taree, going to a Catholic school for the first time and putting so much into my football. It was a real culture shock. Owen Craigie lived about 800 metres down the road and we hung out quite a bit.

I played SG Ball in 1995 and my main aim at school, if I'm totally honest, was to make the Australian Schoolboys side that was touring England and France at the end of the year. I was also keen to play in the under 17 rep teams too; although I was 'country' through and through and would have been a chance of making the New South Wales Country under 17s if I had stayed in Taree, I was regarded as a City player by being at the Knights. I was mainly a five-eighth then, who'd play some centre and halfback. The New South Wales under 17s was to be picked from the City–Country clash and would play in a curtain-raiser to State of Origin, which was a massive buzz. I didn't make the City side – the five-eighth was Craig Gower, from Penrith, and the halfback Keiron Herring, from Parramatta. Owen Craigie made the City side along with the likes of Lee Hookey (Souths), Royston Lightning and David Atkins (Canberra). Lance Thompson (St George) was captain, and Brent Sherwin (Canterbury) and Lee Hopkins (Penrith) were on the bench. City won 34–4 and all of those players mentioned made the New South Wales under 17s, along with Daniel Quinn from the Knights, who went on to play reserve grade for the Knights and a handful of first grade games for the Northern Eagles. They beat a Queensland side that included Shaun Berrigan, Luke Williamson and Justin Murphy 34–12 (Owie scored two tries).

So my goal was to make the Australian Schoolboys. First I had to make the Combined Catholic Colleges Maitland Diocese side to play in the Northern New South Wales Country Catholics, which fortunately I did. From there I made the New South Wales Combined Catholic Colleges side that went to Canberra for the Australian schoolboys championships. We had a pretty good side with Owen, Nathan Cayless, and Trent Barrett, from St Gregory's Campbelltown, who were the big names in our team. I remember the reputations of the gun players we were to come up against. Royston Lightning was just like his surname and he was the 'gun' from the Australian Capital Territory, while Queensland had Shaun Berrigan and Dallas Hood and New South Wales Combined High Schools boasted Matt Gidley and Kevin McGuinness. New South Wales CHS beat the ACT in the final 17–8; we got knocked out in the semis but fortunately I made the Australian side and I was over the moon.

I'd got through a pretty good season with the Newcastle SG Ball side. The competition was played over 13 rounds and that proved a good mental battle as much as a physical test against some good, big teams. We lost to Penrith in the semi-final and they went on to win the final against Canberra; the Panthers had a huge team with Ned Catic in the centres, and Lee Hopkins, Troy Wozniak, Fred Petersen and Craig Gower among their best players.

I was fortunate that year to have Peter Robinson as my SG Ball coach. He was the coach who gave me my first break by choosing me in the team from the open trials, and I have always had enormous respect for him; I was so glad he was at my tribute lunch in 2008 before I left the Knights. He was a great communicator; if I'd had a hard-nosed coach who wanted to 'break' me I might not have responded to that. You have to be a mentor and manager of personalities at that level, in tune with how kids are brought up and where they come from. One of the first things the Knights did was look into my family back-ground and check if I was the kind of kid who could handle being away from home; Robo and Keith Onslow were great with that. They instilled the club ethos in us from the start, all the values which have been so important to me since.

After the SG Ball season finished I was lucky to be called up to the Knights President's Cup team that used to play the first of three games (followed by reserve grade and first grade) on the big match day. It was a real buzz to have 10,000 or more there sometimes to watch us. After sitting on the bench a couple of times, I made my debut as centre against Illawarra at Marathon Stadium in the last round – a day I unfortunately will never forget. Mum and Dad sat on the hill this day, which they never usually did – they always used to sit in front of the grandstand. Anyway, right in front of them, I turned to pass while I had a defender around my legs and, as I twisted, I broke the tibia and fibula on my left leg. I was stretchered off the field and was just shattered – and in a lot of pain. After getting X-rays and seeing a specialist, I was told I'd be out for 14 weeks. I suffered the injury on 6 August, so I got the calendar out and counted 14 weeks from then – 11 November. The Australian Schoolboys were set to fly out on 13 November!

Our Schoolboys coach Bruce Wallace was great and after he saw the doctor's report and spoke to the club, he said he'd give me until as late as possible to get a clearance from the specialist. I was in plaster for six weeks and the leg naturally withered away, but I wasn't going to let the opportunity to tour slip by. Once I got the cast off I swum every day and did a lot of work with a leg-strengthening machine and did cardio work on a contraption called 'the grinder'. The Knights were great in making sure I had access to the best physio treatment, so every day after school I was in the physio room putting my foot in the inflection exercise contraption, which would move the leg up and down, then turn it around and go sideways; it really strengthened my ankle.

I only started running a week before the plane left and it was bloody sore; not that I let on too much. Fortunately, two days before the scheduled departure, I was given the official all-clear, although I think for a couple of weeks before that Bruce had been in contact with the Knights and guessed I would be OK. I still had a plate and screws in the leg but that was all right.

I took my place on the Qantas jet with a pretty good Australian team, captained by David Pearce from Canberra (Erindale College). The full squad was David Atkins, Trent Barrett, Danny Buderus, Nathan Cayless, Kim Corbett, Owen Craigie, Steven Crouch, Ronnie Davis, Matthew Gidley, Keiron Herring, Dallas Hood, Ata Isarabakhdi, Ronald Jones, Brian Leuma, Royston Lightning, Andrew McFadden, Kevin McGuinness, Leigh McWilliams, Duncan MacGillivray, Dennis Moran, Jarrod O'Doherty, David Pearce, Daniel Quinn, Ted Simpson, Bradley Thompson and Shane Walker.

There were some great players in the squad but, just to show what ratio of whiz kids make it through to successful first grade careers, only Trent Barrett, Matt Gidley, Nathan Cayless (New Zealand) and I went on to become senior internationals. Beyond us only Kevin McGuinness, Owen Craigie, Andrew McFadden and Shane Walker played 100 first grade games in the ARL/NRL.

Brad Thompson was a sensational player and an interesting character. Royston Lightning was just unbelievable on his feet, and had the nickname 'The Bolt'. Kevvie McGuinness – 'Buddha' – was also dynamite with the ball and then there were Trent, Owie and Gids, who was man of the match in the first three games on tour, playing five-eighth. Trent Barrett played only the first game, against a French Selection team; he was kneed in the back and suffered a pretty bad kidney injury and ended up going home a week or so later.

My first game was the third match of the tour, against Cumbria at Whitehaven; it was absolutely freezing and I'll never forget how small the dressing rooms were. We won 54–0 but I could feel the metal screws in my ankle freezing up it was so cold! I played in the centres, with Gids inside at five-eighth and Ronnie Jones at halfback.

It was just a fantastic experience to go on that tour. I roomed with Nathan Cayless for quite a bit of the time and he was a determined bugger. He must have read about Wayne Pearce's efforts rooming with Peter Sterling on the 1982 Kangaroo tour – he was religiously exercising in our room all the time; he was very mature and determined back then. It's ironic that I packed into a few scrums against him years later when I played for Australia and he was in the front row for New Zealand, the country of his mother's birth.

Among the duties of the players on tour was that every few days one of us had to do a 'report' for the team diary (which is archived on the Australian Schoolboys Rugby League website, by the way). My contribution was pretty sophisticated, but I suspect someone else tinkered with this; they don't sound like my words and it looks a little bit expansive for me:

Boys are pretty happy about the accommodation at the start of the last week. Only two games to go to keep the record intact . . . want to go home with that undefeated record. Training at The Circle, an absolute belter in boggy conditions but the boys were keen again. We are now used to the routine of life on tour. All the training has paid off and full credit must go to all the staff. The Hull supporters made sandwiches & drinks for the boys which was most appreciated . . . no tuna!! Back to The Royal for a free afternoon . . . pool, sleeping or shopping . . . early dinner . . . off to the movie Batman Forever & Pizza Hut. A big surprise for everyone back at the hotel – a College Ball with girls our own age all around the place. They sought us out but we stood firm . . . game day tomorrow! To everyone on tour there have been a lot of records and

friendships made and it is by far the best team I have played in and I'll never forget this chance of a lifetime.
– Danny Buderus

I wasn't a noted try-scorer in those days (and was less of one when I went to hooker) but I posted four in the 'Test' against BARLA (British Amateur Rugby League Association) at Batley, which stood as a record for a schoolboys 'Test' for a while. I was fortunate to get the man of match and players' player award too.

The game against BARLA was played on the last day of the tour, 22 December, and after a night of celebration and enjoying the hospitality of our hosts for the last time, we had a fairly early start to get to the airport to catch a flight home which would arrive on Christmas Eve. We gathered outside the hotel for the bus trip to the airport and David Atkins wasn't there; he didn't get back to the hotel from the night before. The tour managers decided we had to leave without him and we were all distraught, screaming 'We can't just leave him here'. Some of the players were nearly crying – we were a really close squad. But the managers insisted they had to get us all back to our families for Christmas day and there was no way we could change the bookings so close to Christmas anyway; there would have been few available seats.

So we left the hotel without him and we were all worried that he was going to get back to the hotel and have no idea what to do, wouldn't be able to contact anyone because we'd be on the plane and be stranded in England. You wouldn't believe it, but one minute before the last boarding call David lobbed at the airport departure gate. It was just my luck that the seating allocation was done alphabetically – so I had to sit next to him on the flight. I demanded he went and had a wash in the toilet;

he stank from body odour and good times! At least he slept just about all the way home.

In 2008, to celebrate Rugby League's centenary year, I was very honoured to be chosen in the Australian Schoolboys greatest-ever team, along with Matt Gidley, which made it more special. It brought back memories of that 1995 tour and the great blokes I went away with. Gids and I were the only players from that touring squad to make the 17. We were in good company. The best-ever Schoolboys side is: Tim Brasher, Andrew Ettingshausen, Mark Gasnier, Justin Hodges, Greg Inglis, Brad Fittler, Greg Alexander, Craig Young, Danny Buderus, Les Boyd, Steve Menzies, Paul Sironen, Brad Clyde. Interchange: Tonie Carroll, Ian Schubert, Matthew Gidley, Brent Tate.

I came back from the tour and went into the 1996 season with the Knights with so much more confidence; I jumped the Jersey Flegg (under 19s) and went straight into President's Cup (under 21s) even though I turned 18 in the February. Again I played all over the backline and didn't really know what my position would end up being. I had the tag of still being a kid; I was very shy and was still finding my way and was careful not to get in anyone's way or step on anyone's toes. I was starstruck being around first grade players like the Johnses, Paul Harragon, Jamie Ainscough, Marc Glanville, Tony Butterfield and Adam Muir; I'd see Matt Gidley and Owen go up and train with them and think how great that was and how far ahead of me they were. I was waiting for someone else to tell me in what position on the field my future was; was it at five-eighth, centre, fullback? I wasn't quick enough to be a winger and I never thought I'd ever play in the forwards.

When all the crazy Super League signings came around in 1995 I was offered $15,000 by the Hunter Mariners for the 1997 season when I came off the Knights contract, and

$25,000 for 1998, plus incentives like $3000 for making the Schoolboys tour, and $3000 for making the New South Wales under 17s and a further $3000 if I made the Australian under 19s. I was only 17 and playing SG Ball and my first reaction was, 'Where do I sign?' Ironically the person who made the offer was Keith Onslow, who had signed me to my Knights scholarship but who had gone across to the Hunter Mariners in Super League. A lot of my SG Ball team-mates wanted to sign straight away with Super League, but someone advised me to hold off. I obviously didn't have a manager then – in fact few players did, even the first graders – but somehow I got sent to leading player manager Wayne Beavis, who got me $25,000 for both seasons (1997–98) from the ARL. Keith knew I was happy at the Knights and felt I owed them for giving me my break, so he didn't push it too hard. I have a lot of respect for Keith and I'm glad he finally got back to the Knights in 2008.

But the Super League war, the resulting increase in player payments and the introduction of full-time professionalism created a heap more whiz kids who got thrust into a false sense of security of having 'made it'. They'd virtually come out of school, copped more than $40,000 for their first contract, did not have to get a job and thought the rugby league world would continue like that forever.

I'm glad I had a lot of hurdles put in front of me when I first came into the Knights system; I had some of the best players ahead of me in my preferred position; I had to get a job when I finished school and fend for myself and learn to manage my off-field affairs living a few hours from my parents. I thank them for allowing me to leave home and follow my dream; a lot of kids mightn't have parents who had faith in their kid growing up away from them with the danger of them going off the rails or taking up another interest if it had not worked.

And I look back now and realise how fortunate I was to have Matt Gidley around me too. We're a lot alike personality-wise; he was shy and knew his place too but underneath he had a real desire to succeed, was a good listener, and had a great family around him like I did.

It's no coincidence our parents are very close. We knew we had a lot to prove, that talent would get us only so far, that we had a lot to learn, and that we must always show respect to those who had already achieved what we wanted to. We knew we had to show patience, a big work ethic and a willingness to learn and listen before we had any right to be first graders. I'd like to think we were examples of the attitude young players need these days.

3

MENTORS

IT HAPPENS most sessions, and at most football clubs, I guess. You are doing a fitness drill and the odd player would go over the cone rather than around it; it's only a small shortcut and he's hoping others don't notice. Or it's a hot summer's day during pre-season and you're all completely stuffed and you'll see a team-mate cut an exercise set short by one, believing he's already got plenty of benefit out of driving his body to that point.

'Pepe' was never one of those blokes. Never took a shortcut. Pepe would go two metres around the cone, just to make sure; just so he was nowhere near where he could be lured into cheating himself. If we were on the chin-up bar, Pepe would take his whole head above the bar while others would get their chin just to the height of the bar. He didn't do chin-ups; he did chest-ups.

Before a match he'd be in the dressing shed walking, stretching, and bouncing two balls against a wall into his hands to get his hand–eye co-ordination working. He knew he wasn't the most talented player, but he was the most thorough, the most professional. If the opposition made a half-break in a match and you'd think, 'We're in trouble here,' Pepe would be the bloke who'd come from nowhere on the inside and shut it down. When you're in your own half of the field and sucking in the big breaths, Pepe would be the one who would take the hit up into the teeth of the compressed defensive line, to give his mates a ruck or two to get back into position.

I'm talking about Paul Marquet, a bloke I regard as a great mentor even though he probably doesn't know it. Pepe Marquet never played any representative football – not for New South Wales Country, New South Wales, or for Australia. But he played in two premiership-winning teams – Melbourne in 1999 and Newcastle in 2001 – and has a proud record of 231 first grade games, 137 of them for the Knights.

Billy Peden is another mentor of mine who was cast from the same mould – didn't have to say much; wasn't trying to make an impression on anyone, but always did. He was 24 before he was picked up by the Knights but went on to play 190 first grade games because he was the ultimate professional, ultimate club man and trainer. Billy and I are built pretty much the same physically, so I tried to line myself up against him; I learnt from Billy that despite not being the biggest bloke I could put my body on the line and compete against much bulkier players. I saw the spirit and work ethic he brought to the Knights and I tried to emulate that and pass it down to others over the years.

Mentors are important in professional sport, just as they are in life generally. I am fortunate to have had some very good ones. Not all were the lecturing type; not all were players whose names roll off the tongue as legends of the game. And some of the things that played a big role in moulding my beliefs of how to succeed happened when some of my mentors didn't even realise they were teaching them to me.

You'll find a lot of other footballers who were lucky enough to play for their state and country would rave about blokes like Pepe and Billy who taught them and inspired them; blokes who may not have reached the perceived heights of others in the minds of fans. Because there are fewer 'journeymen' on the books of the NRL clubs these days due to salary cap restrictions, there are probably not as many of these sorts of mentors – and that's a great pity. I think that filters through down to off-field behaviour as much as playing attitudes, but that's a different story I go into later.

One thing I feel strongly about, though, is not to put all your eggs in the one basket and rely on one person as your 'guru'; I think you have to listen to as many people you respect as you can, and then formulate your own character and beliefs from that. I was fortunate I did that. I'd like to think I have been a very respectful person although a bit guarded, and more so after I got badly duped in a business deal about five years ago. (I'll explain about that later in this chapter.)

Naturally the Johns brothers, Matthew and Andrew, had a great influence on me as a footballer and I tried to emulate their attitude. 'Joey' (Andrew) has been such a big part of my life and such an amazing character I devote a whole chapter to him.

Andrew was the one with all the natural skills; Matty was the one who manufactured his skills and talent through sheer hard work. When I was working as a driver for Boots Plumbing I'd come across Matthew and Andrew out training with the ball at Learmonth Park in Newcastle. I had a lot of admiration for the way Matty played the game and carried himself and I aspired to develop the work ethic that took him so far. At first I was too shy to approach him, being just a young lower grader from the bush, but when I did he was great and invited me to do a few sessions with him. I wasn't a natural ball player, so I liked to pick Matty's brains.

I think Matt respected how willing I was to learn and work hard on my game. Matt explained a bit of footy 'science' to me; things like where to direct the point of attack, counting numbers, the best way to get around a defender, how defence would react when you shifted the ball to one side of the field and came back and hit another. He was so willing to impart his knowledge, and on some days off I'd go to a park with Matt and Andrew and do skills work with them. That was absolutely invaluable for a young player like me.

Matty also taught me things like running with the 'chin to your chest' – which gives you more power when you put the step on, instead of having your head up in the air. This proved invaluable when I moved to hooker. Subtlety can change your game a whole lot at times and can be the difference between getting through a gap and getting caught.

A bit later, Joey – as we became closer as mates – started working with me in teaching me passing and kicking skills. I look back fondly on those times when we were young and fit early in my career, and Mark Hughes and I would go to a park and do all those 'extras'. But as you get older and carry chronic injuries, you have to spend so much time on injury treatment and stretching and warming-up and not putting too much strain on your body, so those sort of impromptu sessions end pretty quickly.

I can only encourage young players to show the initiative and go up to the experienced players in their team and ask them if you can pick their brains, because it will definitely be worthwhile. I think these days NRL players tend to do their learning directly from the computer with stats and videos of matches, broken down to individual players' traits and individual plays, and the one-on-one passing down of experience isn't as prevalent as it used to be. I'd rather a young bloke came up to me and said, 'Can you meet me down the park for half an hour this arvo if you've got any time, and take me through this?' I'd really love that, instead of sitting on a computer and pressing buttons, because I know how invaluable it was for me to get that sort of feedback when I was starting out. I was like a sponge wanting to soak up all the information I could from whoever wanted to give it to me; particularly anyone who played first grade.

I suppose my first allocated mentor was Steve Walters, who is still regarded by many people as the best hooker-forward of the modern era. 'Boxhead' was signed by the Knights in 1999 but played only seven games before giving in to a knee injury and retiring. I played three games as centre and a couple off the bench while Steve was with the Knights, but was quickly groomed to take over from him as hooker.

Lee Jackson, the Great Britain Test hooker, and Brett Clements, who was a good, tough hooker, had taught me a lot the previous year but 'Boxhead' stayed around at the Knights for the rest of the '99 season after retiring and became almost my personal teacher. I'm forever indebted to that time I spent learning from him.

The best thing about being halfback and five-eighth in the juniors was that I had a bit of a pass on me; I could throw the ball long. Steve Walters told me more subtle things like where to get your power from when you are passing, where your feet should be, where to position your body to make you more efficient at dummy-half. I still try to pass that on to players today, and in fact am still enjoying repeating those hints to a young hooker at Leeds, Paul McShane.

Boxhead taught me how to read when it was best to run from dummy-half. He used to say 'watch for the dead-ants' – that was the term he used for defenders still on the ground after a tackle. He also showed how to position your head and body when you made a run, to give you maximum force to get through a tackle.

When I made the New South Wales Origin team, I was fortunate that Nathan Brown was on the coaching staff. Being a big Dragons fan when I was growing up, I used to follow Browny's career because he was a surfy-looking kid from the north coast. When I met him in Origin camp I picked his brains and he told me subtle things like how to 'play short' with your elbows high while passing; it's hard to explain but if you try to pass the ball with your elbows straight it will be a hard pass but if you raise and bend your elbows it will be a softer, shorter pass. Later I had former Test hooker Royce Simmons on the Blues staff and he taught me a lot too.

There were other aspects of rugby league that I learned from just observing or talking generally with team-mates. Ben Kennedy was someone you just watched; he had so much passion, worked so hard on his strength and fitness and had so much skill. His determination and loyalty to the team were awesome, and I tried to live up to that. David Fairleigh and Clinton O'Brien were blokes who'd been around and taught me a lot about off-field as well as on-field values and their attitude to maximising every opportunity. Then we had Paul Harragon, Steve Crowe and Tony Butterfield; they set the standards for toughness, club loyalty and treatment of injuries. They also provided off-field direction.

Toughness is a thing that can't be taught through words, it has to come from actions. There is a very strong culture of toughness at the Newcastle Knights that I hope will never die, and to see Andrew Johns, Ben Kennedy, Tony Butterfield, Paul Harragon and others playing 'busted' and putting in so much effort – and never using injury as an excuse – has left a massive impression on me.

So many of those I have mentioned had experience in the facets of football and life I wanted to ask about. It wasn't always about football, because you live and learn your football through your mistakes and the decisions that work; the game is always evolving and you have to keep pace. But in life, whether it is advice on a player manager, taxation, financial advice, who can be trusted in the media or who can be relied on among the back-slappers and associates around the club, I found it was always good to ask a fellow player.

You can't see the world through the eyes of your team-mates only, however, and shut yourself off to other aspects of your life, and I've had a small group of people outside of football I know I can count on. But I believe your family, particularly your parents, are your best and most reliable mentors in life. I wasn't one to have any lengthy discussions with my parents, particularly as I left home at age 16, but they've had a big influence on me in the way they have lived their lives – another example where actions are as good as words. They taught me to treat people as you would like them to treat you; to show respect for others and never forget where you came from and those who helped you along the way. That's why I've always been happy to go back to Taree or Forster, where Mum and Dad moved to, and do coaching clinics or club presentations or help out when I had time.

But you have to be careful whose judgement you take, and trust. Sometimes you take the wrong advice, that's inevitable, and you have to learn and move on. The toughest example I came across was when I met someone at a Knights golf day in 2003 when Matt Gidley and I played in a foursome with two businessmen. This particular guy befriended me; he was a developer and among his projects was a holiday resort in

Thailand. He gave Matt and me his number and said if we were ever interested in investing in any of his projects to give him a call.

We kept in contact and I was holidaying at Phuket in 2005 and decided to ring him, thinking I might look at his development. He answered the phone and said, 'Mate, I'm here now, come and catch up.' So we had a beer at a bar at Patong Beach and he showed me the sights, then next day we had a game of golf. He told me he had a resort development in Phuket and did I want to buy into it for $240,000. All I ever saw were photos and plans, and I said no at first but he kept on at me for about six months and I finally relented and agreed to his invitation to pay 10 per cent, so I coughed up $24,000.

Next thing he was going around the Hunter Valley spruiking that Matt Gidley and I had backed his development and he started using our names to promote it. Matt hadn't even bought into it. Some people put their life savings into it, partly influenced by the fact Gids and I had supposedly 'endorsed' it, but I was just like them and put some money into it on face value.

As it turned out, the whole thing was a hoax and a lot of people lost a lot of money; people were duped out of fortunes. I know some who put over $200,000 into it. When the police investigated, I made it clear he was using Matt's and my names falsely and we had nothing to do with any of his activities – other than being conned like everyone else to throwing some cash into his scam.

Last I heard, the police were still searching for him; he's probably living a comfortable life in Asia somewhere.

I learned a hell of a lot from the experience and it taught me to investigate things a lot more and educate myself to make a lot of business decisions myself. Again, I have some good mentors I can trust there now too.

So life is very much about having the right people to provide advice and to set standards you want to emulate. I don't think there are enough mentors in life these days; the right sort of role models who take time to pass down what they have learned. They talk about well-known sports people being role models and, while some try to downplay that responsibility, I never have. Because whether you are consciously trying to set an example or not, you often are because people observe you and look up to you. I'm conscious of that because of my own experiences, even if I'm more a person who tries to lead by example rather than by words.

Just like 'Pepe' Marquet, who never had to say much to teach me a lot.

4

THE AURA OF ORIGIN

MY FIRST State of Origin coach, Phil Gould, had a massive influence on me. He epitomised what Origin was about and was the person most responsible for New South Wales trying to emulate the Origin passion and spirit that Queenslanders like to think is exclusive to them. He has a record of only one series loss in eight as Blues coach, which proves he knew what he was talking about.

The thing that has stuck most in my mind about what 'Gus' taught me, while educating me that Origin was different from any other football I would play, was his term that there were good plays, good tackles and good players in the NRL and then there were Origin plays, Origin tackles and Origin players. That never left me.

'Origin plays' distinguish themselves apart from good plays, the fancy match-winning plays, or the special things that you see in club matches. Origin plays sometimes are the little things that might go unnoticed by the media but never by your team-mates. And I was fortunate enough to be around Origin football long enough to see the proof of the pudding.

I'm talking about the little things like a team-mate who was out on his feet getting off the ground and coming across from the inside and making a crucial tackle, and then maybe backing up again for another one. Or the guy who was just so consistent in the kick-chase, as enthusiastic in the 79th minute as he was in the ninth.

Of course there were the more recognised moments: Shaun Timmins' left-footed field goal in 2004 in extra-time in my first match as captain; Brett Finch's field goal that won us the opening game in 2006 when he was only called into the team the night before; Johnathan Thurston's show-and-go that set up Billy Slater's try late in my last game for the Blues when Queensland were without Darren Lockyer.

Gus warned me how important those things were the first time I was picked for New South Wales in 2002; in fact on that first day when he looked at me as he addressed the team. Naturally, my first State of Origin match is a special memory; although the build-up to the game is more vivid than the match itself. (New South Wales won 32–4 at Stadium Australia in Sydney, with Andrew Johns – in his first game as captain – winning the man of the match after really pumping himself up for the series.)

My Newcastle team-mates Steve Simpson, Timana Tahu and I made our Origin debuts the same night and it was good to have fellow Knights 'Simmo', Matt Gidley, Ben Kennedy, Joey and Timana in the team with me. Mind you, Gids wasn't in the side until the morning of the match; he arrived in camp at midday after Shaun Timmins was ruled out with injury that morning – then he scored a try with his first touch of the ball. As usual his dad, Geoff, had backed him to score the first try (he always takes Matt and Kurt to score the first and the last tries in all the games they play) and won a pretty handy sum.

I was one of those players who represented Australia before I played Origin. In fact I'd played five Tests by then, after being chosen for the one-off Test against the Kiwis in 2001 (which was played after the Origin series, in which Luke Priddis played hooker for the Blues in all three games), one against Papua New Guinea in Port Moresby, then three Tests on the Kangaroo tour that was almost abandoned.

What I recall most about becoming a New South Wales Blue was the presence of our coach. Gus laid down the law that first day. I remember us all gathering in his suite on level 5 that night at the Crowne Plaza, Coogee, and he rattled off Origin stories like only he can and related them to a few war stories, which really got the blood pumping. The thing with Gus is you notice him testing you out; how you react, what your character is; he was testing me with eye contact. That's something New South Wales players will never forget – Gus looking straight at you, engaging your eyes, and you wouldn't look down, you'd just keep focused on him but feel a wave of relief go through you when he looked away.

The passion Gus added to Origin in that series was phenomenal. Queensland had brought Allan Langer back from England for the deciding game the previous year and he inspired a victory and they were spruiking about the unique Queensland spirit and passion, pushing the impression Queenslanders like to give about the exclusiveness of their passion. It really irked Gus, and the players too, don't worry. I didn't want to let him down.

It was very much a new breed and Gus was out to leave an impression on us. There were Simmo, Timana, Brett Hodgson, Jason Moodie, Braith Anasta, Jamie Lyon, Luke Bailey and me making our debuts, plus Nathan Hindmarsh and Mark O'Meley, who had only come into the New South Wales side the year before.

Gus had this other saying, that you 'don't sit back and be a wallflower'. In other words, get yourself into the thick of action as soon as possible. The other one he hit us with that will also always be with me is: 'Where am I? What's my job? Who's got the ball?' That was his way of simplifying how we had to play as the game got into that rapid tempo that only Origin can produce. Before my first game at the new Suncorp in 2003, we visited the stadium the night before and Gus got us to go out on the playing field and said, 'Go and pick a bit of the field you think you are going to feature on tomorrow night; think about your family, the people that got you there, your team-mates . . . and what you want to do for them.' That was special – a unique moment – to get onto the pitch and visualise what you thought was going to happen.

The Queensland FOGS (Former Origin Greats) would always have a big lunch at Suncorp the day before the game in Brisbane and that happened to coincide with our last training session. They used to sit there and watch us train, and people would come outside and yell abuse at us. Sometimes the sprinklers would just coincidentally be turned on while we were out there; one time someone had a string pulled across so we could only use three-quarters of the field. We used to try to trick it up a bit and practise different plays from what we were going to use; like throwing in the chip on the fourth tackle. It was part of the mental game Gus loved – the mind games that are so much a part of Origin.

There is so much to tell about State of Origin football, I could almost write a book just about that one subject. Instead, I thought I would split it up with some particular topics which best describe my experiences.

My first series

We won my first Origin match as I just described and it was always great for the confidence winning the first game, knowing that you only had to win one of the next two to take the series.

When we went into camp for the second match at ANZ Stadium in Brisbane (Suncorp Stadium was being redeveloped), Gus showed us footage of what Queensland did to us in the last minute of the first game despite knowing they couldn't win. He was saying with real passion, 'They don't rest; they don't give in; never.' We were up 32–4 and there was a scrum with 30 seconds to go and Shane Webcke and Gorden Tallis got their forwards and just ripped in and pushed us off the mark; that really stuck out in our players' minds. Gus then showed us some games when we were ahead by big margins, and others where we were well behind, but we didn't continue to rip in, while they kept the momentum going.

And even though he was nearly 36, we knew we couldn't let up for one second against Allan Langer. 'Alfie' was at his best playing Origin footy; whenever he went for the line he had two runners on the outside and two on the inside and they all just knew how to play it. It was amazing watching it on video; he'd swoop around the other side of the ruck and they'd all follow, giving him inside and outside options; it was a nightmare to defend against.

Gus termed the style Queensland played as 'get on board'. If one of their inspirational players took a lead, everyone around him reacted and 'got on board'. They did this with Alfie, Darren Lockyer and Johnathan Thurston particularly during my time.

Queensland beat us 26–18 in Brisbane, which took us to a series decider in Sydney. And that's when I learned first-hand what Gus had been preaching. When Andrew Johns converted a Jason Moodie try, we led 18–14 with about three minutes remaining and, as Gus commented afterwards, he thought we'd done a Queensland on Queensland. But Darren Lockyer put in a shallow kick-off and the Maroons got one last shot at us. Langer and Lockyer played the leading hands in the lead-up to give Dane Carlaw an overlap on the right-hand side and he scored with 52 seconds to go to level the scores at 18–all. I couldn't believe it.

Lote Tuqiri missed the conversion and we stood there wondering what was going to happen. I thought we'd go into extra-time but there was this long delay with the players and the crowd getting restless before we were told that was it – it was a drawn series and Queensland kept the trophy. There was debate for days about the merits of golden point extra-time but to me there was only one way to go – turn around and play until there was a result. It was just a huge anti-climax to my first series, and to have golden point in the NRL competition, which created some incredible matches, but not in Origin, was absurd. You wouldn't believe that after the ARL made a decision to introduce golden point in 2004 it was needed in the first game and Shaun Timmins kicked his left-footed gem to win game one for us 9–8.

To see Queensland draw the game on the last play and rob us of a series win in my first year in Origin, and for Alfie to be the one to come up with the man of the match award, taught me that what Phil Gould had been drumming into me was not to be doubted. I was devastated that we didn't win the series, and didn't get the chance in extra-time, but when I later relaxed and thought about the series, I just felt so fortunate to have experienced it; I loved everything about Origin – the intensity of the build-up and the match itself, the mateship, the personal challenge, playing in front of massive crowds and the fact that you knew it was making you a better player. I came away thinking I just had to be playing well enough the next year to keep the jersey; I didn't want to be a one-series wonder.

The essence of Origin

The toughest test for a rugby league player comes in the last 10 or 15 minutes of a State of Origin match. Those minutes often produce the big plays that define Origin history and the massive difference between experiencing the pride and elation you get from winning an Origin series and the absolute devastation that hits you when you lose. And as I explain a bit further on, ultimately those last few minutes can dictate the whole rest of your season as a player.

You can have dominant players in club football who are used to the team pattern, intimately know what their team-mates can do and are fit enough and mentally strong enough to make decisive plays and handle 80 minutes of NRL pace. It all becomes automatic in many ways, week in week out.

Origin is so different; you often can't bring your familiar club structure with you. You might be a dominant NRL player in your team who gets the ball twice in a set of six on a few occasions during a game; come Origin the ball might not come your way for ages and the next thing you've got 15 minutes left, it feels like you've been defending endlessly for 25 minutes, only had one touch but racked up 15 or 16 tackles – and you're wondering how much longer you can keep going.

You're playing with and against the elite; you know their games backwards; everyone defends the same, wrestles the same; they have similar set plays; you know the lines they like to run; you know who is good in the air and who is not; who will beat you on the outside with a fend. And you go to bed thinking about every possible move that might beat you.

But when it comes to *that time* in an Origin match, somehow all that knowledge doesn't matter. Freakish talents like Inglis or Folau or Thurston or Lockyer or Slater have that ability to sink you, and you stand behind the goalposts thinking you couldn't have planned better to stop it happening, but somehow it just did. And all you trained for, all the pain you went through to get on the paddock, all the pledges you made to your mates not to let them down . . . where did it all go?

As I went through my 21 Origin matches when researching for this book, I found that in nine of them a crucial score to decide a match came in the last 12 minutes. Unfortunately, six of those came from Queensland:

Game 2, 2002: Lote Tuqiri scoring a try (and converting from touch) in the last minute with the Maroons leading 20–18;

Game 3, 2002: Dane Carlaw scoring in the last play of the game to draw 18–all;

Game 1, 2004: Sean Timmins's field goal in golden point extra-time;

Game 2, 2004: Cameron Smith kicking a penalty goal in the last minute to stop our chance of a comeback for a 22–18 win;

Game 1, 2005: we fought back to lead 20–18 with nine minutes to go, only for Johnathan Thurston to kick a penalty goal in the 78th minute, then Matthew Bowen came up with his intercept try four minutes into extra-time;

Game 1, 2006: Brett Finch landing a field goal in the 79th minute for a 17–16 New South Wales win;

Game 3, 2006: we were leading 14–4 with eight minutes to go and Queensland scored two tries to win 16–14;

Game 3, 2007: we led 6–4 with eight minutes to go and it was anyone's game before we scored two tries to make it 18–4;

Game 3, 2008: it was 12–all with 12 minutes remaining when Johnathan Thurston put on his old show-and-go and put Billy Slater in for the series-winning try.

In Origin the little things count so much; everything is amplified compared to NRL games because of the quality of players across the park and the pressure you play under. You have to kick and chase well for 80 minutes, so much revolves around that; your marker defence is crucial; as is putting pressure on the kickers, and keeping up the speed of the defensive line right to the end even though you're hurting physically so bad in the last 10 to 15 minutes. It's about having confidence in the bloke next to you, knowing he won't let you down but that, if he does, the series can balance on a split second's loss of concentration.

And it's no coincidence that the great players come out in those last 10–15 minutes. Thurston did it to us in my last game in 2008; Darren Lockyer pounced on a stray Brett Hodgson pass in the deciding game in 2006; Allan Langer handled three times in Dane Carlaw's try that squared the 2002 series; Andrew Johns turned the 2005 series on its ear with two absolutely dominant performances in Sydney in game two and at Suncorp, and the Queenslanders seemed powerless to stop him.

You can feel the onslaught coming sometimes, because Origin is about the changing phases of momentum, but you have to get rid of any negative thoughts in your head as quickly as possible. There are no other games I have played in where the momentum going into the last five or 10 minutes is so pronounced – and that is why so many Origin games go down to the wire. What makes a good team is being able to defend that momentum and attack again. You keep probing and looking for a tired big man; you only have to take half a stride in the wrong direction defensively and that is all it takes, because you're up against the calibre of player who can, under the most extreme pressure, put on a brilliant pass at the line, or a chip and regather, or break a tackle with sheer power and pace . . . and then the moment has gone.

That's what makes State of Origin and why people say an Origin game goes so quickly, and why you can feel so devastated when you've fought it out for 240 minutes over three games and know that one split second of wrong judgement cost a series; or that one 'Origin play', by someone in your team who had no right to find the energy or mental strength to put it on, gives you so much satisfaction.

It's those things that have made some of my team-mates and me so close, because you know there is nothing tougher as a player you could have been involved in together, or any greater achievement, than beating fatigue, pressure, the best players from the other state and all the massive expectations – and coming out winners. That's also why Origin takes so much out of you mentally.

It was why I was so desperate to remain the New South Wales hooker after I made myself unavailable for Australian selection in 2006 and why I am so personally proud that I didn't miss a game in seven series.

Meeting Kerry Packer

Another thing that stands out in my memory about the honour of being New South Wales captain was meeting media mogul Kerry Packer for the first time, in 2005, about six months before he died. It was at a dinner at Ravesi's Restaurant at Bondi Beach and it was a bit of a get-together of powerful people like big 'KP', Alan Jones and Gerry Harvey, and with John Quayle also there.

I was seated opposite Mr Packer, as I called him all night, with Andrew Johns sitting next to him. I was pretty anxious being captain at an official dinner with so many VIPs on the table, but more nervous about sitting directly across from such a daunting figure, and wondering what conversation I should have with him.

While we were talking about footy, Mr Packer asked, 'How do you get the injuries out of the game?'

I said something like, 'Ah, umm, Mr Packer, I think we are just playing too much footy and players are getting worn out. I'm just speaking from personal experience – my body gets a bit run-down, especially going on these tours every year and playing a lot of footy during the year; the season just seems a bit long.'

He looked at me and had this real blank look on his face and again he asked, 'How do we get the injuries out of the game?'

I pretty much repeated the same thing – 'We're playing too many games, everyone is getting stronger, fitter and more powerful, and it's taking its toll.'

He gave me a blank stare; I looked at Joey, whose eyebrows were raised, and next thing I felt a kick under the table from A. Johns, signalling that I had put my foot right in this one. I'd overlooked the fact that I was talking to the person who had the TV rights and here I was suggesting he have fewer games to televise – even though I felt I was telling the absolute truth (and the match schedule is still a problem in rugby league).

Mr Packer then said, 'No, no, son . . . son, you're not listening . . . How do we get the injuries out of the game?'

Joey came to my rescue and butted in with, 'It's the intensity of the tackle these days; it's a rut everyone is going through just at the moment, everyone is getting bigger and stronger and the collisions are getting fiercer.'

Mr Packer said, 'Yes, that's right' as Joey looked at me with a big grin on his face. Kerry continued, 'I'll tell you how to get the injuries out of the game: outlaw the bloody three-man tackle. I don't like it; three-man tackles are not in the spirit of the game and that's why they're getting so many injuries.'

I nodded my head and just left it at that before I got myself into more trouble. Then I proceeded to ask Joey did he want a drink, to change the subject as quickly as I could.

My favourite Origin match

So, as you can gather, there are quite a few 'Origin plays' that I'll never forget. But one stands out. It wasn't in the last 10 minutes and wasn't a try-scoring play that people will remember decided a series or even a match. It was a period of play in the deciding clash of 2005 at Suncorp Stadium – Andrew Johns's last game for the Blues. That was the toughest Origin match I played in, and the best victory – even though the score doesn't reflect it.

Queensland, coached by my Newcastle coach Michael Hagan, won the first match at Suncorp on the back of Matt Bowen's intercept of Brett Kimmorley's pass in extra-time – after I was fortunate to score in the 71st minute to give us a 20–19 lead. Joey was recalled for the second game at Telstra Stadium and, after we were behind 12–8 at half-time, Joey got us a 40–20 kick early in the second half and we never lost momentum again; he just dominated the rest of the game, inspiring us to a 32–22 victory.

When we got to Suncorp, we were chasing our first series victory from 1–0 down since 1994. But we had the worst possible start – we coughed up possession and Darren Lockyer and Johnathan Thurston kept us at our end of the field so that we had to defend for 29 successive tackles – virtually the first nine minutes of the game. Queensland hammered our line but our defence was like a blue wall; we just kept on getting up and knocking them over. That can take so much out of any team, but in a State of Origin match that weight of possession would break most sides – whether at the time or later in the match when fatigue sets in.

Suddenly Anthony Minichiello scooped up a kick from 'Locky' and ran 80 metres to get us down their end of the field.

We ended up getting a penalty, which Craig Fitzgibbon landed for a 2–0 lead. That swing of momentum set up the match for us, and broke the Maroons' spirit. It typified everything Phil Gould and anyone else ever told me about the essence of what State of Origin is about. I have never been prouder in my whole career of a bunch of blokes in defence than I was that night.

From that we got a roll on and led 18–0 by half-time. We ended up winning 32–10. Unfortunately, it was the last time I won an Origin series, which is probably more reason why I remember that effort that night so fondly.

Suncorp Stadium – the best in the world

When you run onto the field to start an Origin match and the noise of the crowd hits you, it's the biggest rush of adrenalin you can ever experience. It lifts you off the turf, you feel a chill down your spine and you feel so proud, and so privileged. My thoughts were always the same: 'I'm the luckiest man alive.' There is not a moment in rugby league like it and I never took it for granted; certainly never at Suncorp, where the sound of the crowd lifts you off your feet. I was lucky to experience that nine times.

The euphoria only lasts a few seconds, though; you have to take it in and enjoy it but not let it overtake you; and then your 'footy head' takes over and you look around at your team-mates' faces and see the concentration and focus in their eyes. It's almost like you've put an invisible shield around the field and the volume of the crowd noise suddenly drops.

And running onto Suncorp Stadium after it was redeveloped for the start of the 2003 series is the most special feeling of all. And so is the following hour and a half. I'll never downplay how special it was to play in front of the Knights fans in Newcastle; they are the most intimidating and vocal crowd in the NRL.

But an Origin match at Suncorp always creates a cauldron-like atmosphere, full of hostility, and the noise just seems never to abate for the whole 80 minutes.

The 'new' Suncorp is the best football stadium in Australia. I was fortunate to play in the first club game and Origin game there and I'll never forget either. All the talk in 2003 was about how good the rebuilt stadium was. We were lucky in that the Newcastle Knights went up to play the Broncos in the first NRL game at the stadium, and it attracted what I'm pretty sure was the biggest home game crowd in the NRL then, 46,337. And we got them too; after being behind 12–10 at half-time we scored four quick tries to lead 32–12 only 14 minutes after the break (winning 32–22 in the end). The surface was certainly sandy and you could tell the turf hadn't knitted properly but it didn't seem dangerous at all; however, there was a fair bit of controversy about it leading up to Origin 1, which was played there a week and a half later.

Even that Broncos match, and playing at ANZ Stadium in Origin the previous year, couldn't prepare me for the intimidating atmosphere you get at Suncorp for an Origin match. Maroon hatred was in the air; it was just huge, but rather than intimidate me it made me feel like I wanted to take the 50,000 on. I remember I wore a headband over a cut that match and my first tackle was on a rampaging Shane Webcke, which I found was the best way to get me into the game (if not the healthiest). We won 25–12 that night – two Queensland parties spoiled in a fortnight.

I played eight more Origin games at Suncorp and won only two – the 32–10 victory in 2005 I just described and 18–4 in the last game of 2007 when we'd already lost the series.

It was a great disappointment that we just never seemed to be able to match that atmosphere, or the parochial Queensland support, in Sydney. From the minute New South Wales players set foot in Brisbane after we got off the plane, everyone would remind us that we were in enemy territory; people you passed in the street, cab drivers, people who served you, radio DJs and TV news presenters – even if it was healthy banter most of the time.

Telstra/ANZ Stadium in Sydney is much vaster and while it ensures larger crowds it's not built specifically for rugby league; it's too open and the noise doesn't hold inside. Plus our home crowds just never seemed as vocal and parochial as Queensland's. I hope it changes; even better I'd love to see the capacity of the 40,000-seater Sydney Football Stadium extended to 60,000 (which can be done by lowering the field and adding more seating, apparently), because that would definitely have the potential to rival Suncorp.

The Robbie Farah push

I was at Coogee Crowne Plaza and just about to do the rounds with the media before the third game of the 2007 series. We'd already lost the first two games and, thus, the second series in a row after some critics had written off Queensland as never being competitive again. The media were having a field day looking for selection scapegoats and the captain was not immune, with plenty saying it might be time to put the Wests Tigers' Robbie Farah, who was leading the Dally M Medal count, into my number nine jersey.

Channel 9's Danny Weidler came up to me and said, 'I want to talk to you,' and motioned me to walk a few paces away from everyone else. 'I heard you were asked to stand down [as New South Wales hooker],' he told me.

I said, 'Well, I'm here now, aren't I? I wasn't asked anything like that by anybody.'

Weidler then said he'd heard from 'a reliable source' that people in power – I don't know if he meant selectors, the coach Graham Murray, or someone at the New South Wales Rugby League – wanted me to fall on my sword and let Robbie Farah take over as long-term Blues hooker.

I honestly hadn't caught wind of anything and I told Danny that. He then brought up the Craig Gower affair that had been played out in the media over the previous few weeks. He'd revealed that Gower was going to be released to play rugby union in France; 'Gowey' denied it outright. Weidler kept running with it and, just a few days later, Gower did an about face and admitted he'd signed with Bayonne. Our media manager in State of Origin, David Taylor, advised me that if I did know something I should admit it to Weidler as Craig Gower was made to look silly when the truth came out.

I told Weidler, 'I'm not denying it to put you off; I'm telling the truth,' and asked him who his reliable source was, but he obviously wasn't going to give him up; he just said he was very reliable and almost always was 'on the mark'. Anyway, the rumour grew legs from then and Danny kept running with the story that I wouldn't be in the New South Wales side for the 2008 series.

To this day, I don't know where his 'mail' came from and how much it was discussed by the selectors or the coach. I didn't go to anyone seeking clarification; I just wanted to win the next game and get on with life. But I'll admit I would have been devastated if it had come true; I thought I was still playing well enough to keep my position and didn't feel I deserved to relinquish it. I was confident I could get through another series, even though I'd be 30 in 2008.

We'd lost the '06 and '07 series 2–1, and both could have easily been won by New South Wales, the crucial games were so close. But the focus is so great with Origin that everyone is looking for an angle and there is always a scapegoat and a conspiracy theory not far away; and the pressure to win is so big, selectors are under enormous pressure.

I'm sure what fuelled the rumours was that I played only 60 minutes in the first game and was kept on the bench by Graham Murray when the result was up in the air in the final 10 minutes, despite us having no back-up hooker in the squad. It was fair enough to have a rest when we had Craig Wing, a specialist hooker, there for all but two games from 2003 to 2006; but after he was no longer selected I still often played around 60 to 65 minutes and we had Kurt Gidley having to come on and play hooker a couple of times and Ben Hornby was thrown into the role in 2008. I felt frustrated sometimes that I just didn't get the chance, as captain, to contribute to the team what I felt I was capable of. I believed I could still handle the pace of Origin for 80 minutes (I did play the full match twice in 2006–07).

I was feeling nervous about my position after losing the '07 series but we had a change of coach to Craig Bellamy in 2008 and he called me soon after he got the job to talk about his plans and how we could do things better in preparation. I said to him I'd heard a few stories going around about my position and asked whether he wanted me in the team. He assured me he wanted me there, and as captain, and that was why he was ringing me. That was the best reassurance I could have received and motivated me to make sure I was in good form for the Knights so I couldn't get dropped. In 2008 'Belly' kept me on for an average 63 minutes, but it was always planned when I would get a rest and return to the game and because I knew exactly what he had in mind, there were no surprises and I felt I had a lot more rhythm in that series.

I have a huge rap on Robbie Farah as a player, who was given the New South Wales jersey for the first two games in 2009, before Michael Ennis was chosen for the third. Robbie deserved the first chance and performed well. The Blues have two hookers now very worthy of wearing the jersey, who will push each other for years to come.

The Origin after-effect

State of Origin can make or break a player's season, and a team's if you have quite a few Origin reps in it. The confidence from winning an Origin series, and playing well, can be a major stimulus in winning individual awards, or your team winning the competition or at least making the finals. The adrenalin and confidence you bring back from a winning Origin is just enormous, and the benefit of the experience in taking you to a new level in your career should never be underestimated.

When I won the Dally M Medal in 2004, there is no doubt that the confidence and enthusiasm I brought back from winning the Origin series, and being captain, was a major contributor, despite me having to limp through the last few weeks with a painful toe injury. I reckon Cameron Smith (2006) and Johnathan Thurston (2007) would say the same.

In a team sense, I look at Brisbane in 2006; when they came out of Origin after Queensland had won their first series since 2001, they had fewer injuries than usual and a lot more momentum and confidence, and went on to win the grand final. Melbourne did the same in 2007 when they had five players in the winning Queensland team (and two playing for New South Wales) and they all continued on a high.

Something that is strong now in Origin culture is the belief that, to prove that you're a genuine elite Origin player, you have to be able to go back to your club and back up with influential performances because you owe your club mates that much for the part they played in making you an Origin player. I prided myself on that and never liked missing a game a weekend after Origin, although my coach Michael Hagan made me sit out the next game after the third Origin clash in 2006 – and I realised later he made the right decision.

But the difference in how you feel as a loser, compared to a winner, is just massive. Physically, especially if you are carrying injury, which I did plenty of times, it's tough enough to keep the body going after the pounding you take in three Origin matches and the mental draining you go through. But if you head back to your club after a loss, with your tail between your legs, it can devastate you. It's a huge comedown and if you're suffering a psychological hangover you can get stuck in a rut that is very hard to shift.

After all the mental preparation that goes into State of Origin and the overpowering feeling of relief when you're victorious, it's very hard to enjoy an Origin victory compared to club games. You have a private word with the team and the coach for a few minutes, whack on the ice bags or get a rub-down or physio treatment, then it's off to the media conference for the captain and coach before the doors open to media, sponsors and families and every angle is analysed; your club coach is normally on the phone before you leave the stadium to see how you pulled up and usually it's a case of 'See you at training tomorrow'. You make sure you go back to the hotel for a few wind-down beers rather than a great big night of celebration before, bang, it hits you – you all go in your different directions back to your clubs and have to back up two to five days later.

The Broncos in the end requested a bye the weekend after game three and ordered their Origin players to have four or five days rest before starting the rest of the season. Even though it might have meant surrendering two competition points because you don't get the bye while your Origin players were unavailable during the series, it was probably smart. The demand to change your mindset so suddenly is a massive challenge, especially when the team has been waiting for you to get back and lead the way.

The residual toll on your body from Origin can creep up on you too, especially if you feel the pressure to carry injury through the rest of the season. Again, if you've come off a winning series and your team is still in the hunt for the finals, it's a lot easier to contend with. But the pressure can be incredible, and it can break players – I've seen it happen. A lot have gone down with injury through body fatigue in the first couple of weeks after the series, or hit a lean spell with form, while others can be flying right through to the finals.

In 2008 I came back and went to Byron Bay to chill out for a few days (I missed our game against St George Illawarra) and I really benefited from the little break. I couldn't wait to get back into club footy after that and I was determined to finish the season – and my Australian career – on a high . . . but it didn't end up that way due to a biceps injury.

The ring of success

One special thing about State of Origin has been the distribution of rings that was introduced by Wizard Home Loans boss Mark Bouris, I think in 2004. Inscribed on them is 'Best of friends, worst of enemies' and they would be given if we won the series. It was a really nice touch (inspired by Gus Gould) from Mark, who was passionately behind the Blues. My rings – from the 2004 and 2005 victories – are tucked away in a special box of prized possessions.

5

WELCOME TO CAPTAINCY

I'LL CERTAINLY never forget my initiation as captain of New South Wales in State of Origin. Not just because at that stage I'd only captained Newcastle in three games as third-choice skipper, or because I was following Andrew Johns and Brad Fittler in the role and had played only six Origin matches . . . but because of an incident that became known as 'Gaz Gate'.

Joey did his ACL (anterior cruciate ligament) in the third club match of 2004 against Parramatta, which ruled him out for the season – and Origin. He was the Newcastle, New South Wales and Australian captain at the time. Ben Kennedy took over as Newcastle captain for three games, missed another three with injury (that's when I led the Knights) but was back, as captain, for the last game before Origin 1 – our 17–16 victory against Brisbane at Suncorp from a wobbly Kurt Gidley field goal. So when I was picked to captain the Blues I wasn't even the Knights skipper. 'BK' aggravated his hamstring injury in that game, which ruled him out of the Origin opener.

When we went into camp for a day at Stadium Australia a few weeks before the series began, Phil Gould came up to me in the tunnel and said, 'Mate, I'm thinking of making you captain.' It shocked me, to say the least; I'd never thought of myself as captain material for my club team let alone the state. I said, 'Mate, are you sure you want to do that? Do you think I'm ready?' But Gus told me he thought I definitely was, and for him to put the confidence in me made me feel like I didn't want to let him down. I was obviously honoured that he was even thinking of me, but pretty startled; I was a kid from Taree who just wanted to play Origin; suddenly I was being considered as captain.

I'm not sure exactly what Gus saw in me; I was playing a lot of minutes back then and, being hooker, was always in the thick of the action, so with no obvious leading candidate it was probably convenient to give the job to me. I know we didn't have any regular club captains who were regarded as certain- ties for the team, with Trent Barrett out injured at the time and a fair bit of debate whether Penrith skipper Craig Gower or Cronulla's Brett Kimmorley would be picked at halfback. I walked into the dressing room after training and had a quiet moment to gather my thoughts and said to myself, 'This could be the easiest or hardest job in the world, but whatever happens just relax and be yourself. Don't try to be anything you are not – be the person you are.'

It was a really inexperienced New South Wales side; and that opening game of 2004 was only the second time since 1992 we would field a team that didn't have Andrew Johns or Brad Fittler in it (both were missing for the second game of 1997). Plus we had Ben Hornby, Matt King, Mark Gasnier, Luke Lewis, Ryan O'Hara, Brent Kite and Trent Waterhouse selected to make their Origin debuts, and Anthony Minichiello and Craig Wing, who were in their second series.

I remember being nervous as hell in the first press confer- ence I had to do; that's the part of Origin that fans don't see

– the media part, which is just constant all week leading up to the game. On the other hand, when I got down to the hotel at Coogee, I got my own big room – the privilege Joey had for the previous two series. But I knew I couldn't be like him; leader of the pack with all the socialising early in the camp and the one who lifted everyone and called all the shots at training. To be honest, I never really enjoyed having my own room, I always found it more relaxing to be with people, and having someone to bounce off in the room. As it turned out, the boys soon found somewhere to hang out and make sure I never got too lonely – my room. Nathan Hindmarsh was a prime candidate for that; he'd come in and just wreck the place. Nobody looked at me differently now that I was captain, which was exactly what I wanted.

But my first week as Origin captain turned into a nightmare; I had to learn very quickly how to handle the media and how to become a leader under adversity. On the Tuesday we had a great day and night as a team – gym session, team meeting, a Wizard Home Loans promotion in the city, a training session at St Marys before thousands of people, followed by a coaching session for kids, dinner at St Marys Leagues Club with 200 people who'd won a competition and a pit stop at the Colyton Hotel for about 45 minutes, where we mixed with the locals. It was all about being accessible and whipping up support and interest in State of Origin – and a good image builder.

Before the series Phil Gould had considered an alcohol-free camp but was overruled apparently by the New South Wales Rugby League. Also, some former players told him it wasn't the way to go; that Origin nights out were a special part of the culture and that we should just make everyone aware of their responsibilities and organise everything for the team as a whole and have security guards and good team managers around to ensure nothing could get out of hand.

At 10.30 pm the backs went to the Clovelly Hotel and the forwards to the Charing Cross Hotel, before we all got back together at the Clovelly, ordered pizzas and then went for one last drink at the Coogee Bay Hotel just near where we were staying. We walked back to the Crowne Plaza at 3 am and were told to call it quits after a great night of 'bonding'. I was stuffed and ready for the sack. I know people will ask what we were doing out drinking that late anyway, but we'd only got back to the city at about 10.30 pm, when we could finally relax after all our commitments.

It wasn't until the next morning that I realised something was wrong, with the team management getting called into discussions. All hell then broke loose. What an initiation to the captaincy!

News filtered through late next morning about some of the boys slipping out. Rumours started hitting the media that someone had reported Willie Mason being on a bus at 7.30 am heading back to the hotel and a witch-hunt had started. There were allegations that one of our players had made an obscene phone call to a woman and it had been reported to talkback radio. I went to one of the Coogee cafes for a snack with Craig Fitzgibbon, Andrew Ryan and Mark Gasnier and the obvious main subject of conversation was what the hell had happened the night before and who was implicated. Gaz said he'd just been given a transcript of what was said on the phone to the woman and it sounded like something he would say, but he couldn't remember making a call. He said he'd been called in to discuss it with officials and it looked like he was in a bit of trouble. Later a copy of the tape arrived and it was obvious it was his voice; Gaz was ordered out of the camp by the end of the day.

He had made the call from Anthony Minichiello's phone at 3.41 am, when they were in a cab. We were told not to take mobile phones with us when we went out as a group, but 'Mini' had come back and got it when they went out again. Later there were stories about other blokes being at the casino drunk and some supposedly going to a brothel; we were all called in and asked to spill the beans on what anyone had been up to.

Instantly, the media just went crazy with the story. Later that day we headed to training on the team bus and I counted 14 cameras aimed at us. I was persuaded to go on *The Footy Show* on the Thursday night with our team manager, Chris Johns; my first big public appearance as captain of New South Wales was being belted around the ears about team behaviour and another 'boozy bonding session' and the sacking of the two players. Gaz was dumped on the Wednesday and replaced by Michael De Vere. Mini (who for some strange reason had been picked on the wing, despite being Test fullback, with Ben Hornby picked as fullback) got the boot on the Thursday, with Luke Rooney coming in. By that time other players had been fined for going out – they were Willie Mason ($6000), Trent Waterhouse ($5000), Craig Gower ($3000), Mark O'Meley ($3000) and Craig Wing ($3000). So that was seven out of the 17 players punished.

Chris Johns, on *The Footy Show*, was critical of the players (and himself), claiming it was about time they became responsible for their own actions – which is exactly what I was thinking but didn't say because I didn't want to sound so judgemental. I love a beer and a good time with the boys as much as anybody and have been in a pretty messy state on the grog plenty of times.

Gaz was fined $50,000 by St George Illawarra and his

image took a battering – all from a stupid thing he did when he was full of grog. The girl he called had her life turned upside down for weeks, too, as the media wanted to track her down. It showed just how exposed any high-profile person is if they stuff up like that. Unfortunately, a spate of mobile phone recordings and photos or videos of players followed over the next few years.

It was a nightmare and, coming just a few months after the Bulldogs' Coffs Harbour affair, it was not possible to play down the damage that had been done to the game's image – all because a few of the boys wanted to kick on while they were on such a high being together for the opening of an Origin series.

I beat myself up a bit, wondering if I should have tried harder to get the boys to call it quits and not head out again, but I wasn't comfortable pushing my weight around. A few of the fellas had come up to me before we walked home from the Coogee Bay Hotel and said to ask Gus if they could kick on to a pub in Kings Cross, so I had thought I better represent the delegation and take it to Gus, as uncomfortable as I felt being in that position. He told me the only thing that could happen at that time of the morning, with the boys full of grog, was trouble.

When you're in a drinking environment, it's all about looking out for each other and maybe some of the guys thought they should go out together to ensure one of their mates didn't get into trouble. But in the end it is all about taking responsibility for yourself, and not enough responsibility was shown that night. Unfortunately State of Origin camps changed forever from that time because some of the blokes simply took the wrong option.

You wouldn't believe our luck that Phil Gould had invited *Daily Telegraph* reporter Paul Kent to come out with us for the night, with the idea of portraying that it wasn't all about drunken antics but a real positive story about how tight the squad was and how productive those sort of nights were, especially with so many new players. Well, that backfired in a big way. 'Kenty' was with us through to 3 am and I'm sure he wanted to write positive stuff about us, but when so much went down that night, he had to write about what had happened. We could not have picked a worse night to have a chief sports writer on our 'bonding session'.

Another practice that ended after that camp was the handing of a $1000 cash allowance to each player first day. It was just too easy for some of the blokes to have a big night or to gamble the cash away. From then on, we had the money transferred into our bank accounts and it was less likely that anyone would withdraw the whole amount in one hit.

After that camp, too, we never again split up into small groups and did our own thing out in the bars or anywhere else. It was strictly one-in-all-in in a controlled environment; even to the extent we had a get-together at the Clovelly Hotel in the next Origin camp and black plastic was put over the windows so the media cameras couldn't spy on us. We'd make fun, playing pool, having a laugh and maybe a few bets; we were never allowed to go out separately in public. We got used to having security guards around all the time.

It was quite a drastic change at the time; you want a bit of atmosphere, but now we had to create our own. Some of the boys wanted to get 'out' to have a drink and experience some vibe elsewhere, but we had to all pull in the one direction and just accept it as part of the changing face of the public interest and media interest in rugby league. A couple of times we went to the Scu-Bar near Central Station, which was always pumping on a Monday night; we'd have a great night but it was always a case of ringing them beforehand, checking out the security was good, ensuring we had some space to ourselves – it was a great laid-back place.

One really annoying thing was that there has always been this perception of the players making a tradition of getting absolutely blind on a free-for-all the first night or two in camp before knuckling down to the real preparation. I have to admit we had some really big nights, and some funny nights, but it wasn't about writing ourselves off and not remembering anything about it. Those nights were about breaking down barriers and getting to know each other. But as soon as you make the wrong choice, it will make headlines and affect the image of everyone in the team and the whole game of rugby league. You can institute all the curfews you like, and put in place all the minders you like – and I am not saying they don't help – but it is ultimately up to the individual and his own choices. Alcohol is always at the root of such incidents (and I'll have something to say about that later).

For a while after that match the Origin camps were changed from 10 days to seven days, with players coming in on Wednesdays, not Sunday night. (Now it's back to Tuesdays.) The scale of promotions, including at Harvey Norman stores, and function and media commitments, increased enormously. So did the more scientific approach to our preparations, where we had – I think – a backroom staff of 13 in 2008 and an unbelievably hectic schedule before easing down a little from Monday to Wednesday of the game.

As captain in my first game, I was gutted by what had happened. I wouldn't say I felt let down by the players; I just thought they took the wrong option and maybe that was my fault in a way for not stopping it before it began. It was sad that Chris Johns and his fellow manager Gerard Raper resigned their positions over what had happened and we even had policemen and former police as managers and minders after that.

When we went home for the weekend late Friday, I couldn't wait to get out of there; it was the week from hell and there wasn't much focus at all on footy, just ducking and weaving from the unbelievable coverage from the media outlets. I think all of us needed a break over the weekend to catch our breaths and realise what had happened.

When things like that happen it's natural that you get questions from your own partner and family and friends, who want to know where you were and what you were up to after they'd read all the reports. I turned my phone off and just wanted to leave it behind – what was overlooked was that we had an important Origin game to prepare for and for me that game was even more important because it was my first as captain.

When we got back to the Crowne Plaza at Coogee on Sunday afternoon, it was just a circus. One of the hotel management staff, a guy who really looked after us during my Origin days, rang us all just before we arrived and directed us up some back fire stairs to avoid the posse of media that was camped outside the main entry. The boys stood up and apologised to their team-mates and then we held a media conference where they apologised for their behaviour and vowed to concentrate on winning the match. From that point we moved on and had a really good preparation; the events of the previous week only bonded us together.

The fact was we had a young team and quite a few had never experienced Origin before, but the lessons of that week made them understand pretty quickly what was expected of them.

What hit everyone, too, was how the affair devastated Phil

Gould. He'd driven the promotion of Origin so hard and was right behind taking the camp to country towns and suburban ovals and appealing to the New South Wales public to get more emotionally and parochially behind their team. He wrote a really emotional column in the *Sun-Herald* that weekend, saying it was going to be his last series as coach and how he felt betrayed by some players. Here is some of it, which is worth reproducing because it shows how hurt Gus was.

This will now definitely be my last season as New South Wales coach. I am not a football coach any more and I don't want to be. Some of my players have done the wrong thing and I am filthy.

Two of the players come from my club, the Roosters, and I cannot begin to tell you how much that hurts. With others I knew the risks and, unfortunately, they have lived up to my expectations.

I have never demanded that people show me respect but I am not going to put up with this type of disrespect . . .

On Wednesday word started to filter through about problems with the behaviour of some of our players in the early hours of the morning after our team night out. This news hit me like a ton of bricks. I had a sickness and anger in my guts that I had never felt before. I could see where this was going to take us. I knew what the media would do to this and the damage it would cause. I tried to remain cool.

In the early stages I found it hard to get all the facts and, to be honest, the truth was hard to come by. Perhaps the lies or the misrepresentations are the things that have hurt me the most . . .

When I went to bed around 3.15 am on Wednesday I was a very happy man. I spoke to the head of our team security and he informed me that all players were accounted for and that all were safe and sound.

I said to him, 'That's great, mate. What a great night.'

The whole day had been meticulously planned and well executed. It is always a major concern to me when we plan our now famous State of Origin bonding sessions because I know the dangers and I plan to avoid them. In the current climate in particular I knew we had to get it right.

I also knew that this part of our camp can be a lot of fun for the players and has always been an integral part of helping form relationships and communications.

I had considered doing away with the bonding nights and making it an alcohol-free series, but so many of my past players in Origin told me I would be depriving the players of the best part of Origin and how it would not be Origin without it. They were right, too. This process is important and on this occasion we got it right again. I was so pleased with the way it went and so relieved when we got them all home at the desired hour in good shape.

Now, through the selfishness and stupidity of a few players, our Origin campaign is in tatters.

Fortunately, on the football field, there was a happy ending. Shaun Timmins popped a field goal off his left foot from 37 metres in extra-time to break an 8–all deadlock. 'Timmo' was a real Origin player and he had a great game that night, winning the man of the match award. To finish with an extra-time field goal just added to the drama of an emotional week.

With Craig Gower hurting his knee in that game and being sidelined for a few weeks, and Trent Barrett injured, I was more than glad when Gus made the inspired decision to convince the selectors to bring Brad Fittler back for the final two games after he'd retired from rep football in 2001. Brett Kimmorley was also chosen, adding a lot more experience to the team, but he ripped his hamstring at training on the Sunday afternoon – ensuring there was more drama in that series. Trent Barrett had come back from eight weeks out with his 'hammy' injury on the Friday night and killed it for the Dragons but he was advised he'd be a risk in Origin. Matt Orford was called up but ruled out with a calf injury, so the selectors called in Brett Finch, who was 'Freddy's' halfback partner at the Roosters, for his debut.

At first I felt a bit awkward being captain with Freddy there; he was an icon as New South Wales and Australian captain, was my first touring captain, and had a lot more experience than me; but he was great from the first day in camp. He took me aside and said, 'Listen, you are captain' (although the old boy insisted he had a room to himself), 'I'm not going to take over; I'll just help out where I can.' His selection was an absolute godsend and a master move by Gus. I'm sure there was a degree of having him there to look after me as a rookie captain a bit, considering what had happened in the first game; it was a big plus to have an older head for all the younger boys to look up to. I was only 26 and the same age or just older than most of the players and wasn't comfortable coming down on them but Freddy came along and, just the aura that he had, had every-one's respect at training straight away.

A couple of times he pulled me aside after training and

said something like, 'Mate, what's going on? This is what you should have said then; you have to stamp a bit more authority.' He didn't beat around the bush, but I certainly listened and it made me a better captain. It was more in reference to when there was a dropped ball or blokes just didn't have their heads switched on; I'd be thinking, 'C'mon, that's not on,' but Freddy was right in saying I should be saying it in the right sort of way rather than keeping it to myself. I never had one problem coming down on team-mates during a match, but I was reluctant at training until then and never did it socially, before or after; it just wasn't in my nature.

Anthony Minichiello came straight back into the side at fullback and while Benny Hornby played well in game one, Mini is just a freak athletically and knew how to play off Brad Fittler and Brett Finch. At first 'The Mountain Cat' was much quieter than the Anthony Minichiello we were used to, and he seemed just incredibly focused on making amends. But after a day or two he was bouncing around like the Mini we know and love and he played great. We went down 22–18 in that second game, though – the one best remembered for Billy Slater's freakish try – after I thought we dominated the first half but only led 12–6.

It's funny how you look at historic moments like that. Slater's try, after he followed a Darren Lockyer grubber kick and then chipped and chased around Mini, was just brilliant. But when we went into camp for the third game, Gus showed it in a different perspective. Luke Lewis had anticipated what was happening and came from the far side and put in a magnificent chase and almost stopped Slater scoring. That was an Origin play, said Gus.

I was always confident we could win the third game at home. Mark Gasnier came back into the team and made his debut with Matt Cooper. Trent Barrett was back, at halfback, and Ben Kennedy played his first game of the series, so it was the most experienced and probably best team we had in the series. We blew the Maroons away 36–14 and when Freddy scored our last try it was just the perfect ending for him and Gus in State of Origin.

So I got a win in my first series as captain, and was able to repeat it the following year, when Andrew Johns 'did a Freddy' and came back for the final two games and changed the whole mood of the camp with his presence.

Having two blokes of their stature in the New South Wales side for my first two series as Origin captain was a blessing. I didn't change my style a lot, for New South Wales or Newcastle, and never tried to be a person I just wasn't. I'm not one for long speeches, but became more comfortable speaking in groups and in front of the whole team. And I took on board what Freddy told me and said what I was feeling more often; as a player or senior player you don't want to walk away from a meeting thinking, 'I wish I'd said something there.' On the field, I just tried to lead by example, and although I got trapped into becoming a bit too anxious to question referees as captain, I brought that back a lot too in my last two seasons in the NRL and Origin.

From a pretty rough start as New South Wales skipper I was two from two at the end of the 2005 series and feeling a lot more comfortable with the role, even though Joey was still the Newcastle captain and I filled in only when he wasn't there – which was a fair bit due to his injuries at the time.

I never got the hat-trick. In fact I never won a series again as a new breed of Queenslanders under Mal Meninga beat us in six of the next nine games, including two thrashings (30–6 in 2006 and 30–0 in 2008, both in game two). And that weighs heavily on me; we weren't beaten by much in those series and I had been determined to go out a winner in 2008.

But if anyone said to me I'd one day hold the record for most games as captain of New South Wales in State of Origin (15 games), I wouldn't have believed them – and I still struggle to come to grips with it. It's a massive honour and it was a great experience, even with such a dodgy start.

6

GREEN AND GOLD

I FEEL absolutely blessed that I was selected to play 24 Tests for Australia. You hear a lot of players talk about State of Origin being the greatest test of their ability, and you can't argue with that. But representing your country, especially overseas, is the pinnacle.

Physically, it can be tough. The fact we only play one Test a year during our season has meant that only once (2002) in the past decade has there not been an end of year series, making the season long and taxing. I twice went on tours when I should have been back home treating serious injuries, but that just proves how high an honour I placed on wearing the green and gold.

I was fortunate to make my Test debut with a win against New Zealand in Wellington in July 2001 and I was just as lucky to finish my Test career with victory against the Kiwis six years later, getting my only Test man of the match award. The only regretful memory I had in between was becoming the first Australian captain to lose a series since 1978, and that played on my mind for a little while, although I'm over having that blemish on my career now.

It was no surprise to me that Andrew Johns was man of the match in our 28–12 victory in my first Test. It was notable that Trent Barrett and Matt Gidley, who toured with me in the 1995 Australian Schoolboys, played that night too; 'Baz' was also making his debut, as was Petero Civoniceva, Brad Myers, Dane Carlaw and Lote Tuqiri. I remember looking at my green and gold jersey in the dressing room before the match and thinking how lucky I was and how determined I was to do everything in my power to make sure it wasn't a one-off.

An experience I'll never forget was going to Port Moresby to play Papua New Guinea later that year, before the Kangaroo tour that was almost abandoned because of the terrorism fear. It ended up being my only trip to Papua New Guinea and it was a mind-blowing experience that I thoroughly enjoyed.

I remember arriving there, dehydrated and tired after celebrating the Knights' premiership until the day before, and there were over 10,000 locals on a hill overlooking the tarmac.

As we hit the hot air outside, we could hear them chanting and singing and yelling, plenty of them full of betel nut to get them in a celebratory mood. After we went through the passport check and were waiting to get our bags put onto the team minibuses, we were waving to the fans and they were going berserk. When we hit the road into the city, we had to drive through this mass of people. There was a mob right across the road and I was thinking, 'How the hell are we going to get through them?' It was just mayhem.

Well, the driver had no doubts; he hardly slowed down and just ploughed a line through them and didn't care if he took a few casualties with us. I was sitting on the seats across the back when I heard 'bang' and the minibus jumped up like we'd gone over a speed bump. I looked out the back and we'd gone right over the top of a man who got too close trying to see us through the windows. The funny thing was that he got up as quick as lightning, dusted himself off and ran to meet us on the other side of a park that we had to loop around, waving at us as if nothing had happened.

When we got to our hotel – it was more of a compound, really, with a barbed wire fence around it – there were hundreds more standing around the perimeter of the fence, yelling out and waving for us to come over. They had small bags with gifts in them for us and they knew all the players' names. They were obviously big Brisbane fans; they loved Lote Tuqiri especially, plus Darren Lockyer.

We had a terrible time adapting to the heat; just getting through training was hard enough and when we got to the Test venue on the Sunday we had to contend with more than the heat and the fanatical fans. The PNG side included David Westley, Bruce Mamando and Marcus Bai, who'd all played a fair bit of NRL footy, and Stanley Gene, John Wilshire and Tom O'Reilly who had pretty good careers in England. They were flying at our legs and bashing their heads against us as they tackled; they really rattled us for a while. We led only 18–6 at half-time but got our heads used to it and Mark Gasnier started to carve them up a bit in the second half. We won 54–12 in the end. It was a huge occasion for their players and all the fans; there were bodies hanging out of trees outside the stadium, which housed 14,000. Plenty of the spectators had run about 15 kilometres from the city to get to the ground. At least the police didn't have to revert to tear gas, as they had on some other visits by Australian teams.

They are just such fanatical footy fans up there and they'd jump over each other to get some sort of souvenir; even one of your smelly playing socks. We weren't allowed to give them a keepsake because we were warned it would cause a riot; and riots in Port Moresby often ended up with someone being killed.

It can be an unstable place, but I never felt fear at any stage; I just loved it and took it all in. We went for a drive through a village out of the city and this guy was telling us the village was half Queensland supporters and half New South Wales. He told me to make sure the Blues win the next series; 'People die up here when their team doesn't win.' I asked him what he meant and he said there are often brutal brawls after Origin games because the rival supporters get so wound up about the result. He told us people throw television sets through windows and even spark a village riot because they get so emotional and frustrated.

For the rest of my career I got letters from PNG footy fans. They seemed so knowledgeable and didn't mind asking either: 'Can I have your playing kit?'; 'Can I have your boots?'; 'Maybe you sign a jersey for me and send it to me'; or some would settle for something less valuable like a signed poster. Always the letter would include a reference about me being their favourite player of all time. I compared some with Matt Gidley, who went on the tour with me, and he was getting letters from the same people also telling him he was their favourite player.

We were originally scheduled to leave a week after the PNG Test for a six-week tour of England, but the events of September 11 in New York when the hijacked planes hit the Twin Towers saw an end to those plans. Each member of the 25-man touring team was contacted individually and asked if he still wanted to tour after the world had been placed on high alert and British and American troops invaded Afghanistan.

I was one of the majority who voted not to go. There was just so much confusion and hysteria around at the time and, forced to make a decision virtually on the spot, the thought of being on an international flight to London just seemed too risky. The Australian Rugby League called off the tour; but after things became a bit clearer, and we had time to reflect on what was happening, I'm glad we did tour – even though we didn't leave until early November and the tour was reduced to three Tests on three successive weekends.

I was young and keen, injury-free and full of confidence and enthusiasm, and was fortunate to play all three Tests. My first Test against the Poms wasn't a great memory because we lost 20–12 at Huddersfield, and suddenly there was talk about Australia being beaten in a series for the first time in 31 years. But Andrew Johns, Darren Lockyer and Brad Fittler were just awesome in the next two Tests and we won the series. I came back from that tour with so much more confidence in my ability as a player; and confidence is everything in professional sport. To win a grand final, make my Test debut, then go on my first tour to England all in the one year was more than I could have dreamt of and there is no doubt I became such a better player from those eventful nine months of 2001.

That series was the last time I toured overseas anywhere near fully fit (I go into that in the next chapter), but I looked forward to the end of season trips. We had a one-off Test against the Kiwis in 2002, and for the next three seasons the Kangaroos went back to England, with the city of Leeds becoming our second home.

In fact, when we went on the 2003 tour to England for three Tests against Great Britain, which is unfortunately the last time a full Ashes series has been played, it was the third time in four years the Australian team had been to Britain. There was a lot of pressure on players from their clubs to stay back and attend to injuries and be fit for the next NRL season, and that saw 18 leading candidates for tour positions declare themselves unavailable. I was lucky my coach at Newcastle, Michael

Hagan, and the club hierarchy, were happy for me to go as they saw the value in the experience players gained by such tours.

Players who'd played State of Origin or the home Test against New Zealand that year or in 2002, but were unavailable for the tour, included Andrew Johns, Gorden Tallis, Ben Kennedy, Matt Gidley, Timana Tahu, Brent Tate, Shaun Timmins, Trent Barrett, Luke Bailey, Jason Ryles, Mark Gasnier, Justin Hodges, Chris Flannery, Jamie Lyon, Nathan Hindmarsh, Josh Hannay, Steve Menzies and Bryan Fletcher. Those 18 included nine from the winning New South Wales team.

It was a hard situation for players that year; you have to make a professional decision about what is best for your body and what comes first – your injury or your country. If you say you're fit but risk doing something to the injury and making it worse, you're robbing your club that pays the bills.

I had an Achilles injury but was in a situation where I could get by and I wanted to do everything I could to keep my Australian jersey. And as it turned out, it was just about the most enjoyable tour I went on because we had our backs to the wall with so many players missing and all three Tests went down to the wire in the last 10 minutes.

After we'd beaten a French Selection team 34–10 and England A by only 26–22, there was a fair bit of publicity around suggesting it was Great Britain's best chance of winning their first series against us since 1970. And history will show it was probably the closest they came not just to doing that, but to winning all three Tests. We had to come from behind in all three to win and they are unbelievable memories for me.

Darren Lockyer proved on that tour not just what a special player he is, especially when he puts on the green and gold jersey, but just how suited to the English conditions he is. He'd glide on the soft surfaces and the slippery conditions just made him harder to contain when he had the ball. He was unbeliev-able in those three Tests. Locky has a quiet, laid-back personality (although he can be the life of the party when he elects to), but he still has an aura about him, on and off the field. He just has so much passion for the Australian jersey and to him there was never any thought of whether you're from New South Wales or Queensland. In England, he has been brilliant – and no more dominant than in 2003, when he deservedly won the first of his two Golden Boots.

We were back in England via New Zealand a year later and I'll remember the 2004 Tri Nations tour for two reasons. Firstly, I captained Australia for the first time (when Darren Lockyer was injured) and that was an incredible honour and experience. Also, the 44–4 win in the final at Elland Road, Leeds, was the best Australian performance I was involved in – especially the first half, which compared with the first half of the 2001 grand final as close to the most perfect 40 minutes of football I've seen.

We drew 16–all with the Kiwis in Wellington before heading off to England, and then beat them 32–12 at Loftus Road in London. Locky hurt his rib cartilages during the game, although he still won the man of the match award despite only playing 61 minutes. That meant I was chosen by coach Wayne Bennett as captain for our first clash with Great Britain at City of Manchester Stadium (used for the 2002 Commonwealth Games). Again we got the Poms in the last few minutes; it was 8–all with a minute to go when winger Luke Rooney scored millimetres inside the corner post to give us a 12–8 victory. But two weeks later I experienced my first loss to Great Britain, and my first loss as captain, when they beat us 24–12 after they led 18–6 at half-time. It was a big psychological step forward for them because they'd been so close in the previous four matches against us when they thought they probably should have won and I know that really played on their minds. This time they held tight really well in defence and Danny McGuire, whom I now play with at Leeds, burst onto the scene and gave them someone with pace who could really hurt us with the ball.

We went into the Tri Nations final again with all the British media pumping up the Poms' chance of breaking their drought against us. They had a very good team with Paul Wellens, Brian Carney, Martin Gleeson, Keith Senior, Iestyn Harris, Sean Long, Stuart Fielden, Terry Newton, Adrian Morley, Jamie Peacock, Andy Farrell and Paul Sculthorpe in the starting line-up and Danny McGuire off the bench. But we had Locky back and even though we had some newcomers to the Australian team in Shaun Berrigan, Willie Tonga and Luke Rooney in the backs, we had a good, experienced side.

There were nearly 40,000 at Elland Road with pretty big expectations for a home victory, but we just stunned them. Lockyer, who'd moved to five-eighth that year after being the Australian fullback since 1999, just blew them off the park; it was just about the most dominant performance I saw him put in for Australia – and he put in plenty. We scored six tries in the first 26 minutes with Anthony Minichiello scoring two and setting up another with a grubber kick. The Mountain Cat kicking into the in-goal? Yep, it was a planned move and that was one of the features of that first half; so many of our planned moves worked to a tee.

Some of those tries were just incredible and few teams could have stopped us the way we played that night. We led 38–0 at half-time and the Brits' confidence that they would ever beat us must have taken a battering. Everything we tried just stuck. We ended up winning 44–4 as, to their credit, Great Britain stuck at it in the second half as our intensity obviously dropped. It was their biggest Test loss on English soil and that was devastating after all the expectations that had been built up.

There is no doubt the English players have a mental barrier concerning the superiority of the Aussies, which may be as subconscious as it is conscious – caused by them being in a position to beat us so many times in the past couple of decades but Australia getting out of jail. I had a conversation with a few of the Leeds Test players about this in the locker room and when I asked them why Australia beat them in so many close matches, the answer was brief: 'Darren Lockyer'. They have a very big point; as I have already mentioned in this book, Locky was just brilliant when Australia most needed him and sparked so many tight victories for us in England. The British players have to overcome that and believe that they have the players to reverse the situation. Matt Gidley said to me he felt like shaking some of the St Helens players and telling them to stop worrying about how good the Aussies are, that their best players were just as good. But they seemed to put the Aussies on a pedestal and were sometimes mentally beaten before they played the Kangaroos. I just don't think they have enough confidence; unlike the Kiwis, they don't have enough belief against the Australians. And they don't get the right sort of preparation; their season is longer than ours and they don't have anything like our State of Origin as a stepping-stone to becoming a Test footballer since they abandoned their Yorkshire v Lancashire games a few years back.

Another issue I think is that they have a real deep-seated rivalry between clubs, and from what I hear that can cause cliques when they come together in a Test squad, whereas while we have regular high intensity football with the NRL and State of Origin, we get on well with other players and find it easy to combine in representative teams. They really need to get their structure right if they want to beat us regularly because I reckon they definitely have enough outstanding players to do it, and have had for a few years. I go into that more in chapter 26, on the English game.

The Kiwis, maybe because just about all of them play against the Australian players in the NRL and have a real warrior-like lack of fear with the way they play against us, are a different proposition altogether now. (And didn't I find that out in the Tri Nations final the following year, in November 2005. I got a black mark on my record then, although I had no idea how significant it was until I got home from that tour.)

Darren Lockyer was tour captain again in '05 and I was vice-captain, but unfortunately Locky rolled his ankle at training in France before we played a Test there in between Tri Nations matches, putting him out of the rest of the tournament. We beat Great Britain 24–12 with Trent Barrett at five-eighth to go into the final against the Kiwis. They had beaten us 38–28 at Telstra Stadium in Sydney six weeks earlier, which was the first time we'd been beaten in a Test on home soil since 1992. Then we beat them 28–26 in Auckland, with Locky just brilliant again – the real difference between the two sides.

Brian 'Bluey' McLennan was in his first year as Kiwi coach. He is a really passionate coach and I could imagine how he got them together and had them pumped up. Bluey, who coaches me at the Leeds Rhinos, is just so good at keeping things positive, of having trust in his players that they will gradually improve together on tour. That was definitely the case in 2005; the Kiwis seemed to improve and play harder for each other the longer the series went.

We'd had an incredible run of not losing a series since Great Britain last won the Ashes in 1970 (although we lost both Tests in France at the end of the 1978 Kangaroo tour). We were certainly conscious of, and proud of, that record but there is no doubting that extra pressure was always there because of it and it could be a real burden. I'm not using it as an excuse at all, but it was our fifth tour to England in six years. We were probably ripe for the picking.

I wasn't on the 2000 World Cup tour but had been on the four tours since and the sameness about them, being in the terrible English November weather, and the fact so many of us had so much constant football with no genuine off-season, all contributed to our lack of wellbeing by the end of that tour. We'd got out of jail in plenty of Tests over the previous four years – and the majority of those escape acts were inspired by Darren Lockyer, or Andrew Johns, or Brad Fittler before that period; all once-in-a-generation players.

Meanwhile the Kiwis had gradually improved over the years and found a way to beat us. They played a real aggressive, in-your-face style in the Tri Nations final and often drove us back 10 metres in tackles using the 'fireman's chair' (picking up a player completely off the ground and carting him back, with him being powerless to stop it, until the referee calls 'held'). I think five or six times they pushed us back five or 10 metres into the in-goal for a line drop-out. Physically, they got over the top of us.

The scoreline was what made it such a big story: 24–0. We couldn't even post a point – for the first time ever against New Zealand and the first time in a Test since France beat us 6–0 in 1952. The 24-point margin was also equal to Australia's biggest loss in a Test in history . . . and I was the captain.

I had no idea of this history at the time; I was feeling bad enough about losing the Tri Nations series. I was packing my boots into my bag and was just about to leave the stadium with my tail between my legs when our media manager, Polly McCardell, handed me her phone and asked me to do an interview with Peter Peters and Greg Hartley at 2KY in Sydney. If it wasn't the first it must have been the second question: 'How does it feel to be the losing captain for the first series loss in 35 years?' As I got on the team bus to go back to the hotel, I sat down and it hit me how significant the loss was.

By the time we got home the critics seemed to be after our heads. Then Wayne Bennett caused a stir by electing to avoid the media at the airport after a long flight and a draining tour, only adding fuel to the fire. It seemed to become a free-for-all against the Australian team and our performance. So I was glad I wasn't there to field all the questions in the coach's absence; my wife, Kris, joined me for a holiday in Thailand on the way home, as I desperately needed a break.

It was like no one could accept that we could simply be outplayed or that we couldn't win every Test or every series every year. Admittedly we were without Darren Lockyer and Andrew Johns and a few players in the team had played a lot of footy, but that's no excuse – our players, including me, didn't do the job on the day, while the Kiwis did.

It probably makes it a little easier to accept that now that we were beaten in the World Cup in 2008 by the Kiwis; hopefully the critics have come to accept that we can't be the best all the time and Test football is very competitive now, with New Zealand and Great Britain having some top-class Test players and strong all-round squads. That's healthy, isn't it? It's almost like we're in a no-win situation – when we dominated for so long we'd get comments like 'You're only playing New Zealand and Great Britain, so you've got no one to beat, really; it's not a real international sport' and we also had people saying Test football had become boring because we dominated so much; then we were beaten in the Tri Nations and we needed a royal commission and everyone was calling for heads.

Obviously I blamed myself to a degree for a while because, as senior player and captain, I had to ask myself why I didn't see it coming. To me the preparation was the same as any previous game; the simple fact is the Kiwis were just too good for us over the 80 minutes – and deserved their place in history for ending our run. It was one of the longest winning streaks by any international team in any sport and we are still very proud of that; but it had to end at some stage.

I admit that when I returned from that tour I felt football was becoming a grind for me. We'd got the wooden spoon at Newcastle and I just seemed to be forever working on injuries to stay on the paddock and my body was close to breaking point. And I felt pretty deflated about losing the series with such an embarrassing scoreline.

I started to question then how long I could keep putting in the extended seasons with tours at the end of them. But I wanted one last crack at redemption and we had the Anzac Test the following April, then the Tri Nations was being played in Australia for the first time in 2007. I'd busted my guts to keep my Australian position and had the great honour of being captain when Darren Lockyer was not there. I was just praying to get selected for the Anzac Test the next year; all the boys who took part in the final were.

As it turned out, that home Test was the last time I represented Australia.

7

CHANGING PRIORITIES

A FEW months into Kris's pregnancy with our first baby, during the 2006 season, I started to think more about my life outside of football. I hadn't done that enough previously.

I loved the all-consuming life of being a professional footballer; but you naturally have a very selfish lifestyle. You're constantly thinking about the next game and being as fit and prepared as you can. I was a footy nut; I was very regimented and dedicated to getting ready for a game, treating injury and training, but in 2006 I felt my attitude slip. I slackened off a bit with engrossing myself in doing everything I could in rehab and preparation. Suddenly I was going to be a father and husband and began to put more thought into my time away from rugby league, which had dictated my whole life. I felt older and wiser and the penny dropped that I needed more balance in my life.

Ella's birth was due around 2 November (she arrived early, on 26 October), which meant it was close to Australia's Tri Nations match scheduled on 4 November (v Great Britain). I decided that being at the birth, and being there for Kris in the later stages of her pregnancy, had to take priority. That was the major reason I approached the Australian Rugby League and went through the right protocol to apply to miss the series for compassionate reasons.

But also I could feel my body desperately needed a rest; it was at breaking point. I used to be a bull at a gate on tour, playing with injuries that I knew would need ongoing treatment when I got home. In the back of my mind I knew a few months rest, and often surgery, would get me right when the tour finished. But as I got older and smarter, I started to realise I needed to look after my body to prolong my career. I also realised I'd stopped enjoying the week in week out training and playing.

I am grateful that the ARL gave me permission to miss the series. The irony is that, shortly afterwards, I got suspended for six weeks while playing for Newcastle in the finals (for my lifting tackle on Michael Robertson) and would have been unavailable anyway; I was banned from playing in the series even if I had wanted to.

I was criticised in the media by some people, including former Australian players, for opting out of the Tri Nations; some claiming I showed disrespect for the jersey. I would never do that, for any reason.

I had a long chat with Kris; she encouraged me to play and rush home for the birth. I was fortunate to have played in the Anzac Test against the Kiwis, which was one step towards redeeming ourselves after our loss in the Tri Nations final, but it wasn't a full series victory so there was still a score to settle against the Kiwis at the end of the season. In the months that followed, I did all the parenting courses and couldn't wait for the birth and my attitude towards playing in the next Tri Nations series changed. I decided being there for Kris was more important, and I felt sure I was doing the right thing.

Everyone warned me I might not get my jersey back because Cameron Smith, who was then 23, was such a good player; and that proved right. But I was comfortable with my decision, and still am to this day. I think everything happens for a reason and that you should never have any regrets.

When Ella came along, football took a bit of a back seat; I wanted to do other things with my time, and I felt refreshed, with my body and mind getting much-needed rest. A big part of my make-up is feeling good about life and making people around me feel good. I'm pretty 'cruisey' when I am not playing or training and I just started to realise I needed to ease down a bit with my football too, to enjoy other aspects of my life more.

I'm a person who always looks forward and never back and never thinks of 'what ifs' too much. But suddenly I started to look back a bit and think I could have done this and that in life; I should have taken that opportunity to tick off that experience in my life, and in my career, while I was still young enough. When you're single you just train hard, play hard on the field, enjoy yourself with the boys off the field, and that is your entire life. Ella gave me the chance to breathe a bit and sit back and look at my life. I started to think about playing in England and taking Kris and Ella over there to experience a different life in another part of the world. I got so much satisfaction from other things in life, like just playing on the floor with Ella and seeing the joy Kris and I got out of having her around.

I didn't ever retire from Test football, as some people thought; I just made myself unavailable for the 2006 Tri Nations series. But I knew Cameron Smith was a great player and how hard it was to uproot the incumbent; I benefited from that when I was the Australian hooker. I think it was a great strength in our Test record that selectors stood by players who had proven themselves and were consistent players on the Test stage. I would have worn the green and gold jersey with pride if ever selected again, but I knew that would be unlikely. Playing for Australia was the best time of my life, but I was ready to close that chapter and move on. Origin was a different thing, though; I had a burning desire to continue with that as a major motivation in my life.

I don't think a lot of people, or some officials either I reckon, understand just how much effect the hectic international schedule has on players and how many sacrifices players have made to represent Australia. But I also know there's no easy solution because, with the English season being played at the same time as ours, the only opportune time for Tests is at season's end.

While in France on tour as far back as 2003, a few senior players had a meeting with Australian Rugby League officials Geoff Carr and Colin Love, because there was concern the workload was going to affect a lot of players. They listened to our views and outlined plans that there wouldn't be a tour the following year. In the meantime, though, Wayne Bennett was strongly promoting the Tri Nations concept; and when the first Tri Nations in '04 was seen as such a success, it kept going almost annually. From memory, Shane Webcke, Darren Lockyer, Craig Fitzgibbon, a couple of other players and I were at that meeting. We understood that the international federation had to recoup massive losses from the 2000 World Cup, but at what risk – burning the best players out? One of our issues was that we always went to the northern hemisphere and we felt it would be so much better to play at home where there was less travel, better weather and we could have a day off here and there to go home to see our families.

I knew that I was taking my body past its limits at times – and I was not alone. Having Australian tours to England in 2000, 2001, 2003, 2004 and 2005 came at a physical cost, because too many players just weren't able to give their bodies adequate rest – and paid for it. I think it is no coincidence that Darren Lockyer, Anthony Minichiello, Nathan Hindmarsh, Craig Fitzgibbon and I went through bad periods with constant injuries, largely because our bodies were too fatigued.

I'd like to see less touring because I fear more players are going to get burnt out. When the Australian team goes over to England and France for the Quad Series in October 2009, it will be the first time the Kangaroos have had to go to the UK since we lost the Tri Nations title there in 2005, which I think is good in the sense that it makes an English tour more of a novelty and an opportunity our players really aspire to, just like the Kangaroo tours of the past that used to be every four years.

Australian captain Darren Lockyer hasn't missed a Test series or World Cup since he came into the Australian side in 1999, playing 47 Tests in that time, and that is just phenomenal, especially considering the size of the bloke. There comes a time when you have to restore your body. The injuries you carry throughout the season need to be worked on; other parts of your body take extra strain to compensate for the injured areas, and they need respite too. Whether you want to get quicker, stronger or want to bring new skill into your game, you don't get a chance to work on it if you don't have a genuine off-season. I don't think enough of our Test players have been given that over a long period. And the mental burden can't be under-estimated either; you need to get away from the game and have a genuine holiday and give your mind a period to relax.

I'm all for enhancing the international scene, but to do that you have to cut the competition to allow for it. Look at the Super 14 competition, which has 13 rounds (and it used to be 11 when it was a Super 12). This allows plenty of time for international matches, which attract huge interest. I know we can't go to that short a season, but 20 to 22 club games would be perfect.

I used to love it when I was a kid – the fact there was a Kangaroo tour every four years and the Poms toured here every four years; there was such a build-up of expectation. Now we're playing the Kiwis in-season every year, then at the end of season four out of five years we go to England for three Ashes Tests or a Tri Nations (or a Quad Nations now). The novelty has gone. Players and the fans don't get a rest.

I hope the administrators can find the right balance. The World Cup was a great success in Australia in 2008 and I think it's good bringing France in to make it a Quad Series in 2009; the more regular Test football the French get the better it will be for them. Les Catalans play in the English Super League, and Toulouse entered the National League One (the division under Super League) in 2009, so the game should improve in France.

If officials think the Quad Series is the way forward, then maybe just having that every two years (one in England/France then the next in Australia/New Zealand) with a World Cup say every five years, plus continuing with the one-off Anzac Tests between Australia and New Zealand, is a good schedule. That would offer an end of season schedule of: Quad Nations (England/France) – break – Quad Nations (Australia/NZ) – break – World Cup; then start the revolving schedule again. That would at least give Test players two out of five seasons to rest up and have a full off-season of recovery, and I reckon that would make a hell of a difference to their long-term wellbeing and keep a lot more of our best players fitter and keener.

During the years when there is no Quad Nations or World Cup we could have Samoa and Tonga play one-off Tests against

Australia or New Zealand and maybe they could tour England every four years. There are options there.

Then again, maybe we need to think right outside the square to give international rugby league a whole new dimension that might take the game to places we've not thought of in recent years . . .

8

TAKE ON THE WORLD!

I THINK it's time we revolutionised the international game and made a concentrated effort to develop its 'brand' on the world stage. We've hardly expanded the game during my career – despite the popularity of Samoa, Tonga, Fiji and Papua New Guinea during the 2008 World Cup in Australia. And we seem to always take the easy option of playing games against Great Britain in England (12 of 14 from 2001 to 2008). Until 2009, when France come into a Quad Series in England, the only high-profile Tests were between Australia, New Zealand and Great Britain. From 2001 to 2008 (up to the World Cup), Australia played 34 Tests – 18 against New Zealand, 14 against Great Britain and two against France – all but 12 outside Australia. There is just too much 'same old, same old'.

It's about time we got a bit creative and had a genuine program to expand our markets, otherwise we're going to fall behind competing sports and, I believe, ultimately cause more players to leave the game. Cricket has shown the way with variations of the game through, originally, one-day cricket and lately with Twenty20, which has created a whole new market and dimension. Rugby union for many years has had its Sevens concept, with the 'world' tournaments now being played in Dubai. Countries like Kenya, Argentina, the USA and Fiji are among the best in the world at it – which creates amazing interest, as they aren't equipped to compete at the highest level in the traditional 15-a-side form of the game.

Rugby league is battling for income and some NRL clubs are really doing it tough; I expect there will be massive concerns about the funding needed to sustain the game in coming years. Yet we have never looked seriously at going outside the traditional parameters of two domestic competitions (in the UK and Australia) and three State of Origin games a year – besides the World Cups: 2000, which was a financial failure in England, and 2008 in Australia.

I reckon it's about time we got creative and looked at a Nines version of rugby league – a highly promoted international series with nine players on the field. That was one of the innovations of Super League I liked back in 1996 and '97 – I loved watching it. Yet we don't even have the 'World' Sevens anymore – it was last held in Sydney in 2003.

Imagine the football, and the players, an annual World Nines would create. And I would only play it once every two or three years in Australia or England or New Zealand. In the other years we could take it to the rest of the world. And if the International Federation won't invest the right money and resources (including smart marketing people) to make it happen, I'd contract it out to an external company to organise and promote it; and I'd alternate it between places like Dubai, or Japan, or the USA or other potential new markets for the game. If rugby union can do it, why can't we? After all, we have a better game. I'd call it Super Nines or something like that, or even Rugby Nines International League to cash in a bit on the world identification of 'rugby', as in rugby union. I'd have turnovers where we would normally have scrums and the team surrenders possession if the dummy-half is tackled, so as to open up the game. I would play the games using 20 minute halves.

I think it would be an exciting concept and the major thing is it would attract new fans in new markets; we seem to be watching world sport go by as we do nothing to expand rugby league. And that's a great pity, because it is a great product. I reckon this could be a good way into the American market that we have spoken about for so long, but done little about.

Rugby league has to decide what sort of identity it wants. Does it want to be an international game and develop new markets, and potential new income, or stick to the same old traditional boundaries of northern England, New South Wales and Queensland and a few clubs scattered elsewhere – with regular Tests only between Australia, Great Britain and New Zealand? The 2008 World Cup was seen as a great success and recorded a profit of $5 million. Is there any plan to use that money to broaden the game's appeal? If there is, it hasn't been communicated very well. We don't even have a 'real' inter-national administrative body or office – just the International Federation, which, as far as I know, involves delegates from a few countries meeting a couple of times a year.

It seems as if it has been all about protecting club compe-titions and ensuring they create enough income to keep the players in the game, instead of thinking outside the square a bit. Why do we play so many Tests and World Cups in England – because it seems an easy way to get crowds and make money? Even the World Club Challenge has been played in England every single time except once (Brisbane v Wigan in 1993) – despite it being staged in atrocious weather in February – simply because it's less risky than trying to market it and get a big pre-season crowd in Sydney or Brisbane. All it does is provide an advantage for English clubs to claim they are 'world champions' despite it being a one-off pre-season game with playing conditions very much slanted in their favour. Why not take it to Dubai, Hong Kong or Japan and promote it as the championship for the world 'rugby' football league.

Rugby union's Sevens is fun and it's spectacular and it is attracting new fans. There were 24 nations playing in the three-day series in Dubai in March 2009 that was beamed to 200 countries via 27 international broadcasters, with Wales beating Argentina in the final. For the first time they had a women's world Sevens there too, which proved really popular, with 16 nations competing including China, Uganda, Italy, Nether-lands, Spain and Brazil (it was won by Australia). Kenya and Samoa made the men's Cup semi-finals, ahead of Australia, England and New Zealand. Tunisia and the Arabian Gulf had teams competing. They also had a World Series in San Diego in February 2009, won by Argentina (they beat England).

If we don't do something about expanding our game to more parts of the world, cashing in on potential new markets and revenues and giving our best players the opportunity to pick up good extra money, other parts of the world are going to pick off our best players. A player can go to Japan or France to play rugby and get twice the money he can get putting his body through the grind for 26 to 30 weeks in the National Rugby League – and play fewer games. What are players going to do when they get that opportunity?

We've been to the USA a few times, with a State of Origin game in 1987 and the Kangaroos playing there on the way home from the 2005 Tri Nations. But we've never seriously followed up and we've never attempted to have a crack at other international markets. All it does is put pressure on generating more income out of a cluttered Australian market, which is predominantly based in New South Wales and Queensland (14 of 16 teams), and the restricted British market bordered by Cheshire, Lancashire and Yorkshire (11 of 14 teams).

For starters, in a World Nines we could have Australia, New Zealand, England, Ireland, France, Scotland, Wales, the USA, Samoa, Tonga, Papua New Guinea, Fiji and maybe teams from South Africa, Italy, Russia and other countries – and who cares if some of them are rugby union players? With the popularity and hopefully good income from the tournaments, money could be put into developing the game in other countries and a big bonus payment could be offered to the teams making the final. Our best players could pick up good extra cash if the tournaments attracted big crowds and good television income.

As an example of the line-ups the Nines could feature, here are my squads, based on what I have seen in England and at the 2008 World Cup; but I'm sure there are other candidates I might have overlooked. This is just a sample:

AUSTRALIA: Darren Lockyer, Greg Inglis, Johnathan Thurston, Israel Folau, Justin Hodges, Brett Stewart, Billy Slater, Cameron Smith, Ben Creagh, Luke Bailey, Anthony Laffranchi, Kurt Gidley.

NEW ZEALAND: Benji Marshall, Manu Vatuvei, Lance Hohaia, Greg Eastwood, Isaac Luke, Iosia Soliola, Sam Perrett, Jeremy Smith, Krisnan Inu, Steve Matai, Roy Asotasi, Simon Mannering, Frank Pritchard.

FIJI: Wes Naiqama, Akuila Uate, Jarryd Hayne, Ashton Sims, Jayson Bakuya, Darryl Millard, John Sutton, Semi Taduala plus probably some raw untapped talent in Fiji, where players play rugby union and league.

TONGA: Feliti Mateo, Cooper Vuna, Fetuli Talanoa, Michael Jennings, Tony Williams, Eddie Paea, Mickey Paea, Lopini Paea, Tevita Leo Latu, Willie Manu, Richard Fa'aoso, Fraser Anderson, Louis Anderson.

SAMOA: Frances Meli, George Carmont, David Faiumu, Tony Puletua, Ben Roberts, Lagu Setu, Ali Laui'ititi, Kylie Leuluai, Terence Seuseu, David Solomona, Howard Hansen, Matt Utai, Misi Taulapapa.

ENGLAND: Leon Pryce, James Roby, James Graham, Ade Gardner, Jamie Peacock, Gareth Ellis, Kevin Sinfield, Rob Burrow, Danny McGuire, Sam Burgess, Jon Wilkin, Kyle Eastman, Ryan Atkins.

I can't see any reason not to give it a go. We could go back to the traditional tours to England every four years, or Quad Nations every two years (every four in Australia–New Zealand, every alternate four in England and France), which would give the elite players every second year off. But we could run a three- or four-day Nines tournament every year, offering good prize money and good contract money for the selected marquee players.

I reckon it's a no-brainer. It just needs a bit of imagination and a bit of courage – and probably one big backer. Look at the initial reaction about Twenty20 cricket – it was supposed to be nothing but a one-season wonder that people wouldn't take to. Look at it now. The World Rugby Nines League could be our answer to Twenty20!

9

FROM VILLAINS TO HEROES

IT WAS the only time I got into any public bother, and became the centre of a 'scandal'. It's not something I am proud of; and I deeply regret it even though reports of events were a massive beat-up. But the irony is that the affair steeled the Newcastle Knights and gave us the momentum to win the 2001 premiership.

And I can reveal now that it was a case of mistaken identity that landed me in a bit of trouble. Andrew Johns was the true culprit.

We'd beaten North Queensland in the second-last round of the competition, on a Saturday night in Townsville, and had a cracker of a night out celebrating the win. It was one of those times when everyone enjoyed each other's company and I remember thinking, 'Gee, we've got a good spirit in this team.'

We had a swim the next morning and naturally a few of the boys were pretty seedy; from there we headed straight to the airport for the trip to Brisbane, where we had to pick up another flight to Sydney. The club rule was we weren't allowed to drink at the airport; it just wasn't a good look with so many people around. Joey, always wanting to be a creative leader, had 'invented' the 'alcoholic macchiato' to circumvent the rule. What we'd do is get styrofoam cups at the airport, pour beer into it and think no one knew we were sipping beer instead of coffee. When our plane from Brisbane to Newcastle was delayed for over an hour, and with spirits high from the night before, Joey decided to break out some 'macchiatos' and a few of us went to a quiet bar to have a few stubbies. Still topped up from the night before, a couple of beers soon went to the head and it didn't take much before we got a bit rowdy.

As we were boarding our flight, we were, let's just say, high-spirited – nothing sinister, just enjoying good light-hearted fun. Joey tripped up on the air bridge and when we got on the plane the airline staff went straight for me, and claimed I was the one who tripped over and was drunk. I protested that it definitely wasn't me, but was told not to make a scene. Next moment I was being told, 'Come with me,' and staff went to take me off the plane. A few of the boys followed me and I was taken in for a chat with the captain, who asked me if I knew my responsibility and that no one could enter an aeroplane if they were intoxicated. I told him that I might have had a few drinks but I was fine and I was about to go to sleep, and he wouldn't hear another word out of me. The captain told me to make sure he didn't and he allowed me to go down towards the back of the plane and take my seat. When I sat down, it just hit me what had happened; the boys were giving me heaps and I realised how many people were watching me. Typically I started to stress a bit and, with a few beers on board, became sick in the guts and reached for the sick bag. Now, my team-mates can testify that, when I'm sick, I'm an awfully violent vomiter but on this occasion I was just dry-retching.

I then dropped off to sleep but a few of the boys started

singing songs and were a bit loud and Joey was guilty of swearing at one stage. Once we were well into the flight people were texting or emailing left, right and centre, and by the time we arrived back in Newcastle the news had leaked out that there was a ruckus involving the Newcastle Knights on an Ansett flight. Our media manager, Steve Crowe, said his phone was ringing off the hook. It was the first encounter for me with how quick people are to have their one moment of fame and dob in recognisable sports people. All the media have to do is put 'alleged' in front of anybody's claims and that seems enough for them to run with an allegation, whether it is true or not.

It was on talkback radio that afternoon, and on the back page of the *Daily Telegraph* next day, with a headline: 'PLAYING UP – Passengers, crew accuse Newcastle Knights of misbehaving on flight'. The NRL came down hard on the club, with CEO David Moffett next day announcing the club had been fined $35,000. The *Daily Telegraph* ran a heading on the Tuesday: '$35,000 Knight cap; NRL acts after drunken disgrace on flight', with sub-headings on photos of four players, saying: 'Andrew Johns, swearing, disorderly conduct; Danny Buderus, vomiting, drunken behaviour; Ben Kennedy, disorderly conduct; Matthew Gidley, disorderly conduct.'

One claim was that I spewed over an innocent passenger, which was totally untrue. I dry-retched into a bag and I had only team-mates around me anyway. One bloke was quoted as saying several players were vomiting, plus abusing other passengers and the crew. Someone rang up the radio saying we were spitting. None of that was true. However, Andrew Johns and club captain Billy Peden offered apologies for our behaviour at a press conference on the Monday.

We were out of line. We shouldn't have been drinking at the airport; we shouldn't have been so rowdy; and it would have been annoying for other passengers. It is the only black mark against my character during my career, so I take that very seriously and am very regretful about my behaviour in being under the weather in public. It was a lesson to all of us that we have to be careful how we act in public and how our actions affect the image of not just us but our club and the game. But we were ambushed by people feeding exaggerated reports to the media, who had a field day with it. It was just totally over-blown. Our football manager, Mark Sargent, even spoke to the Ansett security chief and got a copy of the flight log, and spoke to some people who were quoted as claiming this and that, and they all admitted that what had happened was nowhere near as excessive as what had been accused.

There was a lighter side to it. A few people sent me spew bags in the mail or threw them at me at the next game; and I got a few nice letters from fans giving me support.

The players gathered for the game review session on the Tuesday, and we had the newspapers in the room, and we got together and said, 'We were out of line but this is just over the top; we've been ambushed by the Sydney media'. It bonded us together even closer and we developed a real siege mentality and just bunkered down with an 'It's us against the world' attitude, and more so us v Sydney, extending what was already a deep-seated rivalry. We spoke about where we were with just one competition game to go, certain of a top four finish; but what were we going to do about it? We knew that we'd had such a great opportunity to win the competition the previous season but didn't go on with it, and that still hurt. I still believe 2000 was our best chance to win the competition in any season I played first grade, other than when we went all the way in 2001.

We spoke about how we were in the same situation as we had been the previous year when we let it slip and how rare opportunities like this were. We made a pact that day, as a group, that we weren't going to let the chance slip. Amidst all the grief we were copping, and it went on for days, we rallied and said, 'Stuff this, we'll show them how tight we are; we'll answer back with our football.'

Although Darren Albert had been put out for the season with injury the previous week, Andrew Johns returned from suspension against the Cowboys and there was a feeling in the side that we had every team's measure if we just put it together. While Parramatta had broken all these points-scoring records, we weren't far behind them with our attack; they had scored 839 points in 26 rounds and we were second with 782. But we were inconsistent, especially in defence, and had conceded 639 points – 24.5 a game – the worst of all the top eight teams.

But it's all about momentum and having your best players fit at the back end of the season; the return of Joey in Towns-ville, and the extra incentive the coverage of our behaviour on the way home generated, took our momentum to a new level. I always thought we had an extra 'gear' in us that few other teams had that year. When we decided to press the button, we could blow teams off the park.

The following Saturday night we played Penrith, who were running last, at Marathon Stadium and just blew them away. We won 60–18 after leading 30–6 at half-time (and 18–0 after 14 minutes). We were just so pumped up that night and I remember sitting there in the dressing room after the game thinking, 'I know we can win this title; if we play like that again no one can stop us.' We just had this extra edge about us; a catch-us-if-you-can confidence. And no one did stop us.

10

THE NIGHT OF KNIGHTS

IT TOOK me a while to get over how we bombed out of the 2000 season. We led the Sydney Roosters 16–2 at half-time in the preliminary final and should have had a grand final appearance wrapped up, meaning we could send Matthew Johns and Tony Butterfield out in real style. We were beaten 26–20 and it was hard to come to grips with how the season ended so abruptly. I still regard that as a premiership that slipped away; we could have beaten Brisbane if we had stayed alive one more week.

Going into the 2001 season, I felt a combination of determination to avenge what happened in 2000, but a bit of uncertainty about what sort of challenge we would mount. Our three most experienced players had gone, in 'Butts', Matty and David Fairleigh, and we had a rookie coach in Michael Hagan, Andrew Johns reluctantly took over as captain and we had some talented young blokes who hadn't played much first grade.

You could tell from the start of the season, though, that Andrew Johns was going to go to a new level in his career as a senior player. He didn't want the captaincy at first but 'Hages' finally talked him into being the skipper on the field while

Billy Peden would be the club captain, so that Joey only had to lead the team once we crossed the white stripe and Billy could handle the media conferences, and club functions. That took a lot of pressure off Joey and off the team too.

It was Joey's time to shine and he thrived with the extra responsibility; his presence on the field quickly gained this aura to it. It was as if, with Matty gone, Joey's individuality came out on the field and he became comfortable being the person who had to lead us from the front. He just played on instinct and started dominating the team with his own performances and by feeding information to other players on the field about how we should play. He was just awesome that season. So too was Ben Kennedy. To have him and Joey in probably career-best form in the same year was an amazing advantage for us and it was no surprise they were the stand-out players in the grand final.

The biggest question mark going into the season was that we didn't have a five-eighth. When you think of it, since 1989 Newcastle had had either Michael Hagan or Matthew Johns in the number six jersey, and both were dominant tactical players. The only player we had with any sort of first grade experience there was Matt Gidley, who came through the juniors as an outstanding five-eighth, and most people thought he was probably destined to succeed Matty. He was the obvious choice in the situation, especially as we had so much depth in the three-quarters with Adam MacDougall, Timana Tahu, Mark Hughes and Darren Albert. When all were fit, someone had to miss out on being in the starting line-up.

But Gids was earning so much praise for doing some freaky things in the centres, and had such a lethal combination going with Timana, we didn't really want to break that up.

Hages decided to go with Sean Rudder at six. He'd played second row, either starting or from the bench, for the previous two seasons and filled in at five-eighth a couple of times when Matthew Johns was injured. The fact you had the game's best halfback inside him, Ben Kennedy and Steve Simpson either side, smart players in Matt Gidley and Timana Tahu on the right and Mark Hughes and Adam MacDougall or Darren Albert on the left and Robbie O'Davis coming up from fullback, meant 'Ruddsy' had a lot of experience and class around him. So we didn't need someone to create a whole lot for the team; our five-eighth just had to be a good ball distributor, able to get an early ball, be consistent and defend well. That was the best thing about Ruddsy: he became a consistent player that year and really benefited from having an ex-five-eighth as his coach and Joey inside him. He picked up little things from Joey like where and when to run, the 'shapes' we needed in attack, how to utilise our strike-power but not overplay our hand; that was perfect for Ruddsy, who had blokes running in the right holes off him. He had a really good passing game and, like me, didn't have to worry too much about a kicking game because Joey was the master at that; no one in the game could kick effectively as consistently as he did.

It was always amusing to his team-mates that Ruddsy came in for some criticism from the media. The rest of the team had a lot of faith in him and he was really popular, and reliable. He trained hard, put his head down in his own quiet manner and had a really enjoyable year with all the boys.

With a new coach, new captain and new five-eighth, and Josh Perry having to step up to replace Tony Butterfield (who was captain in 2000 and had been at the club since 1988) in the front row, it was only natural it would take us a few games to get into gear. After five rounds we were eighth and had won two, lost two and drawn one and been flogged 42–8 by Brisbane. But we gradually started to find our way and won eight straight. But in the sixth match of that run Andrew Johns tore his medial ligament and missed six games. We tried Matt Gidley at five-eighth and moved Sean Rudder to halfback for five games, then I went to halfback and Ruddsy back to five-eighth for the last one, a 40–0 thrashing against Parramatta. We won the first two games while Joey was missing, then lost four straight, and typically everyone was writing us off as a one-man team.

I thought we'd toughed it out pretty well when Joey wasn't there but, of course, we were going to be down a fair bit with the most influential player in rugby league missing. He had this powerful ability to lift everyone around him, but Joey couldn't do everything on the field himself; he needed 12 players around him pulling their weight too. I admit, though, that we used to panic a bit when he was missing because he had such a dominant on-field personality which our game revolved around, plus the best kicking and passing game in the NRL.

But in that 2001 team we had nine players who were, or went on to become, internationals (Robbie O'Davis, Matt Gidley, Timana Tahu, Adam MacDougall, Andrew Johns, Ben Kennedy, Steve Simpson, Josh Perry and me); plus three more who played State of Origin (Mark Hughes, Darren Albert and Clinton O'Brien); and two New South Wales Country reps (Matt Parsons and Daniel Abraham). People overlook that when they say what a boil-over it was that we beat the hot-shot Parramatta team.

Our problem was our inconsistency in defence; we'd defend well one week and the next week leak a lot of points. We knew the toughness in defence was there, we just had to put it together. In the back of our minds, though, was that we knew we had the ability to put the cleaners through a team.

I knew some teams didn't have that extra gear to go with us. I used to call it 'flat-lining' – when you were just sticking at a level and couldn't play any better; there was no more improvement in you, then the other team goes up another gear and you can't go with them. In 2001 we had all these extra gears and Joey was the one who would flick a switch and take the whole team with him. An incredible statistic from the season was that we lost only three of the 21 games Joey played.

And we had so much belief in ourselves and confidence from the second-last round when we beat the Cowboys in Townsville. We put 60 points on the Panthers the next week, beat the Roosters 40–6 in our first finals match and then made the grand final on a tough 18–10 win against the Sharks.

A lot has been said about the contrasting moods of the Knights and Parramatta players leading up to the grand final, and I can only say it was obvious to us that the Eels looked tense, while we were incredibly relaxed. I'll never forget how their players walked into the grand final breakfast in their black turtleneck skivvies and wouldn't even look at us; didn't acknowledge us. Maybe it was a ploy by them but we were having fun, taking photos of the audience and feeling just so relaxed. Hages and Joey had to front the traditional media conference after the breakfast and all of a sudden there was a cough at the back of the room and this voice came out with, 'Michael . . . is it true you've had a problem with Andrew Johns and you regard Mark Hughes very highly and are thinking of making him captain for this game?' Everyone turned around and here was 'Booze' (Mark Hughes) with his big, cheesy grin. It typified how relaxed we were in the lead-up compared to Parramatta, who couldn't escape all the expectations that came from breaking so many scoring records, winning the minor premiership by five points and being reminded that the club hadn't won a premiership for 15 years.

Joey and BK were revved up straight afterwards, telling everyone in the team that 'we had them' and that we were 'inside their heads'. They were the team leaders and we all just fed off that.

Few people outside of Newcastle gave us a chance, which only acted in our favour. *Rugby League Week* magazine had a front page headline saying, 'UNBEATABLE. Why the Eels are specials'. In the *Sunday Telegraph* the day of the game, eight of 10 tipsters picked Parramatta, with Laurie Daley and Chris Anderson saying they would win by 14. Only Phil Rothfield and Barry Toohey picked us; and Parramatta's popularity with the experts was similar everywhere else.

I don't think anyone expected what we produced in the first half of the grand final. We failed to complete only one of our 20 sets in the first half, and that was a pass from me at dummy-half that was ruled forward. Not one other person made a mistake. Steve Simpson was just devastating on the right side attack, Ben Kennedy was rampaging on the left, Billy Peden – who played most of that season without a medial ligament – scored two tries; Joey's kicking game was just perfect, despite him having a hip-flexor problem that affected his kicking action. Josh Perry and Matt Parsons were just rolling us forward at the start of each set and the score just kept going up in sixes.

Joey just about always had some sort of injury problem and you had to cuddle him and pamper him; be there for him. I roomed with him and he so often questioned whether he'd be okay in the game, and I had to say, 'You'll be right, mate, you'll get through.' I'm not sure if he did it to take pressure off himself, or if it was a mental ploy to challenge himself more. I kept saying to him during the grand final, 'How you going, mate? How's your hip flexor?' He'd reply, 'It's gone,' and I kept saying, 'C'mon, mate, you'll be right.' All the boys had to pat him on the back and build him up. On a serious note, though, Joey was tough and I've never seen someone shut out pain or outside influences then flick a switch and perform as brilliantly as he could. He was definitely inconvenienced by his hip-flexor problem and to win the Clive Churchill Medal was a hell of an effort.

The first half was the most perfect half of football I've ever experienced; it was like poetry in motion: 40 minutes that every player and coach dreams about. Every one of us was in the groove; everyone was hitting the right holes; we produced the match plan to a tee. In fact, we forgot where we were to an extent; it was like you were just having fun with your mates; and you overlooked the fact that there were 80,000 or so watching you in the stadium. It was almost surreal.

It was hard to know what to say at half-time when we led 24–0. It was all about just defending; we could be legitimately accused of shutting up shop too much in the second half. It wasn't good that we let Parramatta come back and we only won by six, 30–24; but it was hard not to take the foot off the pedal a bit. We always had an extra gear if we had to use it; and we did lead 30–12 with seven minutes to go.

It's interesting to look back on that night, and that season, with the benefit of so much hindsight now that I've finished my Australian career and that was the only NRL grand final I won. (I hope I can win the English equivalent before I retire.) I've never been one to reflect; I never go back and watch games or read old articles. My attitude is that it distracts you too much from what is in front of you now. But as my career gets towards the end, I've started to reminisce a lot more, particularly while recording my life in rugby league for this book. I'm starting to appreciate things more and how hard you have to work to achieve them.

I realise now how rare it is for all the circumstances to come together to put you in the frame to win a competition – having a good enough team; having few injuries during the season, to put you in a position to make the finals; having all the key players fit and firing at the end of the season; having a bit of luck; knowing that the bloke next to you is going to perform when the heat is on; and having that special player or two who can pull out the big plays that win a competition. The stars never aligned at Newcastle again after 2001. We had teams good enough to win in 2002 and 2003, and probably 2006, but injury hit us at the wrong end of the season.

I think of the players who have had such great careers but never got the satisfaction of winning a grand final. The one that comes to mind is Nathan Hindmarsh, whom I have so much respect for. No one more deserves to do a grand final victory lap when you look at what he has given Parramatta and what a fantastic, consistent performer he has been for 12 seasons. He's had some great years and played in some very good teams, but never won a premiership. That was his best shot that night, but someone had to walk away without a championship ring. Brian Smith is the same; that was his third grand final as a coach but I think it's fair to say that was his best shot, and he's been coaching since 1984 (including some seasons in England). I can't describe how fortunate I am that that was my biggest shot too, and we won.

I remember being so emotionally drained when I finally got to the dressing room after the presentations, victory lap and all the photos. I caught up with friends, fans and familiar faces as we went around the stadium, and it was unbelievable to see so many people in the crowd who had played a part in my long journey since I started playing football in Taree. When I sat down in the shed, I just slumped to the ground and closed my eyes and stopped for the first time in hours; I was completely spent. Then we had our song to sing, all the media and the well-wishers came and we got pumped up on adrenalin again. It was after midnight before we got away, and had to catch the team coach back to Newcastle.

That bus trip home is probably the most special, and private, memory of winning the grand final. After all the hype and occasion, there were just the boys and the coaching staff for three hours in the confines of the bus. We put the trophy up the back and everyone crammed in the last few rows to be close to it; it would have been a great photo. And the more beers we had, the more deep, meaningful and emotional our conversation became. We were just sitting there as mates, contemplating what we'd just achieved together and how fortunate we were.

But what made it more memorable was the number of cars along the route with Knights flags hanging out the windows and all the vehicles tooting their horns; people reaching out and waving to us with clenched fists as if to say, 'We did it!' Our bus driver from Sid Fogg's, Graham (who is the owner), slowed down so we could take it in; the trip took over three hours. People were stopped on overhead bridges waiting for us to pass and scream support, and we'd slow down and suck up every bit of the incredible atmosphere. Then to have 15,000 at the stadium when we arrived there – unimaginable! Moments like that you never forget.

The other thing that always springs to mind when I think of grand final night 2001 was Joey receiving the Clive Churchill Medal from Joyce Churchill and looking at the cameras and singing out, 'All day . . . all day.' I knew exactly what the message was. There was this bloke we'd come across whenever we stayed in Sydney whose nickname is 'All Day'; he's a bit of a notorious legend in the eastern suburbs. He'd be at training sessions or out and about. He's well known by the footy boys in Sydney and he'd always be at the races too. I don't even know what his real name is, but whenever you said hello or goodbye, he'd respond with, 'All day . . . all day,' meaning he lived for good times all day. That was exactly what Joey was planning to do – well, for three days really. A few days later one opportunist entrepreneur brought these hats to us with 'All Day' written on them and we wore them during our prolonged celebrations; I think Matt Parsons slept in his; he never took it off.

You can never take away the fact that the 1997 team won the Knights' first title in the greatest grand final I've ever seen, but there was always that little criticism that it wasn't a 'combined' competition. By winning in 2001 we set the record straight. And it was also the first night grand final ever played.

I know some people think it's a bit of over-the-top 'blokey' sort of stuff, but you do become brothers for ever when you win a premiership. Of all the years I played footy, these are the blokes I went through the season with when I won my only competition. But it's not just what happens on the field that makes that team special, but the times we shared off the field and the characters we had.

Robbie O'Davis was one of the fittest and most courageous little players to have played the game. He was always thinking outside the square in how to prepare himself physically for a match and in his rehab treatments and was both a genuine footballer and an athlete; he had great footwork, a swerve and brilliant hands and was just sensational as a support player. He hadn't played a lot of games over the previous three seasons and thought he had a point to prove in 2001. He did that.

Adam MacDougall was on fire towards the end of the season and I can still see him and Mark Hughes sitting there in deep conversation talking about how to improve their combination on the left side, while Matt Gidley and Timana Tahu got all the raps on the right. You just knew 'Doogs' would fire in the big games. I loved playing with him; he's an interesting, highly intelligent character.

Mark Hughes was my housemate then, so I knew what he put into his game. He had a physique better suited to badminton but he gained so much respect for the way he put himself into the firing line; I lost count of the times he threw his body in front of a much bigger opponent on the tryline and brought him down. 'Boozy' lived by the club motto 'be the player others want to play with' and he achieved that. He was the joker in the team but he took his footy very seriously, was pedantic in his preparation and would never change a system that worked for him; and he never had any fingernails because he chewed them so much while thinking about rugby league. He was totally all for the team.

I call Timanu Tahu 'the Rolls-Royce' as far as the athletic ability of any player I've come across. Plenty of times that year he ran 40 metres or more to score a try, then slam-dunked the ball over the crossbar. 'T' had freakish talent and a physique to match; it was almost as if he was too powerful for his body and it just snapped at times. He was blessed to play outside Matt Gidley; the 'Gidley flick' to T was their signature play and the best defenders in the game couldn't stop it. Timana scored 18 tries that season, 20 the year before and 21 in 2002 (when he was only 21); that's unbelievable. I mention Gids plenty of times in this book; champion bloke, wonderful player, the best team-mate anyone could ask for and a winger's centre.

When we left Newcastle on the Saturday to head to Sydney for our overnight stay before the grand final, and there were people lining the streets with red and blue paraphernalia all the way to the F3, I looked at Billy Peden and could see how much he was quietly soaking it up. He represented that Hunter spirit better than anyone in the team. No one was prouder of his community than Billy. Pound for pound he was tough as nails, the ultimate team-mate; he was the bloke everyone wanted to play beside. I don't think I can come up with a greater example of a footballer getting what he deserved than Billy scoring two tries in that grand final.

Ben Kennedy scored 17 tries in 2001 – as a second-rower. I reckon Steve Menzies would have to be the only second-rower to have scored more tries in a season (I know he scored 22 in 1995 but he played a few games in the centres) in the past 20 years. BK just had this 'follow me' attitude. He had skill; was a great on-field communicator who said his bit but backed it up with action; he could play busted; he had speed and strength, his athletic ability was awesome and he had the perfect physique for a rugby league player. I used to watch his footwork and the way he got in position to make an offload, and it was faultless. He was just the complete package as a footballer.

Steve Simpson, aka 'The Big Horse', was another bloke who was just the perfect team man who would do anything for the team. He dominated the line he ran on the right edge, running hard and straight onto the ball. Joey told him where he wanted him to run and would throw him the perfect pass and Simmo made that corridor his own; he's just so big and raw-boned he could blow an inside shoulder of a defender apart. He is so competitive at training and takes that into the games, but away from footy is so relaxed; just a humble country character.

Simmo loved fishing and hung around Ben Kennedy and Matt Parsons all the time; we used to call them 'Hook, Line and Sinker'. Simmo and 'Parso' used to room together and were inseparable when we went to away games; it was almost sickening. One wouldn't come down to dinner until the other one was ready to go. If Simmo finished the meal first and went to walk away, you'd hear big Parso bellow, 'Hey, Big 'Orse . . .

where are you going? Wait for me.' They'd be tucked up in their beds at 7.30 because they had young kids and enjoyed getting away and being able to get some extra shut-eye. We'd have a laugh about that.

Parso was just an old pro; the ultimate big, loping country bloke you'd expect to see in a Tooheys New advert. He had one call only on the football field . . . 'Give the *#&!! here' when he wanted the ball. We'd be deep in our own territory and the backs were getting rag-dolled (picked up and driven back) coming out of our half and I'd be at dummy-half and hear this deep voice say, 'Give the *#&!! here, Beds'. I'd throw it to this 120-kilo-plus giant and he'd cart it forward 20 metres and we'd get our momentum off that. He was pretty athletic for a big person and deserves recognition for how he got around the field and competed with a lot more agile players that the game had started to spew out.

Parso has a secret to why he could keep up with the younger, lighter blokes – he never saw the sense in jumping on the band-wagon with try celebrations. While everyone else ran in and jumped over the top of each other when a try was scored, Parso would already be lined up back on his mark, ready for the kick-off. We thought it was hilarious. He reckoned it was an absolute waste expending all that energy; he saw no need at all to run down after a Timana Tahu 50-metre special just to 'high five' his mates. And it was smart. That was something I had to get my head around; not consuming too much by trying to get to dummy-half for every ruck and be in all the action.

Actually Parso did have other sayings he was legendary for. When he felt we (make that he) needed a rest if we were doing it tough getting out of our own territory, he'd yell to Joey, 'Kick the *#&!! out, Cyces' (his nickname for Andrew, pronounced 'sikes' and short for 'Cyclone') and Parso would then stroll to the scrum and be the last one to arrive. His other favourite saying was, 'You're a dickhead'. He couldn't cop anyone lairising around or someone being a smartarse. He took a shine to Clint Newton, but I must have heard him say a thousand times, 'You're a dickhead, Newto.'

Paul Marquet's motivation was to give everything he could to the team. He can look back on his career and say he did everything he could possibly have done to be successful. To him it was all about hard work and discipline. He did things that don't get picked up in commentary, like in the kick-chase when he'd come from 30 metres away to make sure there was no hole in the middle of the defensive line. If you wanted someone to take the ball up on a certain line, he'd take on the role and he trained hard for that one play. 'Pepe' was a very quiet bloke, but you could have a good talk when you sat down with him.

There were other down-to-earth blokes like Clinton O'Brien, who came from Queensland but took to Newcastle and the lifestyle and culture so well and became very passionate about the club and his community. He was an uncompromising front-rower with a good offload, and his partner off the bench was Glenn Grief; we called him 'Chunky' and he was built low to the ground, had fast leg speed and ran a good 'next line', which is when the ball gets turned back inside. Chunky and 'Burger' had to fight hard against their injuries that year, late in their careers, but they soldiered on and were perfect in making sure we didn't lose momentum when Matt Parsons and Josh Perry came off the field. It shows how rewarding the game can be when genuine blokes like them, who worked so hard, win a premiership.

Then we had the newcomers to the team that year in Josh Perry and Daniel Abraham, who were both aged 20. Josh won a competition in his first season and that can be dangerous for a player – they can get a bit blasé and not appreciate how rare that sort of success is, and Josh suffered that a bit although he played for New South Wales in 2003. He had the perfect build for a front-rower in this era and it has been great to see him reinvent himself and win a premiership with Manly and make the Australian team in 2008 after being one of the players squeezed out of the Knights. One of the greatest shames I came across in footy was seeing Daniel Abraham suffer so badly from injury, ripping his ankle ligaments in the Country Origin game in 2003 and the next year breaking his leg, a shocking injury. He was destined to play State of Origin, because he had speed and the right physique and amazing skill. He could kick off the left and right feet, could pass 20 metres left and right, could pass short, had a good offload; he could play second row, lock, five-eighth or centre. But he lost his legs a bit due to his bad run with injury and it was so sad to see his career end like it did.

All those blokes share a common achievement that no one can take away from us: winning premiership rings in 2001. It has always been a special day when we play our last home game of the year at Newcastle on 'old boys day', when all the former players and staff do a lap of the stadium and form a guard of honour to run through. When I get back from England I'm looking forward to being part of those days and catching up with those guys from 2001, shaking their hands knowing they were alongside me on the most special night of my career . . . then having a few beers and waiting for Matt Parsons' first 'You're a dickhead' call.

11

THE PAIN GAME

I CAN understand how people outside of rugby league would wonder why players put their bodies through so much. The best explanation I can give is that it becomes a weekly addiction to work your arse off and beat an injury, then go out with your mates in front of a big crowd and play in the National Rugby League. And I admit I became obsessive about it; addicted to patching my body up and getting onto the field because when I was out there, it was a 'high' that I was willing to go through another physical 'fall' to experience.

There were plenty of days during a season when I struggled to put weight on my legs when I first got out of bed of a morning, particularly after a big training session or a match, because of my chronic Achilles tendonitis, and that went on for close to three years, I suppose. It would kill to walk down the steps of our house and I had the constant nagging pain in my Achilles on both legs; it was like two chihuahuas were biting into my ankles every time I walked. But I knew if I meticulously followed the correct treatment and the right preparation before a match, I could get myself ready to play for the Knights every weekend.

Just about every player in the NRL goes through pain and constant treatment to get the body through a season. It's simply part of the game these days. The most important thing to get out of the game is respect, and being able to handle injury is a big part of gaining respect, in my book.

The hardest part of the season for me was backing up after State of Origin games. Part of being a good Origin player is going back to your club and putting in a good performance with your team-mates a few days after an Origin game. I prided myself on being able to do that. But getting my Achilles, and my arthritic foot in 2004, both right to go into that next club game was pretty tough.

I'm not complaining. I'd do it all again and I'm not seeking any sort of accolade for it. But I thought I'd provide an insight into what I went through over the years as an indication of what so many footballers have to overcome to get out and do their best for the club, state or country. And I'd like to give recognition to all the medical people who work so hard in patching footballers up and getting us out there each week – I am so indebted to the people who have helped me over the years.

Having a good pre-season is so important for a footballer. It's the time to rest your body and get it right; it's when you can develop your skills and hopefully get fitter, faster and stronger. You can always tell the difference in yourself when the footy comes around if you've had a good, uninterrupted pre-season. Unfortunately, as far as I can work out, the 2001 pre-season was the last uninterrupted one I had.

I toured at the end of that year and didn't get back from England until the end of November, had a break until Christmas and then returned to training – with no major injury problem to overcome. In 2002 I had to undergo surgery on my wrist at the end of the season, but was right to start the 2003 season. About halfway through that season I started to have real bad problems with the Achilles tendons on both my ankles and had it diagnosed as tendonitis, something that still plagues me today. In 2004 I suffered a painful foot injury halfway through the season but was able to 'needle' it and get through, but after getting back from the 2004 Tri Nations tournament in England I had to have surgery on that. From then the foot and Achilles problems ensured that I had to modify my training quite a bit, and when I was able to run, at best it would be three-quarter pace.

Unfortunately I tore my right bicep pretty badly three games from the end of the 2008 season, my last with the Knights, and that was a six-month injury, which meant I had to miss the first month of games when I went to Leeds. Over the years I also had a shoulder reconstruction (1998) and broke my thumb (2002); I suffer back spasms that force it to lock up at times, and I broke my leg in July 2009 during my first season with Leeds. When I think about my 11 seasons of first grade with Newcastle and the injuries I've had, at least my knees stayed intact all that time, which I thought was quite a feat. Ironically, I had an arthroscopy 'clean-up' of my right knee a few weeks after I had my biceps surgery and I'd only played 40 minutes for Leeds when I pulled up pretty sore and I had to go in for more minor surgery, which forced me out for a month. It was terrible timing, seeing that I had started my English season late because of the biceps injury. It's fine now, luckily.

Going back over my career, my first major injury was my broken leg after I came down to Newcastle from Taree in 1995, which put me out for 14 weeks. My first injury during my first grade career actually came in my first ever semi-final, against the Roosters in 1998, which was only the second time I was the run-on hooker for Newcastle. I went in for a front-on tackle on the Roosters fullback Richie Barnett as he returned the ball from a 20 metre tap and I came off second best – dislocating the shoulder badly, which forced me off the field. I managed to play with a painkilling injection the next week in the sudden-death game against the Bulldogs. (About half the team went into the game with needles, so bad was our injury toll.) I lasted the whole game, which went for 100 minutes (we lost in extra time).

That was the end of our season and when I went for an MRI scan I found out I had completely wrecked the ligaments and rotator cuff, so I finished my first year in first grade having to have a shoulder reconstruction.

The next big one came when I was caught under a gang tackle on Northern Eagles winger John Hopoate in the round 23 match in 2002. I badly hurt the tendon and ligament in my right wrist and had to miss the last three premiership games. The Knights went into the last round on top of the ladder but were beaten by the Dragons, so we finished second, meaning we had to play the Dragons again a week later in the first week of the finals. I played that match (which we lost after losing Andrew Johns with injury) and the following week against the Roosters, a game we also lost, which ended our season. After three weeks' break, I played in the Test against New Zealand and then went to get the wrist checked out further. Despite MRI, CT and bone scans, it wasn't until I went in for explor-atory surgery on the wrist that it was found that I'd ruptured the ligament and tendon on either side of the wrist and done some cartilage and bone damage, so I had to have two pins put in to reattach the ligament and tendon to the bone. There went a good pre-season, but at least I was fine to start the 2003 season.

Not long into the season the Achilles were playing up badly and really started to get sore, inconveniencing me every time I tried to run. I have tight calves anyway, but the constant squatting at dummy-half and quick take-off when I ran caused further damage. I had all the tests done and found I had tendonitis in both Achilles and it became an injury where I just had to manage it. Rest is the only long-term cure, but I can't do much of that until my footy career is over.

The first 10 or 15 minutes of every game are a bit awkward and I have to be careful pushing off when I run. But after they warm up they are fine. I'm always conscious at half-time not to sit too long, and I do special exercises to keep my ankles loose, but running back for the second half is always a battle until I get the blood circulating again.

The best way to explain the problem is that the Achilles tendon is like a bicycle gear cable with sheaths around it. When it is not used, the sheath tightens around it and becomes rigid, just like a bike cable seizing up and needing lubricating.

It's a fair bit better now that I have had a couple of good off-seasons of rest but for years when I got up in the morning it was just like the tendon had seized and I had to warm it up and work it loose. I'd usually go to the gym early and do a lot of eccentric loading exercises; about 40 minutes of standing on my toes holding weights and dropping down until my heels touched the ground.

I could then do my weight session and if I did a field session in the afternoon, I wouldn't run the next day; I was not allowed to run back-to-back days. I'd get a lot of massage and a lot of physio and put ice bags on both ankles every night before I went to bed, all so I could get my body right to get through 80 minutes on the weekend. I guess there would be six to eight hours a week spent specifically getting my body healthy enough to play. I also wear 'orthotics' in my shoes and I shouldn't wear thongs or anything that doesn't support my feet properly.

When the Achilles gets really bad, I'll wear a special sock on each leg when I go to bed. It's called a Strassburg Sock and it goes all the way up the leg with a strap on the knees which is attached by Velcro to the toe so that it pulls on the toes so they are pointing up. It's not particularly comfortable – and not a good look, just ask Kris!

The day following a game is always a killer. The pain was always bad in the hours after I cooled down after a match and the next day wasn't much fun either. When the tendonitis in an Achilles gets bad enough, there is surgery in which the sheath is cut, but I was fortunate that mine didn't get to that stage while I meticulously followed my management plan; so I soldiered on. Cutting into my Achilles was something I was keen to avoid. Sometimes I'd have an injection of Traumeel, which is an 'inhibitor' that reduces inflammation and lubricates the tendons, and that would really help for a while.

I was a bit stressed going to England to play and not having around me my regular support crew that I had so much faith in at Newcastle, plus I was worried about going from hard artificial inside surfaces to spongy playing grounds early in the season. But so far, so good.

After learning to live with Achilles discomfort, I suffered a painful injury to the big toe on my right foot about halfway through the 2004 season when I took the full force of someone's body when I went to take off on a run. I got through that game but the same thing happened a couple of weeks later.

I had to have a pain-killing injection before every game to get through the rest of the season, but I had no hesitation in battling on because the Knights were without Andrew Johns since round three because of a bad knee injury and we'd lost Ben Kennedy, Steve Simpson, Robbie O'Davis, Daniel Abraham, Timana Tahu and Mark Hughes for long periods. I was captain, and had also been made New South Wales captain that year and we were just inside or outside the top eight most of the season, so I felt a real responsibility to keep playing for the Knights. I received a nice reward in the end when I won the Dally M Medal, although Newcastle finished tenth, just one win shy of the top eight.

The foot injury caused a different pain to the one caused by my dodgy Achilles; it was excruciating after a match when the needle wore off; a real nausea pain. I used to have to lie down on the back of the team bus on the way home from games in Sydney and couldn't wait to get home. I'd lie in a hot bath for an hour with my foot out of the water with an ice bag around it, then I'd put it in the water for a while to get the hot and cold treatment. Sleeping that night was hell; I've never suffered gout, but I'm told it's the same sort of pain – if I had a sheet on it the foot would hurt.

Naturally I had to modify my training more because I literally couldn't walk on the foot, let alone run, without it hurting; my swimming stroke improved that year! At best I could do one or two ball sessions; and that's not something I enjoyed, being away from the team and in the rehab group all the time.

Origin was always tough because you really need to be at every training session if possible, because the team gets so little time together, so I had to do a lot more running. Plus the policy when Hugh Hazard was the doctor was not to take pain-killing injections in Origin games either. The Blues physio Liz Steet, and later Tony Ayoub, were great treating the injuries for me and in the end it became a mental thing to get through. I was fortunate to get different ideas from Liz and Tony on how to treat my injuries.

I got through the full season and played every club match I was available for (when not on Origin duty), although the last round match against the Tigers was a big challenge. Because of the weekly injections I was getting, the foot was really tender and in the end I got a bad infection and ended up in hospital on a drip to get it out of my system. But it cleared up well enough for me to play the last round match and I'd had a month's break before going to England for the Tri Nations tournament, after the Knights missed the finals for the first time since 1996.

By then, though, I knew I was doing a lot of damage, but that's where that obsession of getting your body through the challenge comes into it. I knew I could get through, I got used to it; I'd improved my pain threshold and it was all about not letting the Achilles and foot injuries beat me – no matter what. In a warped sort of way, I enjoyed the battle. You get absorbed in the game by game preparation and feel there is no way you'll miss one because you get so engrossed in putting so much into getting ready for the game. At the time you don't think post-footy; just week to week. Did I ever think it wasn't worth it? Yeah, I probably did occasionally; sometimes I might be sitting there in pain after a game and think, 'Stuff this, how long can I do this? I'm sick of all this routine I have to go through, to the letter, every bloody week to feel like this.' But by the time it came to thinking about the next game, because I'd got through the last one, I'd be motivated to do it again.

Some great work by physio Tony Ayoub on the Tri Nations tour got me through the games, although I could do little of the training. The toughest part was that with the Australian team doctor Hugh Hazard not allowing players to take pain-killing injections to get onto the field, I had to get through coping with the pain by using an old remedy of mixing crushed aspirin and Sorbolene cream into a thick paste and rubbing it into the foot.

I know there is some debate about whether it is right or not to constantly take pain-killing injections to get onto the field. A few clubs won't do it – I know the Broncos and Canterbury, where Hugh was the club doctor for over 20 years until he retired at the end of 2008, don't. We have a great medical team at Newcastle with Neil Halpin and Peter McGeogh and I have had full confidence in them determining when they thought I was fine to play with needles. I always had complete faith in the doctors, physios, chiropractors and others who have helped me over the years.

My philosophy is, 'If it's sore and you can't do any serious damage, you can play. If medically it's a problem and you won't be able to function properly because of the injury and could cause yourself a lot of trouble, you should sit it out.' In the case of my toe, it did do harm playing such a long period needling the injury. But the toe is not too bad now and I'm grateful for medical staff letting me play; I wouldn't change a thing.

I understand each coach and each person is different; I can only comment on my situation but I am grateful for being allowed to keep playing and missing few games, and enjoying my career.

I couldn't believe what Ben Kennedy put his body through at times to get on the paddock; he was never shy in taking needles to get onto the field at any cost, because he was so loyal to the team. I'll never forget the day he had an injection in the sole of his foot before the game; didn't that attract an audience from the players in the dressing room! I couldn't think of a more tender part of the body to get a needle in.

What I saw Paul Harragon go through in the last couple of seasons at the Knights with his back and knee was just as amazing. He probably couldn't run 20 metres today; it was a major mission for him to train, let alone play on the weekend, but he kept putting his body through the mill because representing the Knights was so special to him. 'Chief' used to get emotional driving down Turton Road to the stadium and seeing all the fans waving flags and decked out in their red and blue. He used to pump everyone up telling us how fortunate we were to be the ones they were coming to watch and what it meant to be a Newcastle Knight.

Billy Peden played a season with a partly torn anterior cruciate ligament, knowing his knee could fold on him anytime, but he hardly missed a match. Towards the end he didn't even strap it. He had gone past the point of no return with it; now that's toughness and commitment. The early Knights players always talk about Marc Glanville having surgery on his knee cartilage and running three days later. I had a similar operation after I arrived at Leeds and was out for four weeks.

When I got back from the 2004 tour I went and had tests done and it was no surprise, when I saw foot specialist Martin Sullivan in Sydney, that I was told I'd ripped the ligament off the bone. He stitched it back on (I only had the stitch taken out in 2008) and it ended up putting me out of play for four months, which meant I missed the first five rounds of the 2005 club season – the Knights' toughest, when we had a casualty list bigger than even 2004's and finished with the wooden spoon. The foot had just started to settle down and I could get by fine as long as I strapped it. But it flared up again when, of all people, big Queensland prop Petero Civoniceva stood on it accidentally in an Origin game. As it turned out, it might have been a blessing because it stretched some of the scar tissue and freed it up after that.

While the Achilles problems and the toe (which is now arthritic) were the most constant, and most painful, injuries I had to put up with, I see myself as being lucky because I could play with them. I'm pretty blessed really that in my 11 seasons of first grade, I never had one injury that caused me to miss a lot of matches. The shoulder reconstruction, wrist operation, foot surgery and the biceps tear that finished my career at the Knights caused me to miss a total of less than 10 NRL games. That's a pretty good run.

Of course there were plenty of niggling injuries along the way that all NRL players have to contend with and chronic little things that you know you have to look after. I often had lower back problems and Kay MacPherson was just a magician to go to, as was John Munro up at Mulbring in the Hunter Valley – I would go to him for a rub and always leave feeling better, physically and mentally, from just talking to John, because he always cared so much about your general wellbeing, not just your football or injuries.

Andrew Johns put me on to Kay MacPherson, who educated both of us on how important your 'glutes' (gluteus maximus, gluteus medius and gluteus minimus muscles) are in controlling your body. If Newcastle were playing in Sydney we'd often borrow the car of our football manager and drive to Cronulla to get a treatment from her before a game; it was an unbelievable luxury to have her available. Some weeks we might go down during the week if we had the chance, or if I had to go to Sydney for any reason I'd call Kay and see if she could fit me in. She'd be brutal in finding out the aches and bumps that were putting my body out of whack but 10 times out of 10 she'd fix me up.

One day before we played at Penrith I woke up and could hardly move because my back had seized up. I got Joey to drive me to see Kay and she was like a magician; she loosened it all up and I was able to play that night.

A footballer often finds that certain people and certain treatments work best for him and he keeps going back to those people, and that was the case with me. I can't thank enough those who have helped me, including Dr Neil Halpin; Simon Atkins at Chiropractic Plus, who is the best 'rubber' I've had; and our club physio, Martin Boyd – many thanks go to those guys. I am one to think outside the square a bit when looking for an edge in treating injuries, and in the latter part of my career at Newcastle I stumbled across a bloke called Rod Hay at Booragul who's an Asian-style healer, one of only 12 people in Australia who does this particular type of acupuncture where he aligns your energy; he was great to go to when I was feeling physically flat. The Knights' rehabilitation co-ordinator Adrian Brough was my go-to man at the Knights. I'd get two rubs from him a week; he knew how to treat injuries and was easy to confide in due to his personal approach during what can be a lonely time on the road back to recovery. Robbie Aubin was the person who strapped me for training and games for the best part of a decade. I also had a great faith in head trainer Graham Perkins; there was a bit of ribbing between him and Robbie, who I insisted strapped me on game day. 'Perko' used to drop the bottom lip, but it was all in good fun.

I wished I could go out onto the field for a game and be 100 per cent fit but, outside maybe the first game or two of the season, that doesn't happen; it's the nature of the beast in the NRL. I feel as though I had a good run with injuries; I had to put up with plenty of pain plenty of times but thanks to a lot of people I have mentioned, I have lived my dream. I have been privileged to play the game I love for so long and be paid for it. If I've had to pay the cost physically, it's been well worth it.

12

RULES AND REFS

FIRST WE had referees wired for sound, then we introduced the video referee; now we have two referees on the field in the NRL. They've had to contend with the grapple tackle, untold wrestling techniques in the tackle, the surrender tackle, dominant tackle; having to decide between a strip and a loose carry. You can't tackle a player in the air when he's fielding a kick; you virtually can't touch a kicker now when you go to put pressure on him. There's the benefit of the doubt rule and touch judges coming onto the field to get involved. Policing the rules is a whole new world compared to when I came into first grade.

And after contending with all that, the poor old referee gets every decision scrutinised by one of about 15 cameras during the call or by the media (and often coaches) after the match, and every word he says during the game can be picked up by the fans wearing Sports Ears. Even though I've had my run-ins with refs – particularly when I was learning to be a captain – it's no doubt a pretty tough job.

But I reckon their job, and the quality of the game, could improve if we simplified a few rules. Some NRL games now go for close to 90 minutes because of all the referrals to the video ref and that's not good; we're getting too much like American football; we're even training like the Americans and having players referred to as 'athletes' rather than footballers.

Now these ideas might seem a bit radical, but sit back and think about them for a while.

Firstly, I'd try what Kerry Packer advocated that one time I came across him during my life – let's restrict it to two defenders in a tackle. If a third man comes in to effect a tackle, penalise him. It would make the detection of strips a lot easier, would certainly reduce injuries, I reckon, and the most positive result would be we'd see more offloading of the football. I reckon there would be a lot less wrestling in the tackle, too.

Now I know what one reaction will be: 'It's already become like touch football because the game is too fast with the quick play the balls.' That's fair comment, so why not combine the two-in-a-tackle rule by going back to the defending team having to retreat only five metres rather than 10 metres (which is often 12 or 13 metres). So, three ugly grey areas of the game – wrestling, stripping and holding down – would become easier to detect.

Certainly you'd see a lot more promotion of the football and I'd love for that to happen. The ball carrier getting stripped annoys the hell out of me; some attacking players play for it knowing they'll get a penalty; some defenders get their hands in there and sneakily knock the ball out as the player is getting off the ground to play the ball. Sometimes a player is genuinely trying to lock up the arm and accidentally knocks the ball out. By having only two players allowed in the tackle, you could get rid of the stripping rule and just have 'play on', because there'd naturally be less chance of a strip as you'd have one man high to lock up the ball and the second man going in low to bring the player down (like it was for many years until probably the last six or seven seasons). If you still wanted to keep the stripping rule to eliminate the second man stripping the ball, with two refs on the field and two defenders per tackle, at least you'd get a lot clearer look at the strips.

We would have a lot more genuine 'dominant tackles' being rewarded for being good hits rather than a pile-in-over-the-top free-for-all. To me, a dominant tackle is when one or two defenders drive a bloke back and finish up dominating him with their bodies over the top. A dominant tackle shouldn't be rewarded when it's three or four blokes piling on to a fullback returning the ball when he's trying to surrender because he knows there's no way to gain any more yardage and he just wants to protect the ball and start a new set. Two in a tackle would bring the good one-on-one tacklers right back into the game, rather than having players taught to target the ball area, hold a bloke up and wait for the cavalry to come in and dance around with him.

The surrender tackle is another bone of contention with me. Why have a ref yelling out 'surrender' when a player comes to the defensive line and crashes to his knees. A player doing that is against the spirit of the game; he should be penalised for a voluntary tackle; bugger this surrender bit. You can pick the players who are known 'surrenderers' a mile away and it's another part of the game where it's all about wrestling technique and getting off the ground as effectively as you can. Rugby league should be about tackling technique and offloading skill, not surrendering and wrestling. I know we'd have a wave of penalties at first that would disrupt games but, just like the grapple, which refs didn't crack down on enough at first, it would only take a few weeks to get rid of surrendering from the game.

While I'm listing what changes I'd make to rules and

interpretations, I may as well mention the video ref. While I'm all for taking advantage of whatever technology we have, it has to be within reason. Too many refs are distracted by the constant feedback and instructions they are getting down the line from the video ref, plus chatter from the touch judges. That leads to them getting a feel of the game more from others than their own instincts and contact with the players. I reckon the video ref should be restricted to try decisions, and say a close 40–20 call when referred to them. Now that we have two refs on the field, there should be less reliance on going to the video. As a player, it spins me out how often we go upstairs sometimes and how many times they look at something over and over and still can't come up with a conclusive decision. The benefit of the doubt rule is a joke – there shouldn't be any doubt; it's either categorically a try or it's no try. Sometimes they are looking for something that's not there.

I'd also like to see some changes to the rules around high tackles and foul play. Very few players get sent off these days, which is good because I don't like to see a team play with 12 men on the field. Intentional foul play is just so rare and it has to take a really reckless high shot or kneeing or a king hit for it to be deemed bad enough for a send-off. But I would like to see the sin-bin used more for foul play. If a player comes up with a tackle that looks pretty bad but, as often happens, the ref doesn't want to stick his head out and dismiss the player – put him in the bin for 10 minutes so the opposing team gets an advantage.

The other thing I'd like to see is that if a player is carted off because of foul play, the offending team also loses the offending player for the same period the victim is off the field. While the player who copped the tackle is down being treated, the tackle could be looked at again by the video ref (which doesn't extend the length of the game because play would be stopped anyway while the player is being treated) and if it is deemed a bad enough incident for the player to be put on report, he is out of the game while the player who copped the tackle is out. So if the injury is bad enough for the victim not to return to the match, neither can the offender. The difference between this and the player being sent off is that both teams keep 13 players on the field; they're just down an interchange player.

What happens too often now is if you get a player stretchered off, you're down to 16 while the ref puts the offender on report and the opposition keeps 17 players; that's totally unfair. I believe in an eye for an eye and my system is a good compromise between putting every suspicious tackle on report and letting the video review committee do the referees' job and having send-offs which leave a team a man short.

There has been the odd incident where a player stays down to get a penalty and get an opposing player on report, which I totally disagree with. Playing first grade is about earning respect and that's definitely not the way to get respect in my book. Only the player concerned knows how badly injured he is; if he can get to his feet, he should, and let the referee and video ref decide on the tackle. At the end of the day he can look at himself in the mirror knowing he has the respect of his opponents.

Having said all that, I think the refereeing standard these days is quite good considering the lack of experience in the ranks at present. I think we'll see a lot of improvement in the next two or three seasons. Refs are never going to be perfect and that's more evident with the speed at which the game is played these days. Generally their rapport with the players is okay, although some still have too much of a school-teacher attitude and are hard to approach.

Talking respectfully to the referee in the heat of the battle is definitely a skill; one that I never mastered. Often I thought I had a genuine complaint or need for clarification that required discussion but was virtually told 'Get out of my face'. Sometimes I found the best way was to yell at them and say, 'I need to talk to you,' and then they would blow the whole game up and let you approach them. But that just prompts the crowd to rip into you, a lot of people tune in to Sports Ears to listen to the discussion plus it is often played over the air on radio or television; so it becomes a real soap opera some times. You have to pick your times right; when and how to talk to the referees.

I really don't like Sports Ears; I think it is an invasion into the game that is not required. I'm sure the media love it; I don't know how many times I was questioned about dialogue on the field, whether it was between me and the referee or just something that was said in the heat of battle that had been picked up by the ref's microphone. Some things should be left on the field. I'd be asked about a certain thing that happened in the such and such minute and told that I supposedly said this when I couldn't even remember it. My mum bought a set of Sports Ears one time and she ripped into me because of my language on the field; she could hear everything. She pulled me aside by the ear one time after a game and told me to cut it out; nothing was sacred anymore!

The television cameras often zoom in and it's not hard to read the lips of players and they now have the lipstick-cameras in the dressing rooms; surely that is enough. I know it's all about taking the battle inside lounge rooms and giving the fan as big an insight as possible, but I just think tapping in to conversation on the field is going too far. To have every word the referee utters going out to everyone in the crowd with Sports Ears and also being accessible to all the media puts unnecessary pressure on them as well as giving access to players' dialogue that people off the field should never have access to. It has affected the relationship between players and the refs too; you no longer get any banter and relaxed exchanging of views, instead it has become very formal because the ref knows he is on show and has an audience.

I think Tony Archer is a good example of that. I found him hard to talk to; he's just too formal and too dismissive in the way he'll blow up the game to lay down the law and not let you have a quiet word back to him; he'd be better if he relaxed more.

Shayne Hayne, I think, is the most improved referee in the NRL. He has improved his rapport with players as he becomes more experienced, seems far more relaxed during a game now and because of that they want to work more with him to get a good game of footy. I think that's a tribute to Robert Finch and Bill Harrigan and the process the referees now have in analysing their performances and educating the referees better than before; especially going through their weekly reviews and pointing out specific aspects of their performances, just as the players and their coaches do.

It's great that they do have referees visit clubs in the pre-season and help with different techniques and advise what they are looking for. They also see what techniques we use in the rucks, etc. and I think it helps us to better get on the same page. It has been one of the good innovations under Robert Finch's rule as referees' boss. I had Shayne attend our training sessions a few times, which allowed us to gain a rapport with him and an understanding of how he looks at a game.

A referee I didn't enjoy playing under was Steve Clark; as captain I found him unapproachable and often thought that with Clarky it was about him showing his authority rather than trying to get the teams to work with him. And I often thought he'd go into a game with a preconceived idea about certain players or teams; he'd just hammer a repeat offender over one aspect of the game.

I really felt for the referees when grappling became so much a part of the game; it is hard to police and it became more of a nightmare when everyone became so good at disguising it. In 2008 when the issue really blew up, the refs just didn't get the support they needed in eradicating it when the video review committee didn't come down hard enough and put a few players away for bigger suspensions.

From the games I've seen in 2009, the amount of grapple tackles has been reduced significantly and having two referees on the field has made it easier to detect. But the speed of the ruck is such an important aspect of the game, I'm sure some new tricks will be employed by teams to slow down the play the ball.

I think we have developed too much of an obsession with refereeing decisions. As captain, I have attended plenty of media conferences and there have been very few where a journalist hasn't asked for an opinion on a referee's decision or his overall performance. They lead you, and the coach, into discussion all the time – sometimes it is the first question that is asked – and often coaches don't need much of an invitation to question decisions, although they dance around it to an extent to avoid a $10,000 fine from the NRL. There has become this big pre-occupation by the media with referees and it is hard to escape. I don't know of any other sport where the match officials are so regularly and highly scrutinised and criticised. In the English Super League, where the refs are far below the standard of Aussie refs, the coaches, players, fans and media seem to just accept there will be good calls and bad calls and are happy to roll with the punches and don't highlight every error like we do in Australia. I've found that really refreshing.

No wonder the Australian refs are scared to make a big decision and instead refer it to the video ref; they know it will be dissected by the media for days. There seems to be so much hysteria around refereeing decisions and blaming them for the results, we'll soon be able to challenge a call like they do in the National Football League in the USA (where the coach can make two challenges per game).

I reckon some of my suggestions would relieve a lot of the load and make the game more attractive, less predictable and, ultimately, more enjoyable for referees and players.

13

CONTROVERSIAL CLEAN-OUT

THE 2007 season at the Newcastle Knights was the toughest I went through. It was the year Andrew Johns's career came to a premature end because of a neck injury, and when new coach Brian Smith was given what seemed to be a free rein by the club to change the face of the team. No one anticipated how dramatically a broom would be put through the place. As captain, I got thrown into this incredible emotion boiling around me, trying to see the views of the club and the players as the Knights went through their biggest clean-out in history.

There were some moments in 2007 that I'll certainly never forget. Obviously two were Joey being clipped by Adam Woolnough at training and screaming out in pain and saying, 'I'm gone . . . I'm gone.' Another was Kirk Reynoldson, who was denied one more first grade appearance that would have activated his contract for the next season, being distraught as players huddled around him at training one day; he was in tears saying, 'I don't care about the money; I just want to play with you fellas one more time; I just want to run out there with my mates.'

The season taught me a lot about rugby league and how the NRL had become a cut-throat business. The club obviously thought that, with Andrew Johns set to retire at the end of 2007, it faced a massive challenge and it wanted a fresh coach, fresh ideas and new players. Brian was given a hatchet job to carry out; he had a good reputation for rebuilding clubs, was decisive and confident in his approach, is a smart coach and he knew there was never going to be any easy way for him to do what he was employed to do.

But what can't be disputed is that for any player who had been at the club for any length of time, season 2007 was the toughest period any of us will go through.

First of all we had a big change in personality in coaches, going from Michael Hagan to Brian Smith, who was given the brief to prepare for life after Joey – something that began basically a season earlier than was planned. There was a fair bit of anxiousness amongst the players leading into the pre-season, with 'Smithy' having a reputation of being a strong 'you do it my way' sort of personality. He'd previously shaken up St George and Parramatta and taken both clubs to grand finals, so everyone knew they were on notice from the time Brian got there. And he didn't muck around getting into the job he was hired to do – cleaning the place out of any players he thought could not do the job for him post-Joey.

Brian asked a few senior players to meet him at the Crowne Plaza at Newcastle towards the end of the 2006 season to discuss what we thought we needed to be successful; where we could improve and general feedback about training, facilities and support. I sat with Steve Simpson giving our views to Brian and football operations manager Steve Crowe and it was a positive session.

We had a big off-season – a good off-season – and Brian pretty much stripped us right back to how he wanted us to play; how to carry the football, identifying each player's best skills to go into the defensive line with, your body position, your footwork, how he wanted us to defend. Brian had a lot of ideas and good attention to detail. And he came to the club when we finally had first-class training and injury treatment facilities through the sponsorship deal with the Wests leagues club group, so that further emphasised what a new era it was for the Knights. And he had a great support staff; Brian brought in Trent Robinson and Rowan Smith, and we still had Rick Stone, Scott Dickensen, Adrian Brough, Graham Perkins, plus excellent part-time back-up boys, plus a first-class medical team led by Neil Halpin. It was an interesting off-season that I thought would pay dividends for Newcastle for the next couple of years.

Certainly Brian let everyone know who was boss from the start. He took Joey and me aside early on and told us, 'I don't want to see you chase a referee around the field again,' in reference to our run-ins over the previous couple of years with refs and touch judges. That was fair comment and it took pressure off me because I was never comfortable questioning refs, but felt I had to as captain on behalf of the team. I think Brian wanted to take the pressure off us as well, which suited me.

Joey could get hyped up at training and really ride blokes to train with intensity and would get into them if they made mistakes. I started to follow that lead too, with our input into running the sessions always welcomed by Michael Hagan. Brian was different; he liked having really calm sessions and having things done his way. He said one time, tongue in cheek, during a ball-work session, 'I'll coach the team, you look after yourself.' That highlighted to me he was there to do a job, and he'd soak up all the pressure of how the team played and performed.

The whole atmosphere was just so different from previously and so was the squad. Matt Gidley had been let go to St Helens,

Craig Smith had retired, Todd Lowrie had gone to Parramatta with Hages, Anthony Quinn to Melbourne and the Dally M winger of the year in his only season in the NRL, the real popular Irishman Brian Carney, was also gone (he was supposed to play with Gold Coast but went back to England). Suddenly Joey had pulled the plug on his career after three games and Luke Davico retired a few weeks later, so that made seven players from the previous season's team who had moved on by the time the fifth round came around. But Adam MacDougall had come back to the club, while Paul Franze, Mitchell Sargent and Todd Polglase were signed and Kurt Gidley had really come along as an elite player. Jarrod Mullen also burst onto the scene, so we still had the nucleus of a pretty good side, I thought, even without Joey.

I missed the first three rounds because of a four-game suspension for a lifting tackle on Manly winger Michael Robertson in the finals of '06, and that was hard. Terence Seuseu was coming on the scene then and Brian was really happy with the way he was progressing and wanted to give him some time in first grade, so he proved a really good replacement.

Then came that day at training that ended Andrew Johns's career. We were preparing for the home game against Melbourne, who had won their first three games and were coming off a grand final appearance in 2006, and it was going to be the first time Kurt Gidley (at fullback), Andrew Johns (halfback), Jarrod Mullen (five-eighth) and me (hooker) were going to be in the starting line-up together. We'd won two of the first three games and I remember being so keen to start my season on a good note and thinking that if we were three wins from four, what great momentum that would give us for the year.

We were just doing some simple three-on-two drills at training, a bit of oppose stuff, and Adam Woolnough ran into Joey. Joey just screamed in pain and grabbed his neck. He didn't go down but he was in a lot of agony. At first we were thinking of 'the boy who cried wolf'; here's another Joey episode where he was down for the count and no chance of playing that weekend but somehow he'd be right to play. When I went to him after the session I asked, 'You right, mate, will you be OK?' He told me, with a real helpless look in his eyes, 'Mate, I'm gone; my neck's gone.'

He went to see the surgeon Dr Yeo in Sydney the next day and the rest is history, as they say; he didn't play against Melbourne that (Easter) weekend and the following Tuesday he welled up at training in the gym when he told all the boys his career had finished.

Andrew had rung me before the session and told me, 'Mate, I've got some bad news; that's it . . . I'm done, I'm finished, I've played my last game. I am just about to go to a press conference, I just thought I'd tell you first; then I'm going to come and see the boys.' He came upstairs to the gym at Balance, alongside his fiancée Cath, and made a really heartfelt speech which filled the room with a lot of emotion. After that I thought I should say something on behalf of the team, and the coach also looked at me as if to prompt me to say something in response. With emotion so high, it was hard; words were never going to do the occasion justice. I just said what was in my heart, something like, 'Number one, I feel so sorry for you because I regard you so highly as a mate as well as a team-mate that I didn't want you to go out this way – I wanted you to go on your own terms. But it wasn't to be and we are here for you as a mate, and if there is anything we can do for you, we will, because as a group we owe you so much. You've done so much for all of us in this room and the footprints you've left for us to follow are something we will always appreciate and never forget. Everyone who pulls on a Newcastle jersey for the rest of the season will be playing for you as well as ourselves.'

Joey (I always call him 'Nugget') then went over to the stadium to front a media conference and that was just as emotional. Everyone was stunned, even though for days we had thought it might be coming. Operations manager Steve Crowe, who was great mates with Matthew Johns particularly and close to Joey, was really upset with Joey's sudden retirement. Crowey was a player at the Knights, and worked in media, marketing and football roles, so he knew the impact not having Andrew Johns would have not just on the team but on the whole business, with his extraordinary pulling power gone. It hit him so hard he had to lie down in the office and get himself together.

I woke up the next day thinking, 'Without doubt, this is the biggest challenge I've ever had . . . Are you ready for this?' I felt I had a lot of responsibility on my shoulders but I was also excited about being in a position where we could prove a lot of people wrong – all those who were saying we couldn't perform without Andrew Johns. We weren't prepared for it just yet but, as a club and with a coach brought specifically to the club to plan for life after Joey, we were preparing for it.

We had to change the way we played but the off-season was all about that anyway; the coach didn't want all the responsibility on Andrew's shoulders – where he was spoon-feeding the other boys and if Andrew was out then the whole cast fell apart. It was about building the blocks so that, if Joey was out, we could cover; we could put people in the position to do some of the things he did so well; we could play a different style and each player had improved his skills to take up some of the slack. I looked around at the next training session and took in what a young team I had around me with only Steve Simpson, Adam

MacDougall, Mitchell Sargent and me who were senior players (no one else had played 100 first grade games).

The class and character of Joey was so awesome, you couldn't blame the team for falling by the wayside when he'd been out over the years. In 2003, when he hurt his neck just a few weeks before the finals, it was only expected that we'd struggle just as any team would without their dominant playmaker, especially under the salary cap where you couldn't carry experienced back-up players. But in 2004 when he did his knee in the third game we only missed the finals by two competition points, with Kurt Gidley and Steve Witt in the halves. When Joey was out on the field, there was no better team to watch and everyone just hopped on board; but we had become conscious that we had to lead the way when he wasn't there and we had done that to a great degree.

If he pulled out on a Thursday or Friday with injury, I'd be full of self-doubt about how we could perform. And if we lost, sure enough the 'can't play without Johns' stories would come out. This time I almost felt relieved, because Andrew wasn't going to be there anymore, that was accepted, and I was motivated to lead the club forward and knew with Kurt and Jarrod there, we had two players who, given time, could be as good as anyone in the NRL in taking a game by the scruff of the neck and winning it. But it wasn't going to happen overnight.

The coach would obviously have been disappointed that he didn't get the chance to have such a great player in the team, but on the other hand I think he was excited that the inevitable was already out of the way and he could start his era straight away and do things completely his way.

We were only beaten by Melbourne 22–12, then we won two of the next three with our only loss being 20–16 against the Broncos, who had won the competition the year before. After

10 rounds we were in sixth spot and I was thinking we could definitely make the finals. But then the shit hit the fan, with players really starting to look over their shoulders, wondering if they'd be there the following season, before the big bust-up with the coach and Clint Newton happened.

We were beaten by Brisbane, who were equal last before the match, 71–6 at Suncorp – our biggest ever loss. All the Broncos' seven State of Origin players backed up but only one of our four did, Jarrod Mullen, who was a shock selection for the first Origin match. Steve Simpson, Kurt Gidley and I were carrying minor injuries and were rested, meaning we had probably the least experienced team in all my years of playing having to go up against a strong Brisbane team.

That proved to be Clint Newton's last game, ironically his 100th first grade appearance – which is a record he should be very proud of. He became the first of many casualties of the 'new order'. It was obvious 'Newto' and Smithy didn't see eye to eye and Clint just didn't fit the Brian Smith mould as a player. Smithy's way of coaching is that he doesn't want headstrong personalities in the team who are firm in their own attitude towards how they think things should be done. He's also for the horizontal sort of team structure, with few players on big money. He wants instead the New England Patriots model that he's studied so much – a lot of good competent players on similar pay packets so that when any one or a few are missing, the team can adjust rather than being so vulnerable when a dominant marquee player is out for any period.

I'm a pretty close friend of Newto's and I wanted the best for him because he was so passionate and enthusiastic about playing for the Knights. A few of the young blokes at first could be a bit overcome by Newto's exuberance and his keenness to pass down his knowledge and views. It was something that

Newto had experienced from senior players, particularly me and Joey, when he first came into the side, and he was just passing that on. But maybe younger players today are a lot more sensitive to that sort of talk. The coach picked up on that early and told Newto just to play the game and encourage the young guys with his enthusiasm and on-field actions, not the pump-up talk. I'll give Newto one thing, he's a professional and I think he understands the game and the business of rugby league, having served on the board of the Players Association and learning a lot about the ins and outs of the player environment. When Joey retired he felt he was one of the players who had to stand up and make a stand and lead the way and pump the other boys up. He'd been around the place for quite a while and knew, and believed in, the fabric of the club – be the player others want to play with, be tough in tough times and stand up for your mates. He would have seen it as a whole new challenge for him.

During the warm-up before one game Newto was pumping up for the game and telling the boys, 'Right, this is a massive day, a big day, let's prove we're up for it. On play two let's really get us forward; then we have to get on the back of that. C'mon, it's a massive day . . .' and kept reminding everyone of the job they had to do. The coach heard all of this while the players were stretching and obviously thought, 'Why are you shouting out instructions?' He just wanted quiet focus before matches.

I know a couple of times Smithy criticised Newto's game when Clint thought he'd done really well; he'd picked out a few things he'd tried and said, 'I don't want you to do that,' but Newto was thinking, 'Well, hang on; I've been doing that for years and it's going okay.' It was probably hard for him to take but that's what can happen when you have a change of coach and style; you have to adapt.

Newto was pretty distraught about the way things were going. He said to me one day, 'Mate, obviously I want to stay but I don't know what's going on; I feel the coach doesn't want me.' The personality clash between the two became too obvious and Brian let him know he had no future there. So, next thing, Newto's asked for a release and was gone. Two weeks later, in round 13, he was playing for Melbourne and went on to win a grand final, and was nearly man of the match in that game, he played so well.

I felt trapped right in the middle of the clash of wills. I wanted the best for Newto but I was also captain and obviously had to support the club's stance. And trying to hold that middle ground really got to me; not just with Clint but all the dissatisfied players; it was the hardest thing I'd had to do. More and more players started to feel like Newto did; they just weren't part of the coach's plans going forward and felt they were on borrowed time. In the end, a lot of them couldn't wait until the end of the season.

We came back and beat the Roosters the week after that big loss to Brisbane and winning six of our first 11 games that season, I thought, was a massive effort. But the season just fell apart and I have never had a year in football that was less enjoyable. After Newto addressed the boys to tell them he was out of there, just like Joey and 'Statue' (Luke Davico) had earlier in the season, it was a standing joke among the players, 'Who is going to be the next to give a farewell speech in the gym?'

Everyone knew they were playing for contracts, and that was the way the coach obviously wanted it, as if to keep the players motivated. But it didn't work that way; a lot of the boys were playing good footy but at the end of the day they weren't the coach's sort of players. They didn't have something he wanted, whether it was agility or speed or body shape or whatever, and that was Brian's prerogative as coach.

When it came to the actual tapping of blokes on the shoulder, it was awful because there was just so much of it – too much too soon, I thought. As a group, the players felt isolated – no one seemed to know where they stood. I was getting all the backlash from the players; no one from the club was communicating with the senior playing group, which I thought would have been important. During that period we had a change of CEO from Ken Conway to Steve Burraston; the media was having a field day with stories about dissent and Smithy removing the culture of the club; so I was getting the players' view, the media's view, but no one was balancing that with information about the club's direction and intentions. It was just mass hysteria and it was killing the team environment.

I really felt for Steve Crowe, who bleeds red and blue and had done so much for a lot of the players, including me, in passing down all the strong ethics the club had been built on. Suddenly he was stuck in the middle of this dramatic change of a club he'd devoted so much of his life to since the inaugural year of 1988. Crowey was working long hours and getting caught up in the emotional drama and you could tell it was affecting him physically and really taking its toll on him. It was no surprise he resigned a few weeks before the end of the season.

Surely the administration and the board knew the players were unhappy and that there was a lot of dressing room talk, but they never got involved. It was as if they had given Smithy the job to load the rifle and shoot all the bullets himself and he was the sole face of the whole drama that it caused. It could have been done in a more personable way, with a lot more communication all-round.

Then the Kirk Reynoldson episode happened and that was the last straw for most players; the rest of the season became a waste of time after that. 'Reyno' was a real popular bloke around the place, an absolute champion as a person and he'd been in good form, I thought. The coach must have liked him enough as a player because, in the round 13 game (against Wests Tigers) when I was out on State of Origin duty, he made him captain. Unfortunately Reyno hurt his medial ligament that day and was out for over a month. He had a clause in his contract, reported as being worth $200,000 a season, that if he played 15 first grade games it would activate a fourth year of his contract for season 2008. The day he captained the team against the Tigers was his 12th game. When he came back from injury he played two more games off the bench (round 18 v the Roosters and round 20 v the Warriors) but was then dropped, even though we were struggling for form and experienced first grade players.

In my view, Brian believed Reyno wasn't the type of player he wanted in future and the club therefore did not want the option activated. These are some of the tough, cut-throat business decisions you have to make sometimes; I understand that. But what I didn't understand was how one minute he was at the club, stand-in captain, good enough to play in every first grade game he was available for and was easily going to chalk up the 15 games he needed . . . then, without any earlier indication, he was told he wasn't in the club's future plans.

Reyno was just distraught. For weeks he went through the whole spectrum of emotions: shock, then anger, then helplessness and finally great sadness that he'd been taken out of the team unit. He just couldn't understand why there was such a dramatic change in attitude towards him. When he realised he was gone anyway, he told the club, 'I don't care about the money, I just want to play with the boys one more time. I know you don't want me but I just want to play with the boys;

I want just one last hit-out.' Obviously the club couldn't do that, because they would have relinquished any legal standing they had.

The unbelievable thing was that after Reyno got his lawyers involved, which any player would have done in that situation, Brian told him if he wanted to talk to him anymore he would have to have his lawyer present. Kirk was shattered; I couldn't believe it got to that. The club and the coach kept saying publicly his demotion was only to do with his form and that there were other players who could do a better job. There is no way he could have been dropped on form; that was obvious to all his team-mates and anyone who knew anything about the Knights. And that was a huge emotional drain on the team, watching a mate get treated like that when all he wanted to do was go out there one more time with his boys.

I'll never forget one day at training before our last match against Wests Tigers. We had to beat them to avoid coming last in the competition that year. (We won 26–24 and avoided the wooden spoon.) That was when Reyno was told he would not get the chance to play in one more game with the side and that he had to talk through lawyers from then on. He told the boys what had just happened and was so distraught he burst into tears; the finality of it just hit him between the eyes. We all got in a circle around him to shield him from the large media gathering that was there, so that they couldn't see that he'd broken down. He was just such a popular bloke, just a real quality person, and no one wanted to see him treated like that. After an emotional year, everyone was pretty distraught and drained, but we made a pact to put it all aside and we had to do the best for our town and our supporters. It was tough, but we said, let's get out there and avoid the wooden spoon, win in front of all the Knights 'old boys', who would be present on the last home game of the year; but most of all win for our mate Reyno.

For the last two months of the season it was so hard patching up the team week by week and everyone was just counting down to the end of the season and, for quite a few players, the end of their time at the club. We were trying to act as – and were being told to be – professionals, but it was bloody hard; we'd had the guts kicked out of the long-standing culture. The main incentive the blokes had was to play for each other, for the fans who kept turning up and to put their best foot forward to ensure they got a contract somewhere in 2008. Thankfully, a lot of them did. Kirk Reynoldson signed a one-year deal with St George Illawarra and played 21 first grade games but retired at age 29 after that season, which was a real pity.

Joining the eight players already gone from the 2006 squad (Johns, Smith, Davico, Matt Gidley, Carney, Lowrie, Quinn, Newton) plus my back-up hooker Luke Quigley, these players had joined the clean-out by the start of the 2008 season: Kirk Reynoldson, David Seage, Adam Woolnough, Josh Perry, Daniel Abraham, George Carmont, Brad Tighe, Milton Thaiday, Reegan Tanner, Todd Polglase, Riley Brown and Nathan Hinton – 20 of the 26 players used in first grade in 2006. By the start of 2009, you could add Kade Snowden, Mitchell Sargent, Jesse Royal, Terence Seuseu, Chris Bailey, Luke Walsh and me – and that's a hell of a clean-out. More than half were local juniors. The attitude of the club was obvious, judging by newspaper comments from the new club boss, Steve Burraston, who said: 'We're not fast enough, not strong enough and we don't have enough versatility across the park.'

I know we'd only made the finals once in the previous three years from 2004 to 2006, but did that mean we wouldn't have been any good at all without Andrew Johns? Or was the club saying the game had changed so much we didn't have the right style or shape of player to keep pace? The club felt it had to be ruthless; the directors or whoever were making the decisions had judged that a lot of the players were never going to be successful without Joey there to hold their hands. While all of us will admit it was a lot easier to perform well with Joey in the team than not, I think a few of the discards showed when they moved on that they still had something to offer.

A whole new outside group had come in; the main signings among them were Ben Cross, who had just won a premiership with Melbourne, and Adam MacDougall, who had previously had such an impact at the Knights. Doogs was 31, but keen to prove himself again after playing only 31 first grade games in three seasons with Souths because of injury; and I think he did that. It was like saying we could no longer rely on the fabric of the Newcastle Knights: strong junior development and recruitment from country areas. Brian seemed to be trying to come up with short-term strategies to get us winning in first grade within his three-year contract, at the expense of the formulas the Knights had relied for nearly two decades. Not only were a heap of players bought from other clubs – and it's arguable whether they were better than some who were let go – but part of the strategy was to bring a heap of players from other clubs into the under 20s, at a fair expense, something that had never had to happen at the club before. The under 20s also failed to make the finals in the first two seasons of the Toyota Cup (2008–09).

There is no way Smithy would have got pleasure out of telling so many players to move on; that's not what he is about. He enjoys seeing young blokes improve and grow as footballers and men; I've heard him say that many times. He was just doing a tough job the best way he knew how and he knew it wasn't going to make him popular. He was in a tough position with the Kirk Reynoldson issue, forced to make a decision in order to keep other players who were regarded as higher priorities. Smithy was obviously feeling the pressure, especially with the media and fan outrage around him – as we all were during those few weeks.

There is no doubt there was a fall-out with the fans, just judging by how many people came up to me and said they hated what was happening to their club, and you could see it in the crowd figures – we couldn't crack 16,000 in our last four home games.

I've had a few players who moved on tell me 'Smithy didn't want to coach us from the first day – we weren't his sort of players.' Newto and Anthony Quinn (who became an Origin player) won a grand final with Melbourne; Josh Perry did the same at Manly and became a Test player. I think Brian Smith would have been happy for them having that success; it was never personal for him and he would genuinely be glad they had forged good careers somewhere else. I always believe things happen for a reason; you've just got to move on and there is no use being bitter about it. The change of scenery probably did them all good.

Once 2007 was out of the way and knowing, before the season started, that I was going to end my career in England, I really enjoyed 2008. There was a fresh new vibe in the place with blokes like Scott Dureau, Cory Paterson and Jarrod Mullen full of enthusiasm. It was great to be there to see Kurt Gidley prove himself as one of the elite players in the game and one of the finest, and most consistent, competitors to ever wear the red and blue jersey. After knowing him from when he was 12 and being there when he played his first top grade game, I got a real buzz out of seeing him go from a boy to the man who is now leading the club forward as captain. And Ben Cross has brought a lot to our club; his professionalism and attitude have rubbed off onto everyone, with his Melbourne background. And the new players Brian Smith brought to the club came with new enthusiasm, knowing they had to prove themselves after what had happened.

But I was left disappointed late in the 2008 season when the club let Chris Bailey go to Manly without really lifting a hand to keep him. Here was another player who really wanted to be at the Knights, but he wasn't even approached to stay, with the club citing salary cap issues as the reason.

I loved playing for the Knights, the people at the club, and what the club stood for; and the fans and the area – all those things. And I can't fault how well I was looked after; I was lucky that I always had a new contract in place before the end of my current contract, and had no reason to shop around – plus I never, ever wanted to leave. But I know there were a few times when other players the Knights should have kept didn't stay because the Knights seemed resigned not to match offers. The player would be let go without a fight, even though I knew the player would have stayed for less.

That was the case with Chris Bailey, who I thought was approaching his prime as a player, ready to shine and to be a rep player. He is a country boy from Inverell, a sensational human being with a great family, and the team loved having him around. He wanted to stay but he hadn't heard from the club. In the end he had to ring them and ask whether they wanted him or not and they just said they couldn't compete with the offer from Manly. But how did they know he wouldn't have stayed for quite a bit less? I think he would have.

Again, time will tell if the right decision was made. New-castle picked up Ben Rogers to play five-eighth to replace 'Bails', and with Scott Dureau at halfback and Jarrod Mullen coming off the bench early in the season, they had a few options there.

That's the Brian Smith model: few stand-out marquee players, just a good even squad of players with versatility he can shuffle around when the demand requires it. He's had plenty of success building clubs on that New England Patriots model, so maybe the tough period of 2007 into 2008 will be justified. More and more juniors from the Hunter might come through and replace those of us from the previous era and the culture the club has built might still get passed down to a new generation and a whole new period of success might begin. I know they are working hard on bringing that culture and the Knights' history back to the forefront with the current players.

I still don't believe there had to be so many changes at the Knights, and so many players cut. But it was done with the justification that it had to be done and that the proof would come within three seasons. It appears the plan was: in the first year dismantle it, in the second year rebuild it, in the third year be judged on it.

Brian Smith had got his hand-picked team in 2009. Only Steve Simpson, Jarrod Mullen, Kurt Gidley – who are the three marquee players – and Daniel Tolar are still there from Michael Hagan's last season.

As I put this book to bed, the Knights – after being in or around the top four two-thirds into the 2009 season – snuck into the top eight with a victory in the last match against Penrith, after having won three of the remaining four games after Brian Smith was stood down as coach for the rest of 2009 and Rick Stone was appointed in his place. So at that stage it could be argued that the club was in no better position on the ladder than when Brian came to the Knights – although there is no doubting that some of the systems Brian put in place are excellent. Some people might say that the retirement of Andrew Johns had as big a bearing as anything, and that's hard to ignore.

The shock news hit everyone associated with the Knights, past and present, when it was announced in June 2009 that Brian Smith had decided to quit his job (from the end of season), despite having a year to run on his contract, to take up a four-year contract with the Sydney Roosters. When I received a series of text messages from Knights players, and former players, telling me of the news, I didn't know what to think. Some of the blokes were bitter about him walking away; some accepted it as one of the many business decisions that are such a part of the game today; while others thought it might end up a good move for Brian and the club after the big changes that he was ordered to make were pretty much completed.

It took me a while to get my head around it at first because I had so many different emotions. But after considering it from all angles, Smithy's decision typifies what football is about these days and I can't blame him for accepting the security of a four-year deal on the money that was being speculated (I read $500,000 a season).

As I write this the club had just employed Rick Stone – the assistant coach to Brian and Michael Hagan before him – to take on the job. It was a smart move; otherwise all the drastic changes would have been for nothing. I can't see the point of bringing in another senior coach from outside and inflicting another big culture change on the club three years after what went on. 'Stoney' communicates well with players, is a champion bloke who is capable of leading the club forward, and most importantly he is very familiar with the program Brian put in place.

While I've been in England I've naturally thought of what I would do when I returned to Australia and whether I could get involved with the Knights in some capacity. I was confused – at a bit of a dead end, really – thinking that the Knights'

My brother Broc and I playing backyard footy in the colours of our favourite team, St George. Looks like it's 1–0 to me.

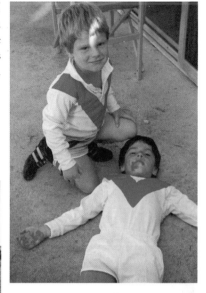

That's me as an eight-year-old at footy training in Taree. What about my mullet . . . what was Mum thinking?

The extended Buderus family at our wedding in January 2007. We would have loved Ella in the photo as well but the occasion became a bit too much for her, as she was only eight weeks old. Kris did an amazing job managing a newborn and organising a wedding. Back: Mum, me, Kris and Dad. Front: Max, Broc, Tianne and Jett.

BEN NEWNAM PHOTOGRAPHY

Welcome to England, my little princess. Ella swinging in the snow.

Ella and me in York, England, on our way to the Wiggles concert.

The most special girls in my life; down at our beautiful local park at Roundhay in Leeds.

You never know what you'll pick up in Darwin: a crocodile . . . and a wife, if you play your cards right.

One of the first shots of Mr and Mrs Buderus; walking down for a photoshoot on the picturesque Hawkesbury River with the bridal party. A perfect day.
BEN NEWNAM PHOTOGRAPHY

Kris and me in the shed at our family retreat, 'The Shack', at Bowhill on the Murray River, South Australia. It doesn't take long to unwind after a day's skiing; that's my ideal family holiday.

That's me on the Murray doing my best on the skis, but I'm still not a patch on Kris – that girl's got talent on the water.

I could listen to Gus (Phil Gould) talk Origin all day. He had a massive influence on me as a State of Origin coach. ACTION PHOTOGRAPHICS/ COLIN WHELAN

It's always a special moment singing the anthem before a State of Origin game. Usually I look for my family and sing as hard as I can. I think Hindy (Nathan Hindmarsh) thought it was me out of tune, but it was definitely Mase (Willie Mason). FAIRFAX/ DARREN PATEMAN

After I'd played my last game for NSW Country, three mates I've always loved playing with – and lifelong friends – sent me this picture of us, with a message from each of them written on it. It's a treasured possession. From left: Fitzy (Craig Fitzgibbon), me, Hindy (Nathan Hindmarsh) and Bobcat (Andrew Ryan). ACTION PHOTOGRAPHICS/ GRANT TROUVILLE

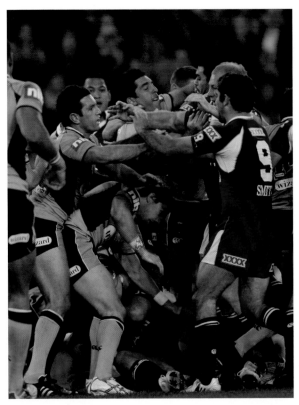

New South Wales v Queensland; it's the greatest test of character. It's a one-in, all-in approach, as this shot shows, with my rival hooker Cameron Smith and me playing rock, paper, scissors while the other boys get it on. FAIRFAX/DARREN PATEMAN

It was a weird moment, me having to present Andrew Johns with his winner's ring after the Origin series win in 2005. Being Joey's Origin captain when he was my club captain always felt a bit strange. GETTY IMAGES/CAMERON SPENCER

Origin 1 2005 at Suncorp Stadium, celebrating the first of my grand total of two Origin tries (the second came in the next match). FAIRFAX/ CRAIG GOLDING

This is an awesome shot of the captains from the first 25 years of State of Origin; one I'm very proud to be part of. NEWSPIX/PHIL HILLYARD

Enjoying some quality R & R in Origin camp preparing for Game 3, 2005, with my great mate Fitz (Craig Fitzgibbon). The door to my room was always open. NEWSPIX/MARK EVANS

Not a happy ending . . . my head bowed in defeat after the realisation Origin football had left my life, after the deciding game (which we lost) at ANZ Stadium, Sydney, 2008.
FAIRFAX/DARREN PATEMAN

Proud Australian players from Newcastle – Simmo, Joey and me – after winning the Anzac Test against the Kiwis, May 2006. It proved the last Test appearance for Andrew Johns and me (not that we knew it at the time). It was some sort of redemption after getting flogged by the Kiwis in the 2005 Tri Nations in England. ACTION PHOTOGRAPHICS/COLIN WHELAN

At the end of every game I played against JP (Jamie Peacock), I always wished he was on my team. He is, now that I'm at the Leeds Rhinos, and a great mate, too, as loyal and passionate as they come. GETTY IMAGES/MICHAEL STEELE

Every young footballer's dream – and it became a reality for me. Singing the anthem as Australian captain at Elland Road, Leeds, 2005, with (from left) Craig Gower, Shane Webcke, bellboy and manager John 'Chow' Hayes. ACTION PHOTOGRAPHICS/COLIN WHELAN

One of our many dress-up days at the hospitable Newton residence in Newcastle. This one was a 'C' party. I was a cyclist, Brian Carney was Christina Aguilera, Andrew Johns was Kane Cleal and Matt Gidley was Warwick Capper.

To take advantage of a mid-year bye, Kris and I went away for a romantic weekend to Byron Bay . . . only to find that staying at the same hotel were three scallywags: Changa (Trent Langlands), Finchy (Brett Finch) and Guru (Eric Grothe Jnr).

Two frustrated horse owners finally get to have a picture with the Golden Slipper. That's me and my best man, Mark Hughes, the day before my wedding, at Strawberry Hill, John Singleton's ranch. The closest we ever got to a Slipper victory was when one of our nags won a maiden at Cessnock.

Gids (Kurt Gidley), me and Lloyd (Chris Bailey) at the Big Day Out, 2008. Attending the gig was an annual event for us.

It's amazing what adrenalin can do . . . I have never jumped that high again. Ben Kennedy had just scored a try to make it 24–0 after just half an hour in the 2001 grand final. What a perfect half of footy by the Knights that night. ACTION PHOTOGRAPHICS/ COLIN WHELAN

This is one of my favourite photos. Every face has a story to tell about how they got to this memorable moment. ACTION PHOTOGRAPHICS/COLIN WHELAN

I'm one for history and what has been done before me, and this is one group of men I never wanted to let down. On our traditional Old Boys day, former players form a guard of honour when the Knights run out for the last home game of each year. Great moment. ACTION PHOTOGRAPHICS/COLIN WHELAN

Winning the 2004 Dally M Awards. Lucky you can't see my bow tie – I had to borrow one from my chairman in the car park before the start of the night. Let's just say it didn't suit me. NEWSPIX/MARK EVANS

Tough times . . . the boys shield Kirk Reynoldson from the media as he breaks down telling the Newcastle team he's played his last game for the club. NEWSPIX/ROBERT MCKELL

A coach with a job to do . . . Brian Smith and I share a light-hearted moment at a press conference in Gosford, 2007. NEWSPIX/SAM RUTTYN

Healthy debating . . . sometimes the refs' calls don't go your way and it can be hard to take. I had my fair share of run-ins with the refs; here I discuss some finer points with Tony Archer, who I didn't find particularly approachable. FAIRFAX/KITTY HILL

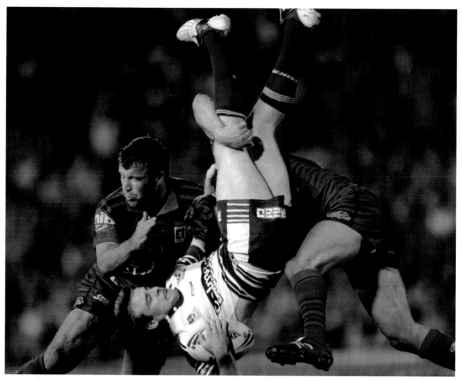

How things can go wrong so easily . . . I copped six weeks for this 'spear' tackle on Manly winger Michael Robertson in a semi-final against Manly in 2006. It ended up being my last finals appearance. FAIRFAX/DARREN PATEMAN

Farewelling the amazing Newcastle crowd on my lap of honour at our last home game, 2008. I wish I could have had my beloved jersey on, but I'd had an operation on my bicep the day before. It was tough and emotional saying goodbye. GETTY IMAGES/MATT KING

In action for Leeds 2009; I love Headingley but injuries meant I couldn't get any real form . . . frustrating. RLPHOTOS.COM/DAVE WILLIAMS

door might have been shut for a few years. But now something inside me is saying I'd love to be involved with the club some day and pay it back for what it has given me – whether in a coaching role or with a mentoring, development role with the younger players. In fact, I feel quite excited about it now, as if I have something to aim for after my playing days are finished.

One thing can't be disputed, however. Brian Smith will leave a legacy at the Newcastle Knights. He has stripped the system right back to the core in a technical sense and introduced a new structure, then reintroduced some of the principles that the foundation of the club was built on. As tough as he was with how he approached things, he has improved a lot of players. The club would be smart to continue the principles he intro-duced, and build on them.

14

UNWANTED HEADLINES

I PUT myself slap bang in the middle of a media controversy in August 2007 over the massive clean-out at the Knights. I didn't know who to turn to during that period and probably turned to a wrong person in the circumstances when I opened up to Barry Toohey, the *Daily Telegraph*'s well respected Newcastle-based league reporter, and a bloke I regard as a mate. The resulting article put me into massive conflict with coach Brian Smith, brought to a head the issue of the manner in which the playing roster was being carved up . . . and ultimately led to my realisation that it was time for me to make plans to leave the Newcastle Knights.

In hindsight, I regret airing my views via the newspapers and the hell it put me, and the club, through. I hate conflict, and I dived right into a storm of conflict. I should have taken my concerns directly to Brian. But I won't deny that my comments reflected exactly how I felt.

My comments were in no way personal towards Brian or anyone in particular; they were more about the process used to rip apart the club without adequate communication with the players. But Brian seemed to take them personally and hit back with what I felt was a very personal attack on me and my right to have my view, and I found that very disappointing. We had our say in a good heart-to-heart phone conversation a few days later, something I wish we'd had before anything came out in the media, but I have to be honest and say our relationship was purely 'business only' after that.

Here is what happened that week.

Barry Toohey, who has been the *Tele*'s league reporter since before I came to the Knights in the mid-1990s and is respected by the players, called me just as the Kirk Reynoldson dramas were starting to boil over. A few players had already confided in Barry before he spoke to me. No one at the club could deny that the morale among the players was the lowest I'd ever experienced during my 11 years in first grade, and Barry knew full well what was going down and how many players were pissed off.

I was pretty candid about what was happening; I made the main points that the players just wanted to know where they stood, that we wanted some clear explanation from the club on what they wanted and that there just hadn't been enough communication. I said I didn't know where the club was heading, we were getting no support, the rest of the season (there were four games left) seemed a waste of time and it wasn't a happy place to be. I did say that the ordeal with Reyno was the last straw as far as low morale was concerned.

The problem was that, knowing Barry so well, I thought we were just having a chat and I was getting some things off my chest; I didn't stop to think he'd quote me so strongly for the story. I don't blame Barry for that; it was a lesson for me, and any player really, that even with journos you know well, if you want something to stay off the record you have to clarify that fact. I didn't do that with Baz and he was entitled to quote

155

me on everything I said. I meant what I said, but I do regret how I said it and, as captain, that it caused conflict within the club.

Barry, as a good journalist would, rang Brian Smith for his side of the story. Smithy defended his attitude, justifying it by saying he was just doing the job that he was brought in to do and that needed doing. Within a couple of hours of my conversation with Barry Toohey, Brian was on the phone ripping into me, asking what the hell I had done. He said, 'I can't believe you could do this to the club; it is the worst thing I have ever heard being said; you have brought so much pressure onto the players, I can't believe you did this,' and so on. I was distraught. I said, 'Hang on, what am I supposed to have said? I've said nothing too bad.' Brian reckoned that wasn't how it was reported to him after speaking with Barry Toohey.

I hung up and rang Barry straight away. I was shaking. I asked, 'Mate, what have you said to the coach? He has just rung me and hammered me.' Barry went through what he told Brian and I thought it wasn't too bad – and to this day I still don't think it was too bad considering what was going on at the club; and Barry agreed with me. Still, I asked him if there was any way of 'pulling' the story, but he said it was too late.

I woke up at the crack of dawn next day and waited until the newsagent opened. There it was, on the back page under the heading 'KNIGHTS PLAYER REVOLT. Exclusive: Danny Buderus reveals how Brian Smith has shattered team morale'.

This is how the story read:

The rocky relationship between Newcastle Knights coach Brian Smith and senior players has reached breaking point as the club battles to avoid the wooden spoon.

Captain Danny Buderus admitted for the first time yesterday Smith's decision to cut a swath through the playing ranks for next season had caused widespread dissent and left morale at the club at an all-time low.

Buderus described the wholesale changes – which has seen long-serving players such as Adam Woolnough, Clint Newton, Josh Perry and a host of others shown the door – as 'too much, too soon'.

The latest moves to try and unload back-rower Kirk Reynoldson, two games shy of activating a retention clause in his $200,000 contract for next season, was the 'straw that broke the camel's back' according to Buderus.

Smith admitted last night he is not surprised at the player unrest because he knew it was coming. 'No one is feeling great at the moment because it is tough times,' Smith said. 'I'm feeling the same way myself. When the decision is made to move people on, and that is what I was hired to do as coach, if it was necessary, there is no nice way to do it.

'I can understand them being upset about it. That is not going to change overnight. It will take some time [for the bridges to be mended].'

Buderus said the uncertainty over the future direction of the club had to be addressed.

'The players are upset, I won't deny that, and club management is aware of it,' he said. 'We just want someone from the club to tell us where the joint is headed – what he [Smith] is trying to do. This club has always been a unique club and the closeness of the playing group is what has made it so special. But we are getting away from what we are about. They can't just keep on wanting the boys to keep turning up each week if we don't know what is going on.'

Buderus described the relationship between Smith and most of the players as 'professional'. He added the playing group was aware there would be changes when Smith was appointed. 'I guess he is doing what the club brought him in to do,' he said. 'He is here to do a job but we were already a pretty good club. We had some good things in place that didn't need to be fixed.'

Asked did he feel Smith's job may be under threat given his failing relationship with the players, Buderus replied: 'It's not up to us. The people who make those decisions must want this to happen, I guess.'

Knights senior executive officer Steve Burraston said: 'There is no question when you make some tough decisions on players that it is going to affect things and with the injury toll we've had and the fact we have lost some games on the trot now, it all affects the morale in the place.'

It was not a personal attack on Brian but a question of where the club was going. And, looking at the quotes now, I still don't reckon what I said was over the top; in fact I watered down a lot of what Barry told me other players were saying.

Nevertheless, looking back, I let my guard down a bit, not thinking to what extent I was unloading on the club when I was pretty emotional about the issue. We'd also had the announcement of the Knights 'Team of the Era' a couple of nights beforehand and a lot of the ex-players were fired up about how the culture of the club and all that it was built on was being ripped apart so dramatically with all the player sackings and most were having a go at Smithy.

I should have gone and spoken to the coach about it but, having said that, we didn't talk much; I didn't find him nearly as approachable as Michael Hagan. I know Brian would not have got any pleasure out of telling a player he had to move on and was not required; it was a tough job for him and the club had given him a brief.

I got a lot of calls from people the next day, including players, saying it was about time someone stood up about what was going on. I was out injured at the time and we were taking on Manly at Gosford on the Friday night. Next day at training, it was obviously a big talking point, with the media surrounding Brian afterwards for his comments. Well, he just hammered me, and I don't think anyone could say it wasn't personal, although Smithy denied that afterwards.

Here is how he responded to some of the questions:

If you really want to find someone who is sad, find the captain of a footy club who's only played 11 games this season for his club through suspension and injury and rep duties and who's seen his club not do as well as he would have liked under his captaincy. I feel very sorry . . . and I'm upset . . . that there's a number of guys in this footy club who I've only known for a short time who I really like who are not going to be here next year. So I can't imagine how hard that is for blokes who are friends of those people and who have done all the stuff that footy players do together and they're losing their team-mates. It's sad but . . . they all know change needs to be made. That's why I was brought here. The board gave me a clear statement of what they wanted done and while it's not a happy job . . . if you want to be happy, then you're hiring. If you want to be sad, then you're firing. It's tough.

Asked about the dramas being played out publicly, Brian said:

> I think Danny could have done it in a different way but like I said, if you want to find someone who's not at the top of their game and is going to make an error of judgement, then you go to someone who is suffering from severe disappointment. Danny's a real proud man. He wanted to have an enormous effect and he has. He's just not seeing and feeling that as the new captain of the Knights after Joey left. He wanted to be an effective and winning captain of the Origin series and it didn't turn out that way. His position as No. 9 in the Australian jersey is probably under threat. For a proud guy who's done so much service for Australian footy, and particularly the Knights, when it's not going well you're likely to find a bloke who is going to say the wrong thing. I wish he hadn't said it. I'm sure he does too but them's the breaks.

When asked about morale, he said:

> Team morale's not so bad, really. It depends if you're talking Monday or Tuesday after a loss. Everybody's feeling it. But if you'd been here and seen our training session the other night – and Simmo summed it up in the end by saying 'that's one of our best sessions for the year' – you wouldn't worry so much. Bedsy wasn't here to see that. Bedsy's missed a lot of sessions this year because he's not been part of the team. Only playing 11 games has made it difficult for him to feel like he's part of that crew at times.

Some of those comments got my back up; I thought what he said was condescending and belittling. And plenty of people obviously agreed; my phone rang hot from people fuming at what had been said, including players from other clubs he had dismantled, who wanted to lend me support. To suggest I was too out of touch to know what morale was like, when I had been at the club for 13 years and spoke to the players more than the coach, CEO or the board did; to suggest I had made wild statements because I was the losing Origin captain and being under pressure for my Test spot, or that I was frustrated by not being a winning captain at Newcastle after succeeding Joey – what did that have to do with what I said? I was the one fielding all the comments from players about how they felt because no one in the club seemed to care; that was the whole issue of my comments.

I went to our operations manager, Steve Crowe, and told him I'd had enough; that I didn't want to be at the club anymore because, like a lot of other players, I no longer felt wanted. I asked him about getting out of my contract at the end of the season even though I had a year, and an option for a further year, to go. I went to Paul Harragon, who was on the board, and asked the same thing. I wanted to go overseas and play because I couldn't bring myself to play against the Knights. What had happened, especially with Kirk Reynoldson, showed that NRL football had become a hard-nosed business and I didn't want to be part of that anymore; I'd had a gutful.

Crowey said not to be stupid, that I'd regret any spontaneous decision and the only way to resolve things was to talk about it. It was just bullshit for the club to be pretending there was no major problem. At least one positive thing that story did do was bring it all to a head.

I went to the game against Manly and sat in the crowd with

Kris and a few people came up to me and were very supportive. We were thrashed by Manly 50–16 and I felt I'd added undue stress for the team who were already affected by injury and up against a strong side. It wasn't a very enjoyable trip back up the F3.

Brian rang me the next day; I knew it was a conversation we had to have but I was nervous as hell picking up the phone. We had a long-overdue chat, which made it a lot easier to go to training on the Monday. Brian said something like, 'I've got this club's best interest at heart and that's why I'm doing this. You know we had to have a change; I have to bring new blood in here and prepare for life after Andrew – I think this is the best way for it to be done.' I talked about how we were getting pulled apart and that we were getting no support from the club.

I said, 'I've got players coming up to me saying I don't know if I am here next week or next year; they're talking amongst themselves. It's tough and no one is helping us out; no one is telling us what is going on – that's all I said.' I also spoke about the way Kirk was being treated and told him, 'All he wants to do is play with his mates.' I said to Brian, 'There is a right way and wrong way to do things; it must be the hardest thing in the world for you to do but, at the least, we need someone to talk us through it; we feel isolated. We need to know what's going on as a team – we are just floundering at the moment. We don't know what is going on week to week – that's all I was saying in the *Telegraph*.' He said I should have come to him and told him that, not gone to the papers, and I said I was the first to put up my hand and admit that.

It was good that each of us was able to tell the other how we felt, and then get on with business. Our relationship as coach and captain was fine from then, if not close. We both moved on and did our best for the Newcastle Knights. We talked footy okay in 2008, but it was strictly the upcoming match and what we had to do, which was a pity as I used to like talking footy generally with him because I respected his knowledge and what he has done in the game.

The feeling in the town was running hot and I was usually defending the club. A lot of people would come up to me in the street saying they'd never support the Knights again. I'd say, 'C'mon, it's not about that; the club is always above the one person – it's the best club in the world. You have to support it and turn up next week.' They'd say, 'No, not while this is going on.' I hope those people have come back. We went better in 2008 and started '09 impressively, with a lot of the newer players going well. The Knights deserve their support.

But I knew then my time was up at Newcastle; it was the right time to move on. I'm glad I listened to the right people and didn't try to bail out at the end of 2007. I had to get away and let the emotion die down and in the end I said to myself, 'If you love this place enough, you can work with Brian fine; new players will come in and start over again; just do your best while you're here and don't get involved in the politics.' In another sense, though, I was proud of myself that I did stand up for my team-mates. Once it all came out, the club's administration was forced to communicate with us about it; the whole place was shaken up. All of a sudden directors were calling up asking to go and have a coffee and talk about the issue.

Steve Burraston, who'd only taken over as CEO a few weeks earlier, came around my place on the Monday for a pow-wow and asked if I could still work with the coach. I said, 'Of course I can; I love the club and I want it to be successful and Brian is the coach and he also wants the club to be successful.' But even that event turned into a charade; journalists and photographers were out the front and I was asked to be in a photo shaking 'Burro's' hand, which I wasn't comfortable with (doing it in front of an audience, that is), but if I had refused that would have given the wrong message and would have been another headline.

During the saga the *Newcastle Herald* hopped into me one day. They ran a headline 'Where is Danny Buderus?' suggesting I had gone under cover after I refused to be interviewed about it in the days after the *Tele* story first came out. I was fuming and thought that was out of order. My first instinct was to fire back but I took a step back, learned from my mistake and realised it was best to have the issue solved in-house. Nothing was going to be achieved by further comment in print. I'd also been instructed by the club not to say anything more.

Before this blew up, I'd already flagged with my manager Darryl Mather about going to England, but this helped make up my mind. I admit there was a chance I could have gone to Wigan in 2008 and finished up at the Knights on that note. I'm glad I didn't. Instead we took our time and decided I'd go to Leeds after one more season at Newcastle.

15

THE CAP DOESN'T FIT

UNLESS WE have some sort of overhaul of the salary cap, I'm worried we'll have an increase in the amount of players picking up more money for less effort in rugby union, or going for the lifestyle change and lesser pressure of the English Super League.

We have to have a cap, otherwise the Broncos would win the premiership every year with the income they have compared to other clubs; but it has to have a lot more flexibility and incentive for clubs to keep hold of long-term players.

The cap has forced out too many good, experienced club men the game needs to mentor younger players both on the field, at training, and in determining the off-field culture of acceptable behaviour. I reckon that has even had an influence on the amount of alcohol-related off-field incidents we've had in recent years.

I have no doubt that the problem we are having with player behaviour is partly caused by the lack of experienced players in the game who would normally have a big influence on the culture of clubs. The culture of a lot of clubs now is being set by 'generation X' players. Younger players are being cast into leadership roles a lot earlier and often they are not well enough equipped to handle it. In 2008, half the NRL clubs had captains who were under the age of 26 at the start of the competition.

The salary cap has also had the effect of seeing so many State of Origin level players join the English Super League, for similar or better money. They enjoy a more attacking brand of football and, despite the competition becoming a lot more even across the board, it's still not as physically daunting as the NRL. Plus a big attraction is that there's not anywhere near the off-field public pressure that exists in Australia. Look at these players, for example, who are playing in the 2009 Super League competition; just about all left, directly or indirectly, because of the salary cap squeeze when they had plenty to still offer the NRL: Shaun Berrigan, who went to England at age 29, Dane Carlaw who was 28 at the time, Casey McGuire (27 when he signed), Matt King (27), Matt Gidley (29), Brent Sherwin (28), Adam Mogg (29), Lincoln Withers (27), Michael Monaghan (27), Clint Newton (27), Liam Fulton (24), Josh Hannay (27), Michael Vella (29), Chris Flannery (27), Paul Whatuira (26), Rangi Chase (22), Brent Webb (26), Clint Greenshield (25), Pat Richards (24), Mark Riddell (28), Phil Bailey (26) and Dean Widders (29). Then there are a few who don't count as imports because they qualify as Polynesian players under what is called the Kolpak agreement. Two such cases are my Leeds team-mates: Ali Lauitiiti and Kylie Leuluai.

Then we have, playing in French rugby union: Sonny Bill Williams (23 when he signed), Luke Rooney (25), Mark Gasnier (27) and Craig Gower (29). I see European rugby and Japanese rugby as being real threats in coming seasons. Why wouldn't you go if you can get a heap more money and have to play only 12 games a year, as is the case in Japan? I think rugby league is being short-sighted if we don't think it is going to affect our game if more players leave when they still have a few seasons left to contribute to the NRL.

I appreciate that the salary cap has dispersed the talent across the 16 clubs and that is why Brisbane is the only team since the NRL began in 1998 that has won the grand final twice and every team, including the Gold Coast Titans, who only came into the competition in 2007, has made the finals. And I know that we're in tough economic times and a lot of clubs are battling to spend to the salary cap limit of $4 million anyway, and a lot have given up running reserve grade teams to cut down their costs, which I find really sad.

My biggest issue with the cap is that it forces out senior players before their time and that has a bigger effect than just bringing the average age and experience of first grade squads down. Those players should be kept in our game to mentor the younger players, and to generate loyalty with the fans. It is pretty well accepted these days that the more successful you are, the less likely you are to keep your squad together.

I reckon the concessions on the salary cap for long-serving players should start once players reach 100 first grade games for the club. Make it that 20 per cent of their salary is exempt from the cap at that stage and when they reach 150 games it is 40 per cent, and 200 games or 10 years for the club should make 60 per cent of the player's contract exempt. And if they reach 250 games they should be completely exempt. I think it is a feat these days to stay at the one club for five years, and that's how long it would take to play 100 games. But that should be a benchmark players aspire to; you want to be on that field for your team-mates and your club and if you do it for five seasons, you're at a club that obviously respects you and that should be rewarded.

During my time at the Knights I had to watch Matthew Johns, Bill Peden and Matthew Gidley, the best club men you could ask for, who were locals, who wanted to stay loyal to the club, leave because of salary cap pressures. They were players Newcastle people wanted in our team – they identified with them as local boys who had come through the ranks. But there was never a good enough system of exemptions to fit them under the cap and the club had to make hard decisions to retain younger players, at the expense of senior players who still had a lot to offer.

We're getting a system where footy clubs are regarded as 'franchises'; they trade players to keep under the salary cap and are forced to let players go they would ideally like to keep. That goes against breeding, developing and retaining players; and keeping them as part of the local community; and developing strong bonds with the club's fans – principles that I grew up with.

Widening the concessions for 100-plus game players would not only help keep those players in the game but it would open up money for the younger players to be kept, and also give them a better apprenticeship because they would have more experienced players around them.

The cap should be geared around keeping players at a club as long as possible and having a mechanism where the rich clubs, or those that don't develop their own talent, can't so easily throw bigger money at them to take them away. I've been blessed to play at a club where good programs were in place to develop talent and for players to want to stay with the Knights. It was all about juniors and bringing them through and for them to aspire to play for the Newcastle Knights, not any other club. But we went away from that for a while and other clubs started to infiltrate the Hunter Valley and the country areas just to the north, which were such a strong breeding ground for the Knights. They started taking away our good young players who hadn't even made it to first grade with offers of an extra $30,000 or $40,000, and when you are 17 or 18 that's a lot of money. We became easy pickings.

The other issue is utilising outside revenue to keep established players. The NRL has looked at marquee player clauses and third-party payments as a way of putting more flexibility into the cap; but it doesn't seem to have worked. I can't see why a club has to go to a company that has no direct sponsorship with it to get extra payments for players ahead of companies that have already shown an allegiance to the club by becoming a sponsor. I wouldn't want to see shonky player sponsorship deals created as a way of cheating the cap but I can't see why players can't get extra income from companies for genuine effort. By that I mean working so many hours a week for that company as an introduction to a post-football career, or doing advertising for them.

I'm like a lot of players in the NRL who signed a contract with a promise of getting third-party payments from an outside sponsor as the only way to pay extra money to keep me at the club. I had two such deals thrown at me. One never came to fruition; the other did, but neither party utilised it. Not getting third-party income that was promised to him by the club was a big issue with Mark Gasnier leaving the Dragons and heading off to France and has caused some conflict between other players and their clubs.

In my case my third-party benefit was worth about $70,000 and I signed, believing that the money would be forthcoming. But a deal between the club and the company broke down when the Knights decided they wanted to go with another company in that 'category'. As it turned out, they renewed their ties with the original company after all, but it was too far down the track – about nine months later, I think – to resurrect my deal. I didn't want to cause a big drama about it and I didn't want to use it as a reason to get out of my contract, because I simply didn't want to play with another NRL club. But it is one of a few examples I know of where those sorts of deals promised during the negotiation of a contract just never eventuate. I think that would happen less often if clubs were allowed to do legitimate deals with companies they already had agreements with. Maybe the third-party deals can be restricted to so many players per club, otherwise Brisbane, who have a capital city to themselves, might get an unfair advantage, but there has to be a way for players to use their image and profile to earn money in association with their current club.

In the end my management, SFX Sports, came up with a 'sweetener' through a firm called Leisure Boating at Port Stephens, in the form of a free membership that gave me access to a fleet of nine luxury boats, which I could have hired. I was keen to take advantage of the deal but as the demands of the footy season kicked in I really didn't get the opportunity. So neither Leisure Boating nor I got much value out of the relationship despite all the right intentions.

But I'm not complaining at all; I was one of the lucky ones in that I was paid very well to do something I loved and was able to stay at Newcastle for 15 years from the time I came down from Taree. I look at someone like Jesse Royal, who broke into first grade with the Knights in 2007, had his best season in 2008 and really came of age as a very good first grader – only for the club to tell him they couldn't keep him under the cap. He was forced to retire because his kids were settled and they had to be his priority; he actually took a job in the mines. Fortunately, the Warriors gave him an opportunity to have one more crack at the NRL and, despite probably not earning any more money than he could have down the pit, he decided to move his family to Auckland to continue in the game. They're the players I feel for; those who work hard to establish themselves as good members of the squad, but whose club can't carry them any longer and they have to move house to keep earning an income from rugby league.

The salary cap has to be geared towards protecting clubs that develop and want to keep their own talent. I can't believe we have an NRL club – the Sydney Roosters – who don't even have their own junior league competition; in fact, they only have four clubs in the area. They have to grab talent from other clubs' junior systems and to do that they have to pay a lot more. That forces up other clubs' costs to keep the players they put time, money and resources into developing into future first graders. I don't agree with that. I know that some clubs with big, strong junior leagues can't give every talented player an opportunity to play NRL and the fact is that other clubs who need to source talent from outside create extra opportunities for them. A sort of junior meat market is not healthy but at least a salary cap in the Toyota Cup and the fact the Roosters and quite a few clubs don't have second-tier teams is changing that.

I don't blame the Roosters for doing it; they've operated very smartly as a business to stay in the NRL and be so successful, but they are always going to have a transit lounge of players coming through because they don't have the junior roots. All they need to do is raid other clubs for Toyota Cup (under 20s) players and cherrypick players at the higher level and they can survive under the franchise system with a salary cap. Look at their 2009 team and how many years they've been at the club (before the season began) – only Craig Fitzgibbon (ten) and Anthony Minichiello (ten) have been long-term first graders there. Then you have Braith Anasta (four seasons), James Aubusson (two), Riley Brown (two), Willie Mason (two), Nate Myles (three), Mark O'Meley (two) who were brought from other clubs, and then a heap of younger players they scouted from outside. Anthony Cherrington and Tom Symonds are their only players who came up through the local ranks. Mind you, the Newcastle Knights at present don't have as much home-grown talent as they usually do but I'm sure that will change in the next few years.

The fact that NRL clubs don't even have a reserve grade now is also sad. They're sort of contracted out to other feeder clubs, not because of the salary cap, but because a lot of clubs just can't afford to carry a second team. And that's because the cost of running an NRL side has increased so much, with a lot more money being put into coaching, training and rehab facilities to give them an edge while all the clubs are so close in talent under the cap.

I think it cost the Knights a million dollars a year to run a Premier League team and in the end they reckoned they couldn't justify that and, like a lot of clubs, decided to scrap their reserve grade. Now they don't even have a feeder side in the New South Wales Cup, so players in the top 25 who might not make the side on any given week go back to the local league where they are balloted out to different clubs.

So we are developing a situation where players go into the Toyota Cup as the stepping stone to first grade. Sure, it gets television coverage on Fox Sports and over 50 players progressed to first grade in 2008, but I'm yet to be convinced the Toyota Cup is going to develop players mature enough for long first grade careers. I think some players will get thrown into first grade before their time through necessity, because the NRL clubs can't carry good back-up talent, and the risk is that some under

20s aren't mature enough, physically or mentally, to handle it and it can ruin their confidence.

The natural progression of coming through your club's junior representative sides, coming into the Jersey Flegg/ President's Cup then into reserve grade and then on to first grade, having experienced players to mentor you along the way and have the fans feel an alignment with the players as they progress through the ranks and then stay with the club, is all being eroded away.

The salary cap wasn't a major reason why I ended my time at Newcastle with a year to go on my contract, but I was certainly conscious that if I moved on it gave the Knights a much better chance of keeping Kurt Gidley and Jarrod Mullen, two very talented local boys who should be kept by the club. Obviously the club saw the benefit of me moving on and freeing up money too, as they did with Matthew Gidley, who was also released from his contract to go to St Helens in 2007.

Another side-effect too is that players get thrust into first grade, and all its limelight, at 18 or 19 and it is a lot tougher for them to handle the sudden attention and profile. Again, they don't have a lot of senior players to advise them at the start of that process.

Generally the young blokes who come into first grade these days are a lot cockier and they are the biggest group in the team dynamic. Even the younger guys outside the first grade squad seem to be a lot more confident around the senior players; I wouldn't have dared try to be 'one of the boys' with the first graders when I was coming through the lower grades. I just wouldn't have felt I'd earned that right until I had proved myself in first grade.

These days the kids get success and good contracts earlier because clubs clamour over each other for the next big thing on the scene, and they've had managers since they were 16 telling them how good and valuable they are; it can easily lead them into a feeling that success will just continue without them having to work hard at it and without realising they may get plenty of setbacks along the way.

I think the NRL club jersey will soon have a two- or three-year lifespan before another player comes in to get fitted for it. And the fans won't feel there is loyalty between players and themselves like they used to. Before, they'd watch them come through the lower grades and then stay at the club as established first graders; now most fans don't know much about their club other than the first grade team and they see the make-up of that team change all the time.

16

LIFE AT 'THE MARRIOTT'

IT WAS a halfway house for the Newcastle Knights players for about four years. For Mark Hughes and me it was our home; well, it was his home at least and I was a lodger. Some of the funniest times have been played out at the house in Myamblah Crescent, Merewether, during a wonderful period of our lives . . . before I was jilted by Booze for his wife Kirralee and tossed onto the street.

I bought my first place in Blamey Avenue, Blackbutt, in 1997 and lived there for about twelve months with Trent 'Poppy' Watson, who I had played junior Knights football with, before he moved out and I was living on my own. Poppy was a great guy to live with; he was studying to be a dietician at the time and it's great to see him running a successful business these days. Boozy and I were starting to hang out a fair bit together; he'd bought a large house in Merewether and one day suggested we should move in together. So I ended up selling my place and we became house-mates from 1999 to 2003 – an enjoyable, and interesting, experience.

I find it ironic that his first 'real job' post-footy was selling beer; it seemed his destiny. He's just a great bloke to be around, and socially he's always up for a beer and a laugh and is the best mate I could ask for. He was called 'Boozy' rather than 'Hughesy' by the boys at the time, but he is trying to shake the nickname now that he's a corporate juggernaut.

My own nickname, 'Bedsy', came about because of a typing error on my boarding pass when we flew to an interstate game, in (I think) 1998. We naturally had a group check-in and our football manager, Dave 'Big Dog' Morley, was yelling out the players' names as he handed out the passes. The established first graders were called by their nicknames . . . 'Joey', 'Doogs', 'Butts' . . . then Dave calls out 'Jonny'. A few of the boys looked around and said, 'Who's Jonny?' Dave looked at the boarding pass and read out 'Jonny Bedsrus', pronouncing it 'Beds-R-Us', as in the bedding retail chain. The penny quickly dropped that it was Danny Buderus and that whoever made the booking for the club had misspelt my name – badly! Next thing the boys were laughing their heads off and repeating 'Beds-R-Us', and somehow it was shortened to 'Bedsy' and it stuck; no doubt as a nickname I could have had worse. That's what I've been called ever since, by just about everyone who knows me around footy. So when our place wasn't referred to as 'The Marriott', it was just 'Boozy's and Bedsy's place'.

Our place became a real home away from home for a lot of the Knights players. I squeezed all my furniture into the place somehow and the big rumpus room downstairs was filled with a pool table and four lounges. After I convinced Hughesy to get a Jacuzzi for the back patio to help with our injury rehab, the attraction of a pool table, big screen TV, spa, a small bar and a fridge always full of refreshments was too much for the other boys to resist. In between morning and afternoon training sessions and a few nights a week there would always be a bit of a crowd at our place. It was named the 'The Myamblah Marriott' by Brett Keeble at the *Newcastle Herald*, abbreviated to 'The Marriott' by the boys – much to the owner's disgust.

'Boozy' charged me $50 a week rent, which was a pretty good deal (which he has never let me forget, by the way). I did offer to pay an extra $10 a week after convincing Mark the Jacuzzi and pool table would be a good investment.

The only downside to living with Hughesy was his bad taste in music; I reckon he has every version of the 'Best of Beer Songs' compilation CDs. The most played record in his collection, however, was *The Best of Hot Chocolate*. When 'Heaven's in the Back Seat of My Cadillac' ('Let me take you there, yeah, yeah') came on, he'd spring up out of the lounge immediately and go into his unique dance routine.

We had a bar downstairs we appropriately called 'Whispers', because Boozy and I were the only ones who 'shouted'. Boozy would put the CD player on random and also provide free entertainment. He would dance with such lack of co-ordination and rhythm we called him 'Jerky' because his body would jerk around with no pattern. But he'd certainly create some atmosphere and before you knew it a few blokes would hit the tiles.

While Booze liked to put on the apron and display his culinary skills, he wouldn't venture beyond meat and three veg or the odd barbecue, although late in our partnership his signature meal became a tuna pasta bake. He'd take the meat out of the freezer and leave it to thaw on the sink (Boozy would say 'faw' because he can't pronounce 'th') until we returned from training. Even when we dined out, 'Boozy' was a creature of habit when it came to his food; he would order the same boring fare, while I wouldn't mind mixing it up a bit.

And he has this strange fetish for bread baked by his hometown baker. Dead set, when we went to his parents' place for one of his mother Denise's great roast dinners, his dad Terry would have the Kurri Kurri baked bread all stacked neatly on a plate with all the condiments lined up beside it. 'Boozy' would have half a loaf (and I must admit I went okay too when it came to the local dough), and then take another couple home with us to get him through the week. He'd often arrange to meet his mum halfway between Kurri Kurri and Merewether to pick up the ironing and washing that she so kindly did for both of us. He'd also make sure she had a couple of freshly baked loaves with her to pass on. Each night he'd have a row of individual slices spread across the kitchen 'fawing' after getting them 'fresh' from the freezer.

Living together, training together, often eating out together and always travelling to training and games together (with a hitch-hiker by the name of Andrew Johns just about every trip) meant we were in each other's faces all the time, but we rarely had a disagreement. Hughesy always dominated the driving – much to his displeasure. The radio dial was fixed to AM station for the oldies, 2HD, and we became avid John Laws fans; it was great to meet him one day at John Fordham's 60th birthday lunch, when he drank me under the table (literally) on Wild Turkey whiskey. It was a memorable day . . . well, others remember it better than I do.

When we used to stretch down after training, a regular discussion was, 'Hey, Bedsy, did you defrost those lamb cutlets we're having for dinner?' 'Yeah; did you drop in the supermarket and get some vegies?' 'By the way, did you vacuum the lounge room . . . what about the washing, does it need bringing in?' The other boys would be giggling and saying, 'Are you two for real? You sound like you're married!' I must admit, we used to play on it a bit because it always got a laugh and a bagging from the other boys. Often, once they'd overheard what was on the menu from our stretch-down discussion, one or two would invite themselves to join us.

Hughesy always liked to be the big brother figure too, looking out for me and looking after me. I must say, he played the part well – particularly this one night in 2000. Steve Crowe, who was media manager at the time, took Hughesy and me for a beer at The Brewery, the harbourside pub in Newcastle, and I was talking about how my contract negotiations with the Knights were affecting me while my manager Darryl Mather was doing the right thing on my behalf by talking to Parramatta, although deep down I didn't want to leave Newcastle. Crowey was asking what was going on and said with a smile on his face, 'What does your other half think?' Hughesy reckoned I should stop mucking around and get a deal done; then picked up the phone and rang our CEO Ian Bonnette. As it turned out, Ian lived about 200 metres away and Hughesy said, 'We're coming around to talk turkey.' Next thing we lobbed on his doorstep and worked out a deal then and there. My management was not at all delighted that I had negotiated without them, as they thought they could have leveraged a better deal, but I was happy it was over. Ian Bonnette couldn't believe how it was done.

I had a dog called Bella, a beautifully bred Staffordshire bull terrier, and fortunately Boozy agreed that I could bring her to his mansion with me. The first week there I took her for a walk around the block and threw a ball across the very quiet street we lived in and got Bella to chase it. She was hit by a passing car and, while she recovered, she never quite had the enthusiasm for 'the chase' again. Unfortunately, Bella took to chewing the bottom of the wooden gate and Hughesy wasn't impressed. I promised to have it fixed before I moved out but, come to think of it, it never did get repaired.

Bella will also never forget her first bath at 'The Marriott'. I put her in Hughesy's shining laundry tub but she was desperate to get out and run out the door. Part of being a good dog owner is letting it know who the boss is, so I kept pushing her back in the water. Little did I know that she had knocked the hot water tap – the bath water was almost boiling and every time I pushed her back in it scalded her. She never let me put her in the tub again. Luckily, I'm better at bathing Ella than Bella.

Somehow Bella devoured one of our well-cooked lamb loin chops. Unfortunately one sizeable bone got stuck in her belly, where it stayed for about four months. We had to give her antibiotics and a lot of love and care but after the antibiotics wore off she became really skeletal in her looks. In the end she had to get an operation; the whole episode cost me thousands and I couldn't cope looking her in the eye knowing I couldn't be the parent she deserved. About that time, Hughesy's parents' dog Benny (named after Benny Elias) passed away, so we struck a deal for them to take Bella off my hands. She's still part of their Kurri Kurri household – and has never looked better, even though she'd be 11 years old now.

We had great neighbours who were a lot older than we were. We were always conscious of keeping the noise down when the boys came around; Hughesy was paranoid about it, and in return the neighbours were always respectful of our privacy. Often, after a match, plenty of the players would end up back at our place and everyone would have to abide by Hughesy's code of conduct. One time one of the boys left the side door open, which meant the noise travelled outside. Next thing, there was a hose being sprayed through the door with an accompanying scream of, 'Keep the noise down!' But those instances were pretty rare. Mark apologised to the next door neighbours and we cooked a big lasagna for them the next day and took it over as a peace offering.

And don't think the place was a refuge only for Newcastle Knights players. Hughesy and I had become mates with Nathan Brown when he was on the coaching staff of Country Origin and, after coaching St George Illawarra's Jersey Flegg team to the grand final in 2002, he and former Test front-rower Craig Young (who I think was team manager) took the team to Newcastle for a weekend on an end-of-season trip. We ran into Browny and the boys in town on the Friday night and said they could come around to our place the next day to enjoy some Newcastle hospitality and the facilities of 'The Marriott'.

Next morning I was downstairs in the rumpus room and here was this parade of 18- and 19-year-olds coming down the steps with every third one carrying a carton of beer over his shoulder. Browny's team that year included Mathew Head, Dean Young, Ashton Sims, Wes Naiqama, Steve Southern and Brett White. We must have had 10 of them in our five-person spa and I don't think they moved for about four hours.

One problem with living so long with 'Boozy' is that he has taken a few 'secrets' that I thought would have stayed between mates and dined out on them as part of his after-dinner speaking routine. Like that I used to take my clothes off when I went to the toilet to do 'a number two'. He claims that the first time we went shopping and he threw in two-dollar 'No-Name' toilet paper that was more like sandpaper than tissue, I threw it back and replaced it with high-quality paper that wasn't scented because my 'cheeks' would react severely to the perfume. I refuse to comment on these allegations because it might incriminate one of us.

Andrew Johns and Mark Hughes created the impression that I am somewhat obsessive–compulsive, which is a massive overstatement. I do like to be orderly, clean and tidy and I will admit my bedroom was the cleanest room in the house.

We organised for a cleaner to come in once a week, actually, because Hughesy wouldn't carry his weight in housekeeping.

For three or four years Hughesy had a weekly column in the *Newcastle Herald* which he was extremely proud of. Tuesday night was his writing night, so I had to keep the television volume down low while he had Kirralee at the keyboard typing in his well-constructed sentences. That was one good thing about the off-season; I could have a conversation with him on a Tuesday evening. The most important day of the week was not game day for this frustrated journo; no, it was Thursday, when his column appeared. Without exception, I'd be woken by the sound of his feet dragging up the driveway in his tartan slippers as he picked up his home-delivered *Herald*. If that didn't wake me, the slamming of the door behind him or the unwrapping of the plastic certainly would. He'd be laughing at his own one-liners if he liked the column; or yelling abuse at the over-zealous sub-editors if they'd cut a line; screaming, 'They've wrecked it, I'll be a laughing stock.' My first task when I got up was to give him feedback and I was never game to say it was anything but outstanding, because I couldn't cope with two days of his sulking.

I was going to say we never fell out with one another, but we did have one argument. We had a big double carport and naturally a double driveway, but one day, as I was stressing a little bit about running late for training, I turned too sharply and drove my car over the water meter. Water started gushing into the air all over the front yard and median strip. Hughesy was recovering from a knee reconstruction at the time and, after coming out to see what the commotion was all about, I yelled that I had to get to training but I'd get hold of one of my plumbing mates on the way and could he stay there and sort it out. As I drove away and saw him sitting on the front steps admiring our new 20-metre-high 'water feature', he didn't look real pleased.

I couldn't have wished for a better close mate during my football days than Mark Hughes because he was just as good a bloke away from football as he was as a team-mate. It was great to have someone you could share experiences with, and to have such memorable experiences to share. While he was seen by most people around the Knights as the funny guy, he is also a very loyal, supportive and understanding bloke and I know we'll be close mates for life.

Boozy finally kicked me out when he got engaged to Kirralee and, although he threw a few of my things on the front lawn in a typical exhibition for the neighbours, it wasn't a messy 'divorce'. We've both since moved on to steady married life with new partners, and into fatherhood – both well prepared after our years at 'The Marriott'.

17

FAMILY TIES

NEVER FOR one day do I underestimate how fortunate I am to have such a great family. I reckon few sports people can achieve what they are capable of without the support of parents and siblings and having a happy home life. It's special to me that Mum, Dad, my brother Broc and my wife Kris – and my extended family – are proud of me.

I've always been conscious of the name I represent. Buderus is not a common name in Australia, in fact the handful you'd find in the phone book are just about all related. It's a French–German name, although I've had a lot of Greeks come up to me thinking it's Greek – especially at my favourite schnitzel shop in Newcastle, where the owner used to say, 'You look Greek, your name sound like Greek.' There is actually a German steel manufacturing company called Buderus which advertises on the fence in the German soccer league (Bundesliga). Dad, who was born in Australia, has operated a family business for many years, with many 'regulars' coming in to talk football, so anything negative that I might have been responsible for would reflect on his business too. I was more conscious of that after the Townsville incident in 2001.

I am very lucky that my parents have supported me all the way with my football career but never interfered or been too pushy. They let me leave Taree before I'd turned 17 to follow my dreams and I have lived away from home ever since. They didn't know much about the game technically, or how to try to get me into rep teams, but they believed in me. That's one thing I love about them, they just wanted to encourage me to fulfil my dreams without being pushy or over-ambitious for me.

There was one time when Mum got a little too involved in my football. I was just nine years old and, can you believe this, she was called to the judiciary for running onto the field during a match. But she did have good reason. Mum actually coached my under eights side because we couldn't get anyone else, then in the under nines she was doing stats for the coach. One day when we were playing Wauchope, I ran down the sideline right in front of Mum and this kid tackled me, then started gouging my eyes. Mum stepped onto the field (she was only about two metres away) and gave the boy a tap on the bum, saying, 'My son needs both those eyes!' Next thing, other parents had pinned her arms behind her back and escorted her off the field. When she had to front the judiciary, other parents, some from other clubs, appeared as witnesses saying she was only trying to protect her son, who was being gouged, and that they had previously had issues with this same team. The coach from Wauchope was later called in and was sacked for teaching his players dirty tactics, so a good thing came out of a bad experience. Dad made sure there was no chance of a repeat interruption from Mum and locked her in the car for the rest of the season!

I think any player will tell you that, when he enjoys success like playing in a grand final, State of Origin or a Test match, one of the first priorities is to have your family there to experience it with you. Whenever I was in a big game I would try to find my family during the national anthem; since 2005, Kris would usually be sitting with my parents, plus Broc and his wife Tianne.

What my achievements have meant to my family was brought home to me after my farewell to the crowd at New-castle the day we played Melbourne in the last round of 2008. One of the experiences I'll always remember was when I did my lap of honour before the game (I only got out of hospital the day before after surgery on my right bicep). I had to keep my emotions in check as I said goodbye to the crowd who had been so supportive of me for so many years, while a vocalist sang 'Danny Boy'. The last home match is always a special day anyway – 'old boys' day', when former players do a lap of honour before kick-off.

The team had a great win against Melbourne, who were minor premiers, and the current players did their traditional lap of honour after the match. As my brother Broc stood under the goalposts watching with Kris, he put his arm around her and just started bawling as everyone was leaving the ground. He was saying to Kris, 'This is the last time I'll be here; it's over.' When I left the dressing room after congratulating the boys on a big win, I met my family out the back of the stand, which was traditional after each game. I looked at Broc's bloodshot eyes and said, 'Are you pissed? Looks like you've had a few.' He replied, 'No mate,' then he fidgeted awkwardly and said, 'I'll ring you tomorrow,' and just walked off in a hurry. I thought something was wrong, maybe something had happened in the crowd, and when I asked Kris what was going on she said he was just upset by the fact my career at Newcastle had ended. It hit Broc even more than it did me at the time, and it made me realise how much joy I'd brought to my whole family and even close family friends, and that's an awesome feeling.

I love Broc and wish we'd done more together during the period I went from an adolescent to a man and was responsible for all the silly things young blokes carry on with, but I'd moved out of home so early. Still, we've remained pretty close, being only 22 months apart. Broc was a good footballer who played under 18s and a bit of first grade as a cheeky halfback; but he was a bit small when the others grew in their late teens, so he stopped playing at the age of 18. I think it was an excuse to sit on the hill and drink a few beers, actually. Plus he's worked hard in the family business, often around 60 hours a week, and that made it hard to concentrate on football. He's still working with Dad in the family business called Town Plumbing Supplies and has been there for 15 years now.

I'd mostly only see Broc when he came down for games; we're not ones for talking a lot on the telephone. Broc, Mum and Dad all used to get a little emotional but Broc and Dad were the most nervous and anxious when I played. Broc gets asthma really badly and gets really uptight at times, especially during big matches.

I know Broc is proud of me and what I have achieved. He was never one to be critical of me or be jealous in any way; he was just rock solid in support and I've appreciated that so much. Kris reckons every time I ran out as New South Wales captain in State of Origin, Broc's eyes would well up with tears of pride. He could also get a bit riled when things didn't go my way; I hear he's thrown a few remote controls at the television. It's nice to know my family is proud of not just my success on the field but how I have tried to conduct myself.

Mum, Dad and Broc came over for the Australian Schoolboys tour in 1995, along with a few other parents, and had a great time. The next time they went to England was when they wanted to surprise me by arriving a couple of nights before the first Test of the 2001 Kangaroo tour. Unfortunately their plans went a little haywire when they organised for a lift from the airport with our resident 'minder' on tour, Gary Haigh. Gary told me he was on the way to the airport to pick up my folks and I remember saying, 'Who, me? My parents aren't coming over, it must be someone else you're thinking of,' before he spilled the beans and assured me it was my parents; he had no idea it was supposed to be a surprise. I'm glad they made the trip; it was the only one they were able to go on and it was pretty special for me to have them over there.

After living a bachelor's life and picking up bad habits from my charismatic housemates (one I hadn't mentioned is Evan Cochrane, who taught me a few things about life), Kris came into my world at the perfect time and has been my rock, and my soul mate, ever since. When we first met – in Darwin – she had no idea about my football background; actually, she thought I was a financial planner. Well, I was, sort of . . .

Andrew Johns, Mark Hughes and I used to go to the Top End annually to do footy promotions – and generally have a good time. It was organised by one of Mark's mates, who was involved in league up there. During our 2003 trip, I got talking to Kris one night at a nightclub called Discovery where she worked. We started chatting and I was telling her what a great place it was and found her really easy to talk to. I quickly sussed out which bar she was working at, so I decided that's where I'd buy the boys' drinks, just so I had a chance to talk to her. She was from Adelaide and didn't know anything about rugby league and when she asked me what I did, I told her I was a financial adviser. I was working part-time at JSA, a finance company in Newcastle, at the time so it wasn't a total lie just to try to impress her.

We went back to the bar the next night, and the next. After I met her during her brief break, one of the glass collectors asked her, 'How do you know Bedsy?' She said, 'Who . . . Danny? Oh, I met him last night; he's a financial planner from Newcastle up here for the week.' He said, 'Bullshit he is; that's Danny Buderus, he's a rugby league player with the Newcastle Knights and the Australian rugby league hooker who's up here with Andrew Johns and Mark Hughes.'

Kris became a little wary after that. On our last night there, we were outside the club and I told her that we were going home the next day and I probably wouldn't see her again but I gave her my number and said, although we were a long way apart, if she ever wanted to ring I'd love to hear from her – you never know what might happen down the track.

When I got home, I couldn't get her out of my head. So I got on the internet, looked up the number of the club and gave it a call. When I asked if Kris was there, the guy on the phone asked who it was and I just said it was a guy she met the other night. He said he'd try to find her, then came back on the phone and said she wasn't there. (I'm sure she was.) I rang again a week later and this time they got her. She was a bit stand-offish, to be honest, and at the end of the conversation I thought, 'Well, I'll forget about that one; she doesn't sound real interested.' Shortly after that I went to England for the Kangaroo tour and I thought, 'Bugger it, I'll give it one more try and call her.' We spoke a couple of times while I was away, but I didn't hear from her after I got home, and thought, 'That's that.'

Kris reckons she was going through her wallet one day a few months later and noticed my number, so she texted me and said whenever I had time I should give her a call to have a chat. You wouldn't believe the timing; I was in camp for Origin 1 2004 and it was the day all hell broke loose with Mark Gasnier and Anthony Minichiello being dumped from the team, and the drama that followed. Luckily, Kris was too far away to read the Sydney papers and listen to radio!

I rang her later that day and bit by bit we talked more regularly and got to know each other at the end of a telephone. When Kris told her mother about us, it was just after the Bulldogs' sex scandal in Coffs Harbour and she was told to be careful about 'these rugby league players; you shouldn't mix with them, they've got a girl in every port'.

Luckily, Kris ignored her mother's words of wisdom and we agreed to meet in Port Douglas for a few days after the third Origin match, when the Knights had a bye and I needed to get away. We were naturally pretty nervous because we'd only met over those few nights in Darwin and hadn't set eyes on each other since, even though we'd talked for hours on the phone.

Kris went back to Darwin and I returned to Newcastle, but we agreed to catch up after the season. Again, it's one of those meetings where I have a good landmark event to remind me of the date: the day after I won the Dally M Medal, I flew back to Darwin and had a few days there before going home to prepare for the 2004 Tri Nations series in England. After I got home at the end of November, Kris came down to Newcastle and I took her up to stay with my parents in Forster, which showed how quickly our relationship was moving. Then we flew to Melbourne, spent a week along the Great Ocean Road and continued to Adelaide, where we had a week with Kris's parents, Marg and Peter Hewitt.

By the end of those three weeks, we knew it was serious and we started planning for Kris to move in with me at Merewether. A year later, December 2005, we were engaged and two months after that Kris fell pregnant. Ella was born in October 2006 – just over three years after we met – and we were married in

January 2007. So it was a bit of an unusual whirlwind start to a great relationship.

Our wedding day was idyllic, taking place at the beautiful Peat's Bite restaurant on the Hawkesbury River near Brooklyn, north of Sydney; it's a restaurant that is accessible by boat only. The day before the wedding was pretty special too. We had hired a houseboat for the groomsmen and the partners of the brides-maids to spend the night before the wedding on, and we dropped in to the restaurant the day before only to find advertising guru John Singleton, rugby league legend John Raper and ex-Wallaby rugby union hooker Bruce Malouf having lunch there. We settled in with them for a while before Singo asked us back to his place on his Strawberry Hill stud farm, at Mount White, and showed us around the property. It was hilarious and a very memorable last day of single life.

I'm sure Kris didn't know entirely what she was getting herself into when she came to Newcastle. Playing in the NRL can be a roller-coaster ride for a player's partner almost as much as for the footballer himself. You bring home all your emotions, physical pain and a total preoccupation with football. When we won a game, I didn't do much of a mental post-mortem – I'd just move on. But I'd beat myself up for days after a loss, going through what I could have done better to avoid the defeat. So I was not the best company at home. Kris is often the one to snap me out of it.

Emotionally, I found State of Origin the hardest loss to get over. You've been away from home for a week to ten days in an intense environment with only the players and support staff around you most of that time. You feel devastated by a loss, especially if you've lost the series; and while there is the chal-lenge and pressure to get back into the swing of club football, the first few days are very tough.

You can come out of State of Origin with a bit of 'camp depression'. It's something Craig Fitzgibbon and I used to talk about openly after camps. Fitzy is in the same boat as me, being a father; he just loves being in camp like I do; being around the fellas every day with a routine of having breakfast, training, attending functions and winding down together every day. You live in each other's pockets, everything is done for you, there is a big build-up to the match then, suddenly, that is cut off and you go home to your family and all the responsibilities of home and it is hard to adapt; it is so different to what you have just experienced.

That's difficult for the players' partners; having us being away for so long and then we're really not 'there' when we get back. So life was a challenge for Kris, particularly with neither of our families close by. Other than Origin camps, there were the 2005 Tri Nations tour, my last, plus we would be away for a night every time the Knights played away. It became a little harder with her also having Ella to look after, but on the other hand it meant she had company and something to occupy her. Kris has always been a strong, independent person and she left home at an early age to travel and has got used to living away from her family geographically, although they've always been very close and supportive. Kris made a lot of sacrifices to move house, change jobs and move away from good friends – and, after four years in Newcastle, moving further away to Leeds. That is something I'll always appreciate and I look forward to paying her back post-football.

While a lot of people think players have a wonderful life, with plenty of time on our hands and not having to work a 'real job', the demands do impact on home life. My treatment of injuries, training and the NRL match schedule – that ensures that you don't know what day of the week you're playing until six weeks beforehand – all had a big bearing on what Kris and I could plan with our time. Often I would have to explain at the last minute that I had to do extra physio to get right for a match and it disrupted the whole week if Kris had something planned and had to change it. A footballer's lifestyle is a very selfish one; you're always thinking about getting yourself ready to play week in week out, treating injuries, often not talking because your thoughts are consumed with the upcoming game.

After Ella was born, Kris and I planned to have a 'date night' every Tuesday and get a baby-sitter in. I always thought it was important for Kris to feel loved and go out for a romantic dinner amidst my hectic, selfish lifestyle that revolved almost entirely around football. Despite all the good intentions, it never eventuated.

I accept it as part of the territory, but something people often overlook is how families feel public opinion about foot-ballers more than the players themselves do. Whether it is when they are sitting in the crowd listening to fans bag the players, or reading what is said in the newspapers, or on radio or tele-vision, or just while out in a pub or restaurant. Then there is the time when you might be out enjoying yourself and some drunken bloke comes up and is all over you. Kris is great; she is very humble and grounded, and like me she sees the privilege of me being someone people recognise and generally want to support, but with that can come the negative of people at times invading our lives.

Also players' partners have to accept the fact that you are public property and, because rugby league has such a passion-ate following, footballers are subject to opinion and often to rumours that are not true. Mum is not nearly as outwardly emotional as Broc and Dad and keeps her thoughts to herself, but she broke that rule a couple of times. She started to listen to talkback radio all the time – and she'd get all upset about what was being said about me. One time, probably around 2001 or 2002, she rang up Ray Hadley on 2GB because someone had called in and said that I never went back to my local area to help out rugby league and I'd forgotten my roots. She got on air to defend me and they made her feel really welcome; she told the panel I'd been in Taree only 10 days earlier presenting awards and attending a coaching clinic. Within 10 seconds my phone rang with reports that Mum had been on the radio; I was relaxing at a get-together at Clint Newton's and rang my mother and said, 'What are you doing, Mum? You shouldn't get involved.' I put her on a media ban after that . . . although I believe she snuck a few calls in to the local ABC radio. When I was suspended for the tackle on Michael Robertson during the finals in 2006, she got very upset about what people were saying about me.

I like to keep things private and keep my guard up, so I wanted to keep my family out of the limelight but I understood that they were just proud of me and Mum wanted to stick up for me. I've had good support from aunties and uncles and cousins too, who always keep in touch with Mum and Dad to lend support. A young cousin, Matt Langham, plays in the St George area and is supposed to be a pretty good player. I'm also keen to keep an eye on a couple of nephews playing in Forster, Broc and Tianne's sons Max and Jett; my unbiased spies tell me Max particularly is a prospect to watch; he's the one scoring tries while Jett is the one providing the commentary. Let's just say Jett, at this early stage of his career, likes the social side of a day at the footy more than playing.

Rugby league is definitely high in the family's priorities. My sister-in-law Tianne, a school teacher, is coaching a footy team at Forster primary school; it's good to see her carrying on the family tradition started by Mum. Hopefully she can stay free of judiciary drama!

Outside of family, players tend to develop close friendships with other players and their partners because we all understand a footballer's lifestyle. Probably our closest footy friends in recent years include Mark and Kirralee Hughes, Andrew and Cathrine Johns, Craig and Nicole Smith, Kirk Reynoldson and Katie, Steve Simpson and Jackie, plus Russell Richardson and his wife Liz, who went to playgroup with Kris (their son Dan is a similar age to Ella). During my last couple of seasons with the Knights, we became close to Ben Cross and his wife Krista.

Kris is like any partner who sees the unglamorous side of footy: me bringing injury home, bracing myself to walk of a morning, being shitty after a loss, looking pretty rough after some knocks. Often I can't help around the house with the housework or with Ella because of my injuries; I'd just want to lie on the lounge and recover (well, that's my excuse, anyway). When that happened we'd call for reinforcements. Kris's mother Marg (a midwife by profession) was just awesome when she'd fly over at the drop of a hat to help out; with Ella being her first grandchild, she was happy to take advantage of some extended time together.

It is hard having them so far away but we really enjoy when we catch up with Kris's family. I couldn't have wished for better inlaws than Marg and Peter, who I get on really well with. They were our first visitors in England in June 2009; they came over with Kris's sister and brother-in-law, Sally and Luke Foster, who are great people that I've also become quite close to. (They have a little girl called Charlotte.) Our getaway is the family shack on the Murray River where we water-ski and have great times just relaxing and not doing much. I took Kirk Reynoldson and Katie down there once and they've become great friends with

Luke and Sally as well. Luke is a keen Port Power supporter in the AFL (Marg is an Adelaide Crows nut, which ensures good stirring between the two). Luke had never seen a game of rugby league until he met me. Now he's right into it with his opinion on tactics and who should win or lose in the NRL.

Luke is also the master of the motivational messages. He'd text me pump-up messages before big games and plenty of them were sensational. He even started sending 'Reyno' some after he met him down on the Murray. I've kept one in my phone it was so good. It reads: 'Great things begin with a single uncertain step . . . your final Origin. Mate, achievement does not develop in a world without challenges. Tonight is your biggest challenge yet and you know, better than anyone, that achievement involves three things: a sense of purpose, the capability to pursue that purpose and the resilience to continue when the going inevitably gets tough. There is nothing you can't have if you will reach for it. Look inside yourself, Beds, you are more than what you have achieved in football so don't measure yourself by what happens tonight – there's no certainty, only opportunity. Experience will tell you what to do, confidence allows you to do it and it will happen for you.' He sends some great things, Luke; there's always a positive message in his texts, and it's great to have someone who takes time to send motivational messages like that to someone who is a mate more than a public football figure to him – it sort of personalises it even more.

I've got a great extended family and I'm looking forward to the time when we're back from England and have the flexibility of time to catch up with them more often. What I'm realising now as my career nears its end is that Kris's and my time together when I was playing rugby league will only be a small part of our lives as a married couple, so it is Danny Buderus in a role other than as a footballer that Kris will see the most of.

18

MENACED BY A 'SUPERMODEL'

LOOKING OVER my scrapbook, I came across the most bizarre stories written on me during my career. I can't believe this long, crazy episode made the newspaper gossip columns, one article having the heading 'Danny Boy and the super-model'. Here is a brief summary of what went on over more than two years; a surreal attempted con by a very weird but clever woman; a 'journey' that took threats by the police to finally bring to an end.

I'll start at the start. The Knights were in Melbourne for a match against the Storm in 2002. Mark Hughes said to me, 'You wouldn't guess what just happened; the Knights have just made contact with me and passed on the number of this model called Amy Taylor; she saw us on *The Footy Show* when Ryan Girdler did his "Our House" segment on us.' Boozy told the office staff to tell her that he had a girlfriend but his housemate, who was also on the show, was single. So I played along and said to pass on her details and through curiosity I emailed her. It went on from there, just an unbelievable saga I thought would never end.

After an exchange of emails, her story changed: Amy became Courtney, who was Karolina Kurkova's cousin, and eventually I received a phone call from a woman claiming to be Karolina. I looked her up on the internet and found out that she was the emerging supermodel at the time in Europe and America – and way out of my league! A little while later I found that my former Knights team-mate Darren Albert, who was playing for St Helens in England, was getting the same photos and same story fed to him by the same woman.

I was obviously pretty suspicious about it anyway; she was telling me how she'd send me some photos and she was spot on with the details about her career. She then asked if I would like to catch up next time she was in Australia. She rattled on and the stuff she was coming out with was just mind-blowing, she knew a bit about our football and she'd seen us on 'Our House', and might be doing a bit of modelling work in Sydney and Melbourne. Then she said she'd send her cousin round to meet me.

I knew Karolina was Czech, so I immediately smelt a rat, especially after I'd watched Karolina Kurkova on *You Tube* being interviewed and it sounded nothing like the voice I had heard over the phone. So next time she rang I said that she didn't sound like the same person, but she kept trying to convince me it was and said she'd fly me over, first class, to America and we could hang out with P. Diddy, the American rapper and fashion designer, and we'd go shopping. It was obviously 'Courtney' putting on an accent.

Eventually this girl arrived at our place unannounced, an American in her early 20s, and introduced herself as Courtney Taylor and said, 'Karolina wants me to give you this,' and she started showering me with presents, like clothes, and also photos of Karolina. It just got weirder as time went on. 'Karolina' called and said she was in Australia and was going to go to one of our games. I tried to call her bluff and said that we had to meet.

I arranged a place and a time, and as I had expected, she didn't turn up. Later she said she was at one of our games; I asked her the score and she rattled it off. It became a real game and I was laughing it off on one hand, but was intrigued and amused on the other hand – until it got out of control.

Courtney reckoned she had to set up a place for Karolina in Newcastle because she wanted to come and live here for a while. She said she had to arrange a unit for her in the city, so I went around to have a look at it and it sure didn't look like a supermodel's penthouse to me. Some of the things she rattled off over the phone were bizarre and far-fetched – like when she claimed she wanted to do a movie on our relationship, how opposites can attract, and Bruce Willis wanted to direct it. I'm just thinking, 'This is getting ridiculous now.'

I even heard from her when I went with the Australian team to England at the end of 2003 – a year and a half from when she first contacted me. I was in Paris and she claimed she was in Paris too. I tried to catch her out by asking her to meet, but she claimed she had to go home the next day. She asked where I was and I told her I was at such-and-such pub. She reckoned she'd been there and said that if I went outside and to the right there was a beautiful bar called the such-and-such. She was spot-on and that got me thinking, 'How would she know that?'

Courtney Taylor kept coming around to our place and it would get real heated. I'd tell her, 'I know you are a fake. What are you doing here?' and she'd just bolt back out to the car. I'd just order her off our property and threaten to call the police.

In the meantime, all the boys were as intrigued as I was about the hoo-ha that was being created and that it just wouldn't stop. Rebecca Wilson at the *Sunday Telegraph* got hold of it from somewhere (I think 'Courtney' contacted her). One week she was saying in her column how two supermodels were chasing me.

She obviously swallowed Courtney's story, just as I did at first, because she could be so convincing; and being such a bizarre tip it was obviously a pretty good column par. But she was made aware of the real situation and printed a different slant on it a week later. Here is what was in her columns (April 2003):

Danny boy and the supermodel

TWO American supermodels have lobbed in Newcastle this weekend to watch Danny Buderus play for the Knights. One of the models, who adorns the covers of the world's leading fashion mags, attended a local yoga class and was asked why she was in town. She said she was there for the footy but wouldn't say who her player mate was, before whizzing off in a silver Porsche. We can confirm Buderus and the supermodel have been in touch for a while.

Danny hangs up on love-struck fan

POPULAR Newcastle star Danny Buderus has put an end to one of the most talked about relationships in rugby league. As we revealed last week, the Test hooker caught the eye of an international supermodel last year and she has bombarded him with phone calls ever since. Amazingly, the woman involved was believed to be 2002 *Vogue* model of the year Karolina Kurkova, but her New York agent denies this. In the meantime, the phone calls kept coming but Danny has had enough. 'The calls started more than 12 months ago after we played in the World Club Challenge in England, which she said she watched,' he said. 'We talked about meeting up but it never happened. It got to the stage where it became a massive distraction and last week I told her it was going nowhere and that is where it ended – full stop.'

It still makes out that I was actually talking to the real Karolina Kurkova, rather than someone pretending to be her; so I could imagine all the gossip.

It went on into the 2004 season, although the phone calls became more irregular; and while Boozy was quite enthralled by it, watching it unaffected from the sideline, it got out of hand when she contacted my parents and said I was going to father her child. When it got to that stage, I thought, 'This is way too much,' so I got a private investigator, a lawyer and my manager involved.

'Courtney' contacted several people in the media, and even the Newcastle Knights, with these bizarre claims. Danny Weidler did a big 'exclusive' on it in the *Sun-Herald* under the heading 'Knight Stalker' after she contacted him by phone and email, claiming I had fathered a child with an American heiress (the same claims she had contacted my parents with). Luckily, while some other media organisations got sucked in initially, he saw it was a big con. His story revealed that she wrote 17 emails under the name of Taylor Gerber, claiming she was representing an American woman called Courtney Taylor. She said we had a child we had named Paris after her friend Paris Hilton and she wanted me to go to the USA to do a DNA test, which would prove I was the father. But wait, it gets more ridiculous; she then claimed Paris Hilton wore a T-shirt to a fashion launch with 'Danny Buderus' printed on it, to gain publicity for Courtney's case.

She even left an overseas phone number for the media to reply to her. Then she contacted the National Rugby League asking for them to intervene and arrange a meeting with her. I told the NRL she was a lunatic and to ignore her. The police said nuisances like that just move on to the next person once they're exposed. When I described her, they told me they had a file on her and she'd just move on to another person.

My manager called her and said the charade had to end and that she was causing a lot of grief. You wouldn't believe it, a couple of weeks later he was getting hoax calls from a woman claiming to be the daughter of an American who owned a series of casinos in Las Vegas and wanted to do business in Australia. He met her once and when he described her to me and what she was wearing (a New York Yankees baseball cap), he couldn't believe it; it was definitely the same person.

Fortunately, after being exposed as a fraud in the stories, the calls stopped. I was at Bondi, in camp with the Australian team, a few months later and I laid eyes on 'Courtney' in the street, but she didn't lift her head up to make eye contact. A huge wave of emotion came over me; I wanted to go over and have it out with her and ask, 'What the hell is your go?' But I kept walking and she scurried away. I never came across her again, although others have.

Apparently she tried the same thing with some of the Manly players and got on the VIP guest list at a match as the daughter of an American billionaire; and also got on the A-list for other events in Sydney. She had a long list of 'targets', including at least three more high-profile rugby league players and an AFL player who have been 'taken' by the habitual trickster. I believe she is still doing it; obviously she chases people via Facebook or media stories and concocts some fantastic story. The world is a strange place.

19

THE SCIENCE
OF NRL FOOTBALL

THE SCIENCE involved in preparing for a National Rugby
League match has developed unbelievably in the past decade.
The advent of the computer stats and video package that all
clubs have is a major catalyst. Plus, with the salary cap spread-
ing the talent so evenly across the 16 teams, any edge you can
get in fitness, preparation and knowledge can prove such a
difference when it comes to results.

An individual priority for an NRL player is that when he
puts his boots on he has to feel, physically and mentally, that
he is ready to play; ready to get the best out of his body. So
having a good preparation is first and foremost in your mind.
I had little systems I'd do, like going for a swim the morning
of the game, eating different food, doing particular stretches,
and having the same people give me particular massages to get
my body in the best shape possible to go into 80 minutes of
physical battle. The strapping on my ankles had to feel perfect,
Robbie Aubin was spot-on doing that just about every time.
I would also use a 'compex machine', a device which would
get blood pumping into my Achilles.

On top of each player's idiosyncrasies and superstitions,

which just about every NRL player has, there is the ever-evolving team preparation. I'll take you through a typical week at the Newcastle Knights from about 2001–05 to my last season in 2008, as a guide to how things have changed.

The most important thing after a match is the physical recovery, and these days it starts the minute you walk off the field. In about 2002 or 2003, I think, we introduced the ice bins to the dressing room after a game: big green plastic bins which we would stand in for about 30 seconds at a time and do that three times. We'd then go back to the club and have a beer with family and friends, do the official presentations, then head off to the Burwood Inn and have a few quiet beers there. When we used to have a lot of Friday night games, we'd have a recovery session on Saturday mornings and while there we'd plan the weekend, which often involved a good day at Newcastle races that afternoon, followed by a quiet day Sunday before starting preparation on Monday for the next game. I am a believer that you need to blow off a bit of steam over the weekend, whether or not you hit a golf ball or have a couple of beers, or go to the races, or spend time with your family. The day at the races was a great way for us to have a laugh and ease down after the intensity of a match and the build-up.

On Monday we'd get back into training; do a light session of game component skills in the morning to flush out the soreness in the body, then go through the team review (watching video and being fed stats) and some individual feedback on our performances from the coaching staff. On Tuesday we'd have weights in the morning, sprint work, then a hard field session in the afternoon, a bit of conditioning and having physio treatment in between or first thing in the morning.

Wednesday would be a day off and Thursday we'd do the game preview and then go out and do ball work. In between that we might do a blast of weights, which is an explosive 25 or 30 minute section of weights; then we'd go out and do a team run-through of our plays. We'd have Thursday afternoon off and have a light ball session Friday morning before departing for the match Friday afternoon (if we had a Saturday night game). Of course there could be three to six hours of physio, massage and injury management on top of that, and sometimes we'd attend club promotions.

Match day would start with breakfast followed by a game of cricket, which was always fun – but quite competitive at times. We had some good cricketers – Andrew Johns was always bloody competitive, as was Mark Hughes – then some really bad ones. We used to call our football manager Mark Sargent 'The Sunflower' because of his bowling action. I was called 'Straight Arms' because I only had one shot, the lofted shot to 'cow corner'. I was hopeless, always had my head in the air when I went to hit the ball.

On game day, I used to arrive about an hour to an hour and a half before kick-off, watch a bit of reserve grade, do a quick team talk to go over the main tactical points, then each player would go through his individual ritual of getting himself ready. To add to the atmosphere, music would be blaring in the dressing room almost up to the warm-up. At the start of each season each player would submit his request as part of the song list. There were some cracking tracks from all sorts of genres. Tony Butterfield would sit with his earphones on listening to the soundtrack from the movie *Titanic*. It was a weird choice, I know, but to be honest, he played it for me one day and I found it really calming and the type of music that would help me focus. So I bought the CD, knowing it would be a good companion in the CD rack for Boozy's Hot Chocolate collection, and it made a big impression on me when I played it at home one night; we must have been caught in a melancholy mood at 'Whispers' and reached for the 'classics'. It was one of those touching moments that neither of us will ever forget – the sight of Boozy swaying to Celine Dion singing 'My Heart Will Go On' is a magical 'Myamblah memory'!

A lot has changed in the past few years, and specifically at Newcastle since the arrival of Brian Smith as coach, which coincided with us getting use of a gymnasium and outstanding training facility at Balance, which is part of the Club Phoenix club at Mayfield West, owned by the Wests leagues club group. Players these days are even starting to wear 'sat navs' (satellite navigation sensors) at training and apparently they can now be used during games to measure how many times you sprint, how far you run in metres, how hard you get hit, and so on. That enables the coaching staff to determine how you are going to recover for next week's training and what you have to do for the following week's preparation. They'll measure a player's heart rate when he tackles, and look at different techniques to expend less energy.

It is amazing what goes into preparing football teams these days; not only do you have the technology, but there can be five or six coaches – a forwards coach, backs coach, speed coach, wrestling coach, defensive coach and head coach.

A typical week, starting on Monday, is like this now (or was for the 2008 season before I left for England):

Monday: We'd come in and stretch, do light team skills to flush some of the soreness out of the body, rehab and 'pre-hab' weights, take supplements before and after weights, then go over to ice baths – usually three lots of having two minutes in ice followed by two minutes in hot water. We'd have a healthy buffet lunch provided for us by the staff at Balance, then have some massage and do the video review of the match. Rick Stone, who is a great communicator and clever footy brain, would show video on defence and Rohan Smith, Brian's son, who is also really astute, would cover attack. Brian Smith would then do his overview.

Tuesday: We'd have breakfast provided and we'd do stretching, a speed session, a bit of fitness work and skills drills plus some individual game-specific work for players in different positions, and probably some wrestling technique work. Again supplements and lunch were provided. We'd have ice bath treatment again, an afternoon weights session, and also individual massages were provided at allocated times during the day.

Wednesday: A stretch session, massage, then the rest of the day off.

Thursday: On Thursday we'd have a good video preview session where we'd be split into left field, right field and middle positions and discussion would be encouraged. Brian introduced the good idea of one of the players doing some research and presenting his preview with points of how we should play them. Then we'd go into the coaches' preview, Rick Stone going through the defence and Rohan Smith the attack and Brian doing an overall preview. After that we'd have a good field session with specific defensive work, including wrestling technique.

Friday: We'd have a morning 'blast session', which would involve field power exercises like throwing a medicine ball under-arm and over-arm; and this one particular exercise where we would have a ball on the end of a rope and throw it into the ground from side to side in a wood chopping motion; it was very hard, very good for your core muscle group. Then we'd have a brief field session with the ball. This was a light day, as we'd taper off as we got closer to match day. If we were playing away, we'd leave on Friday afternoon.

Saturday: Initially, in 2007, Brian Smith – always looking for an edge and wanting to learn from other sports – liked his team to train the day of the game; I think he got that from a British soccer or NFL (American football) study that suggested that if you get your heart rate up the day of the game you get more out of your body during the match. Before a home match we'd train for up to half an hour at Townsend Oval; we'd run through a couple of sets and check the fitness of players who had question marks over them. On some away games we'd find somewhere to train too. With so many in the squad having to cover different positions and the make-up of the team often not finalised until that day, it was good to see the frame of mind the players were in, who was running in what position and generally getting a fine-tune the morning of a game. But the game-day session (which most players didn't like) was finished by the end of the season, when it was found it hadn't got the desired results.

After we'd arrived at the ground we'd stretch, do a bit of last-minute video on the opposition, get stripped, warm-up, get weighed and take some supplements and cramp tablets. There are a lot of boxes to be ticked before you play these days. You can lose up to 5 kilos of fluid during a match, so hydration testing has become a big thing in the game.

Sunday: Recovery in the morning, the rest of the day off.

Video analysis is very important in the modern game. During the preview sessions we'd look at the opposition's game from the 'eagle cam' view – which is a camera in the grandstand which provides a good, elevated overall aspect. We'd watch how the opposition numbered up in defence, who they put in different positions – like a halfback who might defend out on the wing; we'd study their wrestling moves in the tackle and how to combat them, and their overall structures and what tactics to use to overcome them. We'd look at their attack; things like who kicks left foot or right foot, where they kick from and kick to most of the time, and how far they could kick it.

The technology today is mind-blowing. The young players are so keen to learn and improve and they love looking at the computer and video technology all clubs have at their fingertips.

Preparation is everything, but that can be a very individual thing at times, too. Players are different in how they prepare; some might not even get a sweat up for the last two days of the week because they want to save themselves so they can go out and rip into the game. I found the best way for me was to train like I play, in every session. In the hooking position you're involved in just about all the play and I had to prepare as if I was playing, so that I was mentally and physically switched on to the workload I would have in the match.

Ben Kennedy would walk through the last training session, but we knew how destructive he would be on the field. Andrew Johns prepared like he was playing; he wanted every pass to be right at training; everyone to be at high intensity; that was his way of getting himself, and the team, right. Kurt Gidley is like that too, he does a lot of running. But when you look at a lot of the big boys, it makes sense for them to cruise through training. It's the hardest job in the world to run into brick walls all day in a match, so they are going to slant towards the mental preparation for the battle whereas the quick players need to build up physically and agility-wise too.

The review of your own performance is much more detailed than it used to be. You'll get reports on your attacking game like hit-ups, yardage and support play, plus defensive aspects like how many dominant tackles you made, how many of your tackles were effective, how many were misses or ineffective. A lot of coaches look at how many tackles the team was forced to make in a game (usually 280–360 tackles), which would indicate how often the ball was in play and what percentage of possession you had. Also individual tackle counts, and just as importantly missed tackle counts, would be analysed.

When Michael Hagan was coach, he brought in a system where you would receive a cumulative total of points for different components of the game – like how many runs you made, how many metres you made, your support play and kick-chase. There would be certain points attributed to each component and it was multiplied by the amount of 'effort', with points deducted for missed tackles, ineffective tackles, dropped balls, etc. My goal was 200 points because I was on the field and involved in the play for a long period as hooker; that became my benchmark to indicate if I'd put in a decent performance. A front-rower who played only 30–40 minutes might have had a benchmark of 100 points.

You often hear coaches and players say, 'If we get our defence in order, everything starts from there,' and it is true. Most teams have almost identical structures in defence but it is the detail behind that which makes such a difference – the wrestle, the 'peel' (defending players peeling off a tackle), communication and individual judgement.

Warren Ryan brought the numbering system into rugby league. I remember when he joined Newcastle as coach in 1999 and we turned up to training one day, and there were all these numbers across the field and we thought, 'What's going on here?' But he explained the science behind it and everyone uses it now in most levels of rugby league.

There are usually 10 players in the defensive line, plus the two markers and the fullback. The theory in defence is that when you are in the middle of the field, you're at '50 per cent' and have to have five defenders either side of the play the ball. When you're at '80 per cent', which is the description for eighty per cent across the width of the field to the left, you'd have two defenders on the left of the play the ball and eight defenders on the right. When you're at '60 per cent' (just to the left of the middle of the field), you'd have four defenders on the left and six on the right.

If you follow that system and adjust to those numbers as the play goes across the field, your defensive system should work and it is up to the attacking side to create hesitation or doubt, or do things so quickly that you can't adjust to that numbers shift required in defence.

Tackling technique is obviously also very important, and again there is a basic structure there that everyone follows. If you are in front of the attacking player's arm that is carrying the ball, your job is to get over the ball and use his momentum to pull him around. The second defender always comes from the inside, from where the play the ball was, and he has to try to get him around the midriff. The third man would come in and slow the play the ball down and use aggression to get him on his back. The effectiveness of each defender is measured in the review. It's important that the second man in comes from the inside, otherwise your defensive structure and numbering from the outside gets puts under pressure.

Wrestling has become such an important part of rugby league, and while some people associate that with the 'grapple tackle', there's more science to it than that. It's about countering any wrestle moves of opposing players, co-ordinating your movement with your fellow tackler, and how much energy is expended in a tackle. After all, you don't want to waste energy fighting against the force of a team-mate also trying to effect the tackle.

There are different systems of how to combine to nullify certain strengths and styles of ball runners. For example, there is one technique for someone who backs into a tackle or hits and spins; one for someone who drops down and tries to find the ground quickly like a surrender tackle; another for someone who can get up and play the ball quickly. We'd work on perfecting the different techniques during the pre-season and then, as the weekly games rolled around, we'd look at specific players and what technique to use on them.

If we were playing the Warriors, they have Steve Price as their main 'go-forward man'; he steps off his right foot, then right foot again, then backs into the tackle and tries to offload – so we'd need to use a certain technique. Sam Thaiday finds the ground really well and never gets caught on his back; we'd have to slow him down by using another system. Every player has a technique that they find effective. Greg Inglis palms off with either hand; you have to use a three-man tackle and be effective with him because he's so hard to put down. Petero Civoniceva has a good right foot step and he sort of comes square on at you and spins right at the end as he meets a tackler, and he plays the ball very quickly.

When it comes to defence, peeling off the tackle is the starting point of a good structure. The hooker, who is obviously the main dummy-half, is looking at how the teams peel off the tackle. All the good teams peel off exceptionally well but if the defenders peel slowly or get caught on the ground, that blows the defending team's system out of the water and brings into play the quick men – the hookers, halfbacks or fullback – who try to exploit that area behind the ruck.

Communication is important in making the tackle, but also after completing the tackle. There will be the dominant tackler – that's the bloke over the ball – then the one around the legs and the one around the waist. The player around the ball is the one who controls the tackle and peeling off afterwards. He is last one off and takes the marker role, the one around the waist usually takes the second marker position and the one down low would get back into the defensive line. The player with the weight on top of the ball, which is the focal point of the tackle, has the role of slowing down the play the ball, so that the third man can peel off and have enough time to get back in the line.

The hooking role has certainly evolved a lot since I came into first grade, too, and most hookers these days are converted halfbacks or five-eighths. You can't just fire the ball off the deck from dummy-half and make a heap of tackles; that went out a decade ago.

There is the familiar 'two-steps-and-deliver' system aimed at trying to suck the marker in to create space down the centre of the ruck; it's a technique of shaping to or stepping one way as if you're going to pass the ball that way, then going the other. The call for the marker is 'don't sink in' – he needs to hold his position until the ball is delivered or the dummy-half runs. When the hooker comes out and puts two steps on to the marker and he 'sinks in' and the runner gets into space behind the ruck, that's regarded as a 'no-no' from the coach's perspective. Teams are coming up with different plays all the time to try to create something from the play the ball.

The hooker these days invariably has a good kicking game too, because dummy-half is such an advantageous position to kick from. I would have liked to kick more but, to be honest,

I wasn't a natural, plus I had the best kicker in the game in Andrew Johns, so I gave the ball to him 10 times out of 10.

The game today is very structured and pre-planned and the plays are usually well rehearsed and very effective, so it's smart to stick with the plan of a certain set play at a certain part of the field for a certain situation.

But, as has always been the case in rugby league, what sets the good players and good teams apart is being able to play off the cuff as well. You look at Matt Bowen – he's off the cuff. Kurt Gidley likes to follow his instincts. Billy Slater, Brett Stewart and the mercurial Jarryd Hayne are other examples of fullbacks who are possessed with pure speed and great anticipation. You can't coach speed or natural ability; or instinct. And these sorts of players bring crowds to their feet and have them wanting to come back the next week.

Players know the familiar plays that are centred on certain players. Take Darren Lockyer, for example. He has a standard play that defenders know is coming but he is still so effective because of the way Brisbane (and Queensland, who use the same play) execute it so precisely and with so many options. Locky gets a long ball from the dummy-half or first receiver and has someone coming under him (inside), someone hitting a straight line and someone out the back. Most often he'll have Tonie Carroll short off him, Karmichael Hunt off the back, or Justin Hodges there for the long ball. Every player knows it's Locky's bread and butter play, but they do it so effectively. With the options it creates – pass short, pass long, pass out the back, kick or run himself – and with the strike-power around Lockyer, it's very hard to defend.

You don't have many plays coming out of your own half. When you get some field position, the plan is to isolate a player one on one who is not the best defender – although they are becoming fewer in the NRL. It used to be about putting someone into a hole but defensive lines are so compressed and disciplined these days it's harder to get that space, so it reverts to attacking a player one-on-one; big man on smaller man or faster man on bigger, slow man. For example, we'd try to get to a part of the field where we could run Steve Simpson at them; that was our go-to play for years. If we were rolling forward effectively, we would try to give Matt Gidley good early ball, enabling him to draw two players in with his signature 'Gidley flick' to Timana Tahu. Most times that would see T race away and put the ball over the line. The science is to make a player make a wrong move in defence; to come in when he shouldn't have come in, or to stay back when he should have come forward, or come out of the line when he should have hung back in the line. Joey was the best at it; he'd look at the video and say, 'Look, he turned in a little bit, so I'm going to put a play on him' and make a mental note of it. Joey could attract three defenders, which was always good for someone like Steve Simpson who could isolate a player and beat him with his size.

That's what so many attacking plays are based around, and why most teams run decoy runners and have players joining in from 'out the back', to cause doubt in defenders and for them to break their well-rehearsed structure, or get more numbers than they have on that side. Every team would have certain plays they work towards; sometimes you'd have a whole set you'd play out to make one certain play work. But most times it's a case of getting forward and shooting from the middle of the field, and running good options either side with the halfback on one side, and the five-eighth on the other.

Sometimes the best place to shoot from is down the short side; it's something I looked for when I could. A good dummy-half looks for an advantage down the short side, looking for a three-on-two. Whenever I saw a centre make a tackle and get caught at the ruck, I'd go down his short side trying to get one of their players caught out of position covering for the centre, hopefully creating an opportunity for one of our quicker fellas to go one-on-one with one of their big boys.

As I said, most teams have similar attacking and defensive structures, with variations that every opposing team is aware of. So the issues which become integral to where a team finishes on the ladder are: the skill of execution with which a team runs its plays; their fitness and ability to fight fatigue; repairing injured bodies and the team's ability to cover for injured players; the ability to get the players mentally at their peak as often as possible during a long, hard season; team morale – and the confidence that comes from managing all those things.

Under the salary cap, where you simply can't carry enough specialist players in the one position, it is about manufacturing versatility in players; having players in your squad who can cover many positions but are an expert at one. Kurt Gidley is the perfect example of that new generation of player; he can play fullback or anywhere in the backline and do an exceptional job. Under Brian Smith, Newcastle have done that well; they've spread the money across the positions. You can't have more than one player on $400,000 to $500,000; you have to disperse the talent and money across the squad.

In years gone by, if the Knights lost our best and most experienced player, Andrew Johns, we'd often crumble; everything revolved around him – you just instinctively waited to hear his voice on the field. That's changed now; if one player slips out, the fullback can go into halfback, or the halfback to five-eighth, or you can interchange the forwards through the positions. But even with that versatility, it's all about having the same team on the paddock in as many back-to-back weeks as you can; the confidence and familiarity from that is so important.

That's where high-tech preparation and rehabilitation has become so important. I have no doubt more players go onto the field better prepared physically than 10 years ago and certainly better prepared mentally and tactically. It's getting more scientific, more specific and more important.

20

IN THE MEDIA

I'D LIKE to think I had a very good relationship with the media – even though I must confess I rarely gave a 'fully frank' interview because I was worried about how the media would interpret what I said. And I regret that now, in a way.

I know I represented much of what you get from the modern-day footballer – saying nothing controversial or anything that might be regarded as inflammatory. I wish I had spoken more from the heart and passed on my real opinion more often rather than being so worried about the consequences if I did, or how my comments would be portrayed in the media. That may sound a little hypocritical considering the regrets expressed earlier in the book over my heartfelt comments that led to the run-in with Brian Smith in 2007. But other than that one time, I wish I had shown a little more confidence to come out with what I was genuinely feeling, while not being disrespectful or arrogant.

At times I was boring; I remember thinking that some-times when I'd have to front a large media scrum or formal media conference when I was State of Origin captain and some journalists would switch off their tape recorders before we'd finished. I'd think, 'Gee, it must be getting boring now.' When I look back, though, I was probably most honest and forthright after Origin matches, when the adrenalin and emotion were still running and I was more likely to tell it exactly how I felt.

It took me a little while to grow into the role of regularly fronting the media as New South Wales captain; I was nervous and a bit uncomfortable at first. I had to front big formal media conferences at the start of each Origin week, then a big one at the end, and had endless small group interviews or one-on-ones in between. There was always the worry about how Queensland would pounce on something that was said, so I was pretty guarded. When you stopped to think about it, neither side needed any help with motivation but you dared not say anything the least bit inflammatory anyway, in case it gave your opposition an edge. We used to hang on the wall clippings of stories that may have criticised our ability, especially if the comments came from anyone in or close to the Queensland camp. I know Queensland did the same; it all just adds to the atmosphere in camp.

On the drive down from Newcastle to Sydney to join the camp each year, I'd be excited about catching up with all the boys and getting into Origin mode, which was always such a special feeling. But going through my mind was what was going to happen with the media bombardment when I got there and what they were going to ask me.

I got on well with the media guys and we had to be thankful Origin attracted so much focus. But it was mind-boggling just how intense it was and I know it was something that absolutely astounded Craig Bellamy when he came into his first camp in 2008, and Graham Murray before him. When you add the promotional activities and functions we had to be available for, and media conferences after each open training session, it was a really exhausting task for the coach and captain.

The ARL would appoint a full-time media manager to be with us, provided by the NRL, which was Polly McCardell for my first four seasons, then Tristan Hay, and David Taylor during my last two. We'd go through all the media requests over the first couple of days. Dave showed me the list of requests he'd received for the first game in 2008 and it numbered over 160 over five days. That was a job in itself for Dave, replying to them all and deciding which ones we could and couldn't meet. There would be regional radio and television on top of the national networks and Sydney and Brisbane papers, plus regional papers and *The Footy Show*, *NRL on Fox* and the magazines. It was a bloody hard job for the media managers; they'd have a heap of pressure from journos saying they wanted to promote the series and thus wanted access to the players, but the coach would naturally not want them to be weighed down by all the extra distractions.

Players quite often didn't want to do certain interviews, or even get in photos, and give Queensland a sniff of something they could apply their siege mentality to. Plus, they just wanted to keep their footy heads on and focus on nothing but the game.

Ultimately the media would go to Willie Mason, because Mase was a natural human headline. There was no better example of this than his 'stadium full of 50,000 nutbag, redneck Queenslanders' line before the second game in 2008. It was a throwaway line, but I reckon Willie was smart enough to know it would get a big send-around, and just didn't care. The Queenslanders probably got off on that; God knows how it would have been received if Chris 'Choppy' Close had still been the team manager, but I don't think it would have made one iota of difference to the result of the series – both teams were highly motivated anyway. But when you look at it, stories like that are great for Origin and Willie was only saying what most of the players would have been thinking but would not say.

I just always felt guarded; not wanting to give anything away that I didn't have to. I'd downplay any potential weaknesses in the Queensland side, give them a rap as much as possible and downplay any refereeing controversies (before the game at least; in an emotional environment after some losses I gave my opinion on some decisions).

Starting Origin week standing in a huddle of 30 or 40 media people sort of signalled 'Game on, Origin has arrived'. I never wanted to give a boring interview, but I would be nervous and guarded. So it was often, 'Yeah, yeah, Queensland are going to be tough; they're a great team . . .' At the start of the week it felt as though the media sometimes were more interested in what we did on our 'bonding night' rather than how the new team-mates were fitting in and more positive stuff relevant to the match. I'd be second-guessing what angle journalists were aiming at or where they were coming from, but I'd work it out after a while.

Most NRL players don't feel comfortable or trust the media entirely. The fact is we live in a very invasive society these days and any controversy is pounced on and blown up and then regurgitated for days and days, in the press, on the internet, on television and on radio. The media all compete like never before against each other. It's hard for players to know who can be trusted, so at first they usually trust no one, put up the barriers and become inaccessible whenever they can. If they thought about it, this doesn't help their situation, because it leads to the media thinking they are being evasive, presumably because they have something to hide. That's a pity, because I found most of the media good to deal with. My attitude was always to be up front. But even when players do talk with the media, the first instinct is to talk in clichés and play it safe, not wanting to inflame anything; they sort of talk without saying anything.

The only way to work it out is through experience and advice. You learn whose phone calls to return, and I made a point of returning calls because I appreciated the job the media had to do. Also, if you don't get back to them it's an invitation to write the half-truth. I showed the media respect by always returning phone calls and being accessible when I could and I believe the media gave me great respect in return, which I appreciated. It blew me away how many attended my tribute lunch in Newcastle. That was something I was very pleased about, because they didn't have to do it. The local guys like Brett Keeble (*Newcastle Herald*), Barry Toohey (*Daily Telegraph*), Craig Hamilton (ABC radio) and Jim Callinan (NBN Television) – and a few of the Sydney guys – are blokes I learnt to respect and trust, while appreciating their job was to criticise when they saw fit. To my way of thinking, it was all about being objective and not running any agendas, and I think that's all any footballer asks.

I must say, though, that the world NRL footballers live in today is becoming more invasive, more aggressive as far as the media is concerned; they never quite know when they are safe from anyone spying on them and reporting it to the media, who quite often run with an 'alleged' occurrence without fully checking it out. It's tough, but it's the world we now live in and footballers have to learn how to cope with it.

21

IN THE PUBLIC EYE

OFF-FIELD behaviour of rugby league players has become a big public issue, maybe the biggest issue holding the game back, judging by the series of events and bad publicity they created in 2009. It's about time players took responsibility and woke up to the fact that they are public property 24/7 – and no matter how unfair they might think it is, it's a fact of life.

And just as importantly, it's about time an independent disciplinary commission was set up to deal with off-field misbehaviour. That's how big an issue I believe it has become for rugby league, with the hungry media going overboard to divulge every possible angle of an event.

There's no doubt that a higher percentage of players act sensibly and responsibly than when I entered first grade in 1998. But the few who do step out of line are highlighted to such an extent that it is affecting the image of others and leading to general assumptions about the game itself.

It's nothing new to suggest that alcohol is at the root of most unsavoury events that happen; or that binge drinking is a big problem in society. We've heard all that. I like a beer as much as the next bloke; and I've had a few too many plenty of times. But there is a time and a place; and a degree of responsibility and respect you have to show yourself, your club and the game of rugby league when you get in that situation. It's hard to show clear judgement when you're blind drunk, so don't allow yourself – or your football mates, if you can – to get into a situation where it can all go wrong. There is too often someone out there who wants his or her five minutes of fame and will dump on you.

The bad publicity is taking a major toll on the game's image at a time when sport generally is struggling for sponsorship dollars. Thankfully crowd figures have stayed up, probably due to a great season in '09 by the heavily supported Dragons. Rugby league has proven again to be resilient, but how many times can we shoot ourselves in the foot and get away with it? The ravenous media coverage of the incidents are almost as big an issue; it's almost like the Super League days, when there seemed a constant search for off-field scandal – particularly in the News Limited media, who are half-owners of the game. I think too many agendas, and rivalry, in the media only adds to the problem.

The NRL and the individual clubs are doing their best to educate players, and I think attitudes are gradually changing. Players are far less likely now than they would have been three or four years ago to go out in public for a bender and put themselves in a situation where if they even sneeze the wrong way it can end up being front page news.

However, there are the minority who are plunging the game into a terrible image problem through their irresponsibility. And leaving it up to the clubs to take action – even though they are the employers of players – is not the answer, despite David Gallop maintaining it is. It has gone beyond that; players at *all* clubs and the game *generally* suffer from the stupidity of a few.

What happens now, it appears to me at least, is that the clubs report incidents to the NRL and then, on the surface, they are left to hand out their own punishments. The NRL watches closely, often warning clubs to come down hard and pushing them into a corner. The clubs often act to save face. It becomes very rushed, with a decision sometimes made on emotion, and in haste. And then there are inconsistencies between clubs, who naturally have to balance the need for strong deterrents with the realisation that suspending players affects the club's livelihood in very tough times.

Take the decision-making out of the clubs' hands. Set up a panel to deal independently with poor behaviour, at all senior levels of the game. Include a policeman or former policeman, a lawyer, two former players – maybe one with an untarnished 'cleanskin' image and another who is a 'reformed rogue' who could play devil's advocate to some extent. Put a long-time rugby league sponsor on that panel; and I'd ensure a woman was there too. An inquiry should be conducted quickly and thoroughly, with all players and witnesses interviewed privately. Penalties could be decided with some sort of structure of penalties, with the prime deterrent being that players are stood down from matches, rather than the current most common penalty of monetary fines.

We've had an endless number of fines handed out to players, yet the penny hasn't dropped with very many. You ask any footballer and the biggest penalty they feel is not being able to play football; they hate being spectators and letting their mates down. When players get fined, it comes out of future earnings anyway, so they never physically see the money being ripped from them. But being put on the sideline affects them straight away and it affects the whole team – which should create peer pressure to behave themselves.

There has to be an example set by the senior players, a culture governed by them, in which the players who are outed for mucking up are made to feel awful for letting their mates down. If one player gets suspended for three weeks, then another a few weeks later, then another, the rest of the team will look at them and say, 'You're costing us a chance to make the finals, and thus representative teams, or increased contract money; but on top of that we are all getting bad reputations for what a given few are doing.' There is a lot of peer pressure in sport and that peer pressure has to be applied to ensure that rugby league regains some of its image. I reckon there are some players out there in 2009 who are probably ashamed to be known as rugby league players, considering some of the bad publicity that has been whipped up.

Respect from your team-mates is a big motivator in professional sport and it's about time some of the good citizens in the game made a bigger point of the lack of respect shown by the minority who get themselves into trouble. And senior players, who are fewer in the NRL now because of the salary cap, can play a big part in pushing that point and being the ones who let the younger players know that such behaviour is not on.

The classic case of why punishment should be taken away from clubs was the incident involving the Broncos players Darius Boyd, Karmichael Hunt and Sam Thaiday in 2008, when they went into a toilet at a bar with a woman who later alleged they sexually assaulted her. They were cleared of any criminal conduct. It happened after the first week of the finals series and there were calls for them to be stood down from playing. I'm not sure any club would have sacked three players during the finals, although I am not saying it was right not to suspend them; but that is the issue. The pressure would have been taken off the club if the case had automatically gone to an independent panel to rule on and the punishments would become consistent right across the board.

Most clubs, and the NRL, are providing course after course about behavioural issues, but in the end it is up to the individuals and the peer standards set by those around them. The number of off-field dramas that gained publicity in 2008–09 without doubt would have turned potential sponsors (and current ones) away from the game at a time when we can't afford it. On top of that, the general reputation of rugby league players took a battering. Unfortunately, as players, we all seem to get tarred by the same brush – regarded as 'boofhead footballers'. I know that often what actually happened gets beaten up, but if players didn't put themselves in a position to have anything written about them in the first place, the degree of publicity wouldn't be an issue.

The game has always seemed to rebound, but 2009 might have given this theory its biggest test after the culmination of so many misdemeanours. I've had a lot of people who support the game tell me they don't have any interest in it anymore. They say, 'You blokes just don't learn.' That's pretty hard to take.

It is a big emotional roller coaster these days, with so much intensity put into a game in the NRL, and players feel they have to 'come down' and to do that they want to throw a few beers down them. I certainly did. You feel as though you need some stress release; you have this intense preparation, a massive adrenalin build-up and, after the match, you think, 'I've got through that one; I feel all right, so I'll go a few beers.' But players have nowhere to hide these days and they seem to be greater targets for the smartarse on the street, and a media which delights in latching on to any bit of scuttlebutt and running with it, no matter how trivial or how unjustified it is.

There is a skill involved in being a public figure, and players have to be taught it as early as possible in their careers. There has to be a degree of risk assessment – and it's just too risky now to let your hair down in a public place. A lot of players don't like it when people come up to them in public and act as if they know them; and they have to know how to handle that situation in a non-confrontational way, even if the person who confronts them is drunk and obnoxious.

I often think of that TV commercial in New South Wales aimed at drink driving; the one where a bloke leaves a pub over the limit and is paranoid that he is going to be breath-tested, and the voice-over says, 'Every police car is a mobile RBT, so if you're worried about being caught . . . you should be.' The commercial finishes with the words on screen, 'Mobile RBT; you don't know where, you don't know when.' Well, that could be applied to players in regard to the media these days. Every person in a crowd is a potential photographer or 'reporter' who might snap a shot on a mobile phone, or take a video on a mobile phone, and sell it to the media. Or someone will call a radio station or a newspaper and tell a story about you; all it needs is the word 'alleged' and it seems open slather to run with it. You don't know where; you don't know when.

Although I was at Leeds at the time, I heard that in March 2009, Brett Seymour was videoed on a mobile phone by a passerby; he was doing nothing illegal or even causing any nuisance, just being drunk. He should not have put himself in such a position – but what is the world coming to when someone can get thousands of dollars for getting a few seconds of a footballer being drunk put on television? Seymour was fined $20,000 and stood down for two matches.

The amount of media focus on rugby league these days is just astonishing, and the media can pay big money for a big story. I've been told there is a guy in Newcastle who scans the police radio and also has a strong link with all the cab drivers. As soon as something comes up, he is on the phone to media organisations. I'd hate to think how many stories he's tried to break over the years.

We had a policy at Newcastle that if there were any potential problems you had to report to the club straight away. If you were caught drink driving or in a fight, you had to let the club know and work out a strategy. The worst thing is if something is in the papers and you don't tell the truth about it straight away, or think you can hide it.

Footballers should be able to unwind and have some fun like any other young person, on the few occasions when they can have a good drink; but that's becoming less and less possible. Most married senior players these days would go somewhere quiet for a few beers, or just go home and have a few there if they wanted to. The next day you wake up feeling a lot easier in the mind (and better physically) knowing you hadn't been anywhere, or been involved in anything, that could have incriminated you. But you can't blame the young blokes for chasing the bright lights; we've all done that.

I've been put in situations where someone who is drunk has tried to antagonise me. You just have to leave. I've had blokes spitting in my face as they talk shit; it's not enjoyable, so I just take myself out of the situation. If you say, 'Piss off, mate, I'm having a beer with my mates, do you mind?' – and sometimes you have to say that – they may respond with, 'Sorry mate, that's fine.' But sometimes they want to carry on and get in your face and you have to know how to handle that without aggravating the situation.

I think the younger players these days are being educated a lot earlier about the environment they now live in, yet they are in an age of binge drinking and that's a big problem in society. We're lucky at Newcastle that Russell Richardson, a former team-mate, owns one of Newcastle's hot spots – the King Street Hotel – and he looks after the boys when they go there. It's the same at the Burwood Inn at Merewether, where the owner 'Baz' Bradley ensures the boys get their own space, and he'll put them up for the night in one of the hotel rooms if they have had too many drinks.

I think 99 per cent of NRL footballers are good fellas. But they have to learn the skills of coping with public attention. One of those skills is the simple task of taking five or six seconds to respond to someone who recognises and addresses you in public, and then asking them how they are going. It is a privilege to be in that situation. It's not all about training hard and playing hard; part of the job is also carrying the image of the game and yourself.

An issue that received plenty of negative publicity in 2009 was the attitude of footballers towards women, and the question of group sex. I couldn't say there is a culture of group sex in rugby league these days. Like most players, I've heard stories going back a few years of several players having sex with willing women, but I think it would happen very rarely now. I think players have become much more aware of the dangers of that sort of behaviour. Once others enter the room, things can get out of hand, no matter how willing the woman appears to be. It's too dangerous. People can wake up the next day and start to consider, 'What happened there? Why did I do that?'

Generally, I think it has to be said that there are two sides to the footballers/women issue. Sure, the attitudes of some footballers towards women need to improve, but footballers are targets too, of opportunistic star-gazing women who openly prey on them to have a 'fling'; 'trophy hunters' as they are often called. They don't care if a player is married or in a steady relationship and when footballers, and the women, are affected by alcohol a lot of judgement is washed away.

It doesn't just happen at the club after a game or at a nightclub any more, but through Facebook and other sites on the internet. The invention of Facebook has made it even more dangerous for players because it's easier for women to contact them and chase them, and vice versa. It's a very hard thing for a young footballer to resist when he sees no harm in it; which often there isn't. But he has to know the possible consequences if things get out of hand – or out in public.

What annoys a lot of footballers who do respect the game – and women – is that they all seem to get tarred by the same brush when incidents occur and people can look at you at functions thinking, 'Oh. He's a rugby league player; we better be wary of him, judging by what we have heard. I wonder if he does those sorts of things too.'

That's unfair. But it's real. We have to apply pressure to those who break the rules of good sense and come down hard on them – with the back-up of a strong, independent tribunal which players can't escape when they step out of line. The sooner that happens, the better off rugby league will be.

22

THE MEN IN CHARGE

I FEEL lucky to have had a good cross-section of coaches at the Newcastle Knights, New South Wales and Australian teams. All had different strengths and traits, and I learnt something from each of them.

Malcolm Reilly was the coach who introduced me to first grade but he made an impression on me long before that. My first year at the Knights was 1995 in SG Ball and that was when Mal joined the club too. A year or so later, Malcolm came up to me in the gym one afternoon when I was sitting on an exercise bike. He said, 'Righto, lad; I'll put you through your paces. You look like you are just rolling your legs over; I'll give you some targets to hit.'

Malcolm doubled the resistance on the bike, set a program and started pedalling. His eyeballs were hanging out and he was off the seat pedalling furiously, his body shaking. He stopped and said, 'That's my score; you've got to try to beat that.' I tried but could get nowhere near it; it was absolutely killing me; I lasted about 10 minutes. Mal said I had to set my targets and improve every time. Whenever he saw me in the gym after that, he'd ask me how I was going with my bike target and I'd hop on the bike and he'd watch me. He probably wouldn't have known me other than that I was just another young Knights player, but he took a bit of interest in me. I'd watch him in the gym and he would pretty much use every machine and walk out physically spent – and he was 47 years old!

Any physical challenge thrown at him, he'd tackle. There are plenty of legendary stories, including the time at Newcastle when he watched us doing an underwater challenge in the pool and said, 'Give me a set of togs and I'll show you.' He got changed and went the whole 50 metres of the pool underwater. He didn't even dive in to get some momentum; he just pushed off the wall of the pool. We thought he was going to die, but he was one of those blokes who would never give in. I've never seen a redder head than his when he got out. A few of the boys tried to do it after that, and we'd been swimming for an hour, so our lungs had expanded. But we couldn't match him.

Mal's boxing challenge with Steve Crowe is also legendary; it was pretty brutal. It started off as a bit of fun – all the boys were standing around, and Mal and Crowey had smiles on their faces. Then, bang, Mal put one on him and Crowey got one on Mal, and it became quite vicious. You could see Mal wanted to do everything but box to pretty much get Crowey down. In the end Matthew Johns jumped in and said, 'That will do.'

Mal introduced me to first grade in 1997 off the bench against the Queensland Crushers, after I'd played reserve grade. I was a skinny fellow and only went on for the last 10 minutes, but I remember Tony Butterfield terrorising opponents with his physicality. It was early the next season before I got some regular time in the first grade side, but Mal included me in the first grade squad for the 1997 semi-finals and that was a huge buzz, to feel I was on his radar. I got suited up for the semi-final against Manly and, when Matty Johns went down hurt, they looked at me to replace him but thank god Matty got up because I don't think I was ready for it at that stage.

Mal brought me off the bench against the Warriors in Auckland in round seven in 1998, to replace Lee Jackson at hooker. I was playing behind a big pack, and I scored a try from one of my first touches from dummy-half, which was a buzz. One thing I remember vividly was Robbie O'Davis returning the ball from a kick with no fear and bouncing off big defenders left, right and centre. The ferocity of the hits was something I'd never experienced; I'll never forget the sound of bodies crashing together.

I'd never played hooker in the lower grades but Mal obviously saw a future for me there, with the Johns brothers having a mortgage on the halves. Mal appreciated that I could play a few positions; I filled in at centre and fullback in first grade as well, before I was the starting hooker at the end of the season, so I have a lot to thank Mal for: introducing me to first grade, switching me to hooker and showing confidence in me. In my short time under Malcolm, I learnt about mental toughness, about driving yourself in order to succeed, playing with injury and living up to the club motto of 'being the player everyone wants to play with'.

When Malcolm announced he was going back to England, most of the players thought Peter Sharp – who had coached the Knights reserve grade to the premiership in 1995 before going to Parramatta in 1997 – would get the job. Instead we were surprised when the club announced Warren Ryan was taking over; he hadn't coached for a few years after finishing with Wests in Sydney, but had a massive reputation as an innovator and technical genius. 'Wok' put a few noses out of joint with his manner but set up a lot of things for the Knights' future and taught me a lot about the game. Another significant signing that year too was strength and conditioning coach Scott Campbell, who came to the club from St George.

The Wok just lived and breathed rugby league. You would often see him at the Cricketers Arms Hotel with our football manager Dave Morley and some mates, comparing crosswords and exchanging their knowledge of different things. The players were down there regularly and if Warren saw you there he'd come over and place a few glasses or salt shakers on a table, move them around and say, 'Right, we are going to do this or that this week; what happened was this last week and we should have done it this way'. Even if you were with your girlfriend or on a first date, it wouldn't worry Warren; he'd call you over because he was always thinking football.

Most weeks he would have a move designed just for that opposition, and that takes a lot of coaching and thinking about the game. We'd get to training and he'd have these moves ready to go. But he built his team on defence essentially; defensive structure and attitude. At training he'd line up four big sleds with tackle bags stuck on the end of each one and we had to line up in groups of five and use good leg drive and tackle technique to push them up and down the field, moving them about five metres at a time. It was all about footwork and timing. Apparently, when he was coaching Canterbury in the 1980s when they hit the tackle sleds, he'd say, 'I want to hear it like the waves crashing on the sand,' and then he'd turn around and the tacklers would hit the bags in unison. The other saying he had was a twist on the famous Mohammad Ali quote, 'Float like a butterfly; sting like a bee.' Warren would say, if he felt we weren't physical enough on the bags, 'You boys were floating like elephants and stinging like moths.'

To Warren, rugby league was a science and that's why a lot of coaches look to him for guidance, and many NRL coaches still contact him for advice. But Wok was abrupt and ruthless in his attitude and a few of the players didn't appreciate that. I was still earning my stripes as a first grader, playing any position the coach wanted me to, and I was soaking it all up. He used to say that the ruck was the focal point of the game, the pebble in the pond. He had a saying: 'Why go around the back door when you've got the front door kicked in?' In other words, why throw the ball wide when you are having success going through the middle.

While Mal Reilly first put me to hooker, Warren made me a hooker. He saw me as a person who would relish that role of being in the middle and getting the team going forward from dummy-half and being able to play a little bit with the ball. Bringing Steve Walters in at the end of his career to hold the position for the 1999 season and teach whoever the designated successor was going to be was a smart move. As it turned out, Steve only lasted eight rounds because of his chronic knee problem, but he stayed around to teach me plenty. I'd played all over the backline as a 'Mr Fix It', really, before then but I let Warren know I was keen to take the hooking role once Boxhead retired and I think he respected my enthusiasm. I was just bouncing in to training every day looking forward to learning new skills from Warren Ryan or Steve Walters.

Warren said to me, 'You've got an opportunity here, son; but do you love defending? Do you like the contact? Because we can teach you plenty of things, but that has to come from you.' I told him I was definitely up for it.

While I soaked up everything Warren told me, a fair bit of discontent grew in 2000 when Matthew Johns and Warren were bluing badly, and Tony Butterfield also fell out with the coach. There was a big revolt and it got pretty ugly at one stage; some players just didn't like the way Warren communicated with them and he didn't mince his words; he was very honest with people.

One of the issues was that Warren and Dave Morley came up with a scheme called 'White Knights' in which special rings were made, to be sold for $1500 or $2000, I think, with proceeds to go towards player retention and recruitment. It was generally a good, creative idea but, to sort of increase the validity and marketability of the rings, the players were pressured to buy them too. Each ring had a blue and a red gem and was numbered; I can't remember how many were made, but quite a few fans bought them and it raised a bit of money for a player retention fund. For some players not on a great deal of money, offloading a lot of money for a ring they would hardly ever wear didn't go down too well. That caused a lot of disharmony, with Tony Butterfield, as the senior player in the club, at the heart of it. I thought I'd do the right thing and buy one (it's been sitting in a drawer for years), but some players were filthy on being told they had to acquire one each.

When Michael Hagan took over as coach for the 2001 season, although we'd lost Matt Johns and Tony Butterfield had retired, some good systems were in place, ready for us to progress as a football team. Hages was the perfect person to follow on from Warren; his strengths were his man-management. He was a great manager of personalities, had a great passion for the Knights as the first former Newcastle player to coach the first grade side and, having been a first grade playmaking five-eighth (who played for Queensland), he had some smart plays and also allowed Andrew Johns to blossom as a leader and tactician. They formed a really good partnership, with Hages allowing Joey to have a big input at training and how we played the game, which I think was clever coaching because Joey was just about the smartest player in the game.

Hages was a lot younger than Malcolm and Warren, too, and would mix with the players socially – although he handled very well the fine line of being a mate as well as the coach; we always knew he was the boss. And I think he struck the right balance with Joey as well, who was going through a tough time in his life in those first few years under Hages's coaching – his divorce from Renae and his issues with bipolar disorder. It's no secret he'd have Joey on the other end of the phone in a real state at times, but he handled that well and gave Joey 'stress leave', as we called it – time to get away and get himself right – and probably no one else could have got more out of Andrew Johns as a footballer at the time than Michael Hagan did.

Hages was an approachable, personable bloke who was always interested in our lives outside of football too and wanted us to turn up in the right frame of mind. Being new to first grade coaching, he would listen to the players and he understood that he and the team would have to learn together.

As I started to feel the pinch physically from playing so many club and representative games, Hages was terrific in recognising when I needed a rest or to alter my training. He'd see me dragging the chain and know I was mentally tired as well as physically. He'd ask how I was and I'd always say, 'Okay, mate,' not wanting him to think I wasn't prepared to put in; then he'd see me walk away and my shoulders would slump down and he'd know that I wasn't feeling on top of the world. He would look at how I should be balancing my football and everyday life and how my personality was handling the stress, because he was aware of what was required to get the best football out of me.

As I have already mentioned in this book, there is a real culture in State of Origin about backing up for your club team the weekend following an Origin match, and that was certainly my mentality. But one time Hages insisted I was stood down for the weekend match and that I had to get away and freshen up. We had a few words at first but he said it was not negotiable, so I went up to the Gold Coast and didn't come back to training until the Monday. I felt I was letting my mates down, but he was right; I had a spring in my step again the following week and was better value for the team after that.

I know there was a perception from some people outside the club that Andrew Johns coached the team as much as Michael Hagan, but that was not true; Hages was just being smart in giving Joey plenty of input. There was no doubt who the coach was and who had the final say. I felt sorry for Hages in that sense. In 2004 and 2005, we had Joey and a lot of senior players injured, plus we lost Ben Kennedy to Manly and Timana Tahu to Parramatta, so it was a tough period for the club. Hages was under pressure then and in the end the club seemed to become undecided whether he was worth keeping. I think he showed what a good coach he was when Newcastle came back and made the finals in 2006, and when the Eels made the finals in 2007, his first season with them.

I know I speak for a lot of players in saying I enjoyed playing for Michael Hagan, and that's the best way to describe it – we were playing for Hages rather than under Hages. A lot of players could say they played their best football when he was coach.

I have spoken at length elsewhere in this book about Brian Smith. When he came to Newcastle it was a large change of personality, as it was from Malcolm Reilly to Warren Ryan to Michael Hagan. I found Brian hard to get to know closely and a little unpredictable. We never had a relationship in which I would feel comfortable walking into his office, sitting down and having a chat. But I liked him and he is a good coach.

I think, with me being a senior player near the end of my career, he probably didn't put as much attention into me as he would have with the younger players he was trying to mould as he focused on developing a new era for the Knights. Even though I was captain, he never asked my opinion much. That is just Brian's style; as head coach he's prepared to take on that burden himself and live and die by the results of doing things his way. He's been around a long time and built some very good teams, so that's fair enough.

One stand-out feature about Brian as a coach is that he is the boss. He wants to carve the structure of the place as he sees it and tries to mould players into the kind of players he feels he needs to do the job; he strips them back to what he wants them to be and goes into a lot of technicality. He brought some players to Newcastle who are doing a great job and showing tremendous fighting spirit. If the players don't fit the mould, they are moved on. Brian is also about being the head of a coaching team and consults with his assistants very well; he lets them concentrate on a lot of the specifics with players while he takes on an overseer's role, distancing himself from the players a little while using his assistant coaches to do the more personal stuff.

Smithy is certainly smart when it comes to football and has some really good ideas; I think he picked Andrew Johns's brains a bit when he first came to Newcastle. We changed our defensive formation under Brian and that took a lot of the first off-season to perfect. It would have been interesting to see how Brian and Andrew mixed had Joey not been injured so early in the 2007 season. Joey certainly had a lot more 'pull' under previous coaches in terms of how we played the game and the off-field culture and I think there might have been some conflict at some stage.

When it comes to my representative coaches, again each was quite different. I have also spoken at length about Phil Gould in previous chapters. He is the perfect Origin coach, so good at bringing people together as a group, and instilling passion into the team, because he is such a great motivator and orator. He also has a very astute football brain and he brought in some good set plays but was also smart enough to know you have to keep things fairly simple with the limited preparation time we have in Origin. 'Gus' knew what it took to win Origin games; he built a warlike, comrade-style atmosphere in camp.

Ricky Stuart succeeded Phil Gould as New South Wales coach in 2005 and I found him right up there with Gus from a motivational viewpoint. Technically, Ricky had a couple more big plays than Phil – scrum moves and tap moves. Motivationally he was really intense and driven as a person anyway and he brought that into Origin.

When Ricky took on the Australian coaching job, we went to Graham Murray for 2006–07. 'Muzza' encouraged a more relaxed approach after there'd been some conjecture that it had all become too intense for a few seasons. It was noticeable that we went into games without the off-the-field intensity of the past. This was a strategy which worked well for him with the City Origin team for a few years, and obviously at North Queensland, where he took them to their first finals campaign and a grand final the following year, in 2005.

It was a distinctly different period being a New South Wales player then; there were a few games where I wasn't sure whether we'd done the required work or not. Personally, I preferred the intense build-up because that is what Origin is about, 80 minutes of high-paced intensity, but I could understand others wanting a more relaxed approach, because Origin camps had become so hectic.

Muz wasn't big on motivational speeches like Ricky and Gus, but he brought a lot of technical things into camp. I think Graham found the media intensity surrounding Origin a real eye-opener, as Craig Bellamy did in 2008, and there was a media campaign against Muz that gained momentum in his second year, with some reports saying he didn't have the confidence of the players. The fact was that we went very close to winning the 2006 series, only beaten in the last couple of minutes of the deciding game in Melbourne when Darren Lockyer scooped on a loose pass to score.

I never had any problems with Graham Murray; I liked playing under him, but he was in a different mould from Phil Gould and Ricky Stuart, who seemed to have that extra experience and edge when it came to State of Origin passion and understanding. I think a few players found the jump in style – from the full-on, emotional, intense build-ups from Gus and Ricky who had been around the Origin scene for a while (Ricky as a player in five series, Gus as coach in eight) to the more club-like, low-key approach from Muz – too big a jump and they might have said so privately. That leaked out and it grew from there. Muzza became very sensitive about it, particularly that players might have been talking out of turn. A few of the senior players told him not to read the papers and just ignore it, but he was pretty cut about it.

Each coach has a different style, but players have to look at themselves and they couldn't blame the coach for losing those two series. We lost the next year under Craig Bellamy, who was regarded by many as the new 'guru' of coaches.

I'd played under Belly previously when he was New South Wales Country coach and the assistant Australian coach, and he was the boss for my final Origin campaign in 2008. It's obvious he was a sponge when it came to rugby league information, having played under great coaches like Tim Sheens, playing with some great players who became coaches like Ricky Stuart and Mal Meninga, and then been Wayne Bennett's assistant at Brisbane. He gathered all he could from them, then went about forming his own ideas about the game. I've never seen a coach work harder; he is meticulous in his preparation.

That was shown when he brought John Di Stefano, a strategic manager, into Origin camp in 2008. John is a specialist in analysing such areas as team meeting structure; the best way of getting maximum results from the limited preparation period the team had; the efficiency of internal communication; and the effectiveness of leadership.

It just shows how smart Craig is. He's also a bloke who will sit down and have a beer with you and is always up for a chat. I have the utmost respect for Belly, because of everything he stands for – work hard, prepare well, play well.

He looks through a lot of video from different angles and is good at slightly adjusting a set move to make it more effective. He is very particular with ruck play – getting quick play the balls or slowing down the opposition's play the balls – and that's why he had a wrestling coach in a New South Wales Origin camp for the first time. Even with the wrestling, it was a mental thing as much as anything and a fitness component to our training; we weren't doing WWF moves. I learnt some new things about wrestling technique and being more efficient in the tackle.

We sure didn't lose the 2008 Origin series, Craig's first as coach, because of lack of preparation; we were like a racehorse trained to the minute, but we were run down in the last 100 metres of the straight.

There were also some excellent assistant coaches in the New South Wales camp during my time with the Blues. John

Cartwright was outstanding and I'm not surprised he has impressed so much with the Gold Coast Titans and has been a big component of their quick development on and off the field. He was mostly our defence coach and he had some great ideas, but he knows how to be a skilful ball runner, because he was one of the best in his playing days. He is very knowledgeable on the lines to attack, getting the right body position to offload and what players to 'spot'.

My first Test coach was Chris Anderson, on the 2001 Kangaroo tour. I regard 'Opes' as a sensational 'tour coach'; which is a difficult job, very different than coaching at club level. To be a good touring coach is about giving the boys responsibility, knowing their limits and making them train hard. Chris let the players enjoy themselves and let off some steam, which you have to do after a long season and being so far from home. He'd have a beer with the players and is a real man's man, but he'd come down hard on you if you didn't aim up at training the next day. It was important to show respect for the jersey and each other and he understood that pivotal to that respect was putting in at training and not losing sight of what we were there for – to represent our country with honour.

Chris simplified things tactically but had us all on the same page. You don't want to over-coach with the best players in Australia in your team; we had a basic formula and stuck to that. We had no right to win some games on the tours I went on, especially in 2003, when we had our backs to the wall and had to come from behind in the last 10 minutes to win all three Tests. The spirit and closeness of the team got us through and a lot of that was due to how Opes managed the team.

I'll never forget the feeling when we learnt Chris had had a heart attack and was rushed to hospital during the Ashes-deciding third Test on the 2001 tour at Wigan. We went in at half-time and someone said, 'Where's Opes?' Assistant coach Greg Pierce got up and said he wasn't feeling well before our captain, Brad Fittler, stepped in and said, 'Right, what is wrong with him?' We were told he had a suspected heart attack and Freddy just asked, 'Is he going to be all right?' We were assured he'd be fine and the doctors just thought it was wise to take him to hospital for tests. Freddy stood up as the great leader that he was; he virtually took over the coaching role at half-time and with real authority told us how we were going to play the game. I was blown away by how calm and decisive he was, considering our coach had just been rushed to hospital in the middle of a game. We led 12–6 at half-time but we came out and put it all together for the second 40 minutes and won 28–8.

On tour in 2003, we played a French Selection, England A and Wales before the Tests against Great Britain. With so many players having pulled out of that tour, we were down in experience, with 14 of the 23 players on their first Kangaroo tour. Ryan Girdler was hurt earlier in the tour and missed all three Tests and after Craig Gower was ruled out with injury for the third Test, Opes was the centre of a selection drama when he used Darren Smith, who was playing with St Helens. Mick Crocker went from an interchange forward to five-eighth and Smithy was put on the bench, which meant Joel Clinton, Shannon Hegarty, Luke Lewis and Richard Villasanti were overlooked – even though Craig Wing had already been shifted to centre to cover for 'Girds'. It was a controversial move; no one had ever been picked from outside the squad on tour before. Opes was criticised mercilessly for the move, particularly as we'd already won the first two Tests and retained the Ashes trophy. He expected to be bagged, but he didn't care what anyone thought; he believed that was the best option to win that game. You've got to give him credit; he stuck to it and didn't care about the backlash. He wanted Smithy in the team he knew was experienced enough to do the job.

I felt sorry for the guys in the squad who missed out, and I know I would have been pissed off if I was chosen for the tour and saw someone else brought in from outside. In Luke Lewis's case, he has still not played a Test for Australia. But I had no beef with the decision and, as far as getting the most balanced and most experienced team out there, it was a good decision. It turned out to be one of the most memorable Tests I played in. We were down 12–6 with three minutes to go but somehow scored two tries to win 18–12. On the last play of the game, Darren Lockyer was looking for a 50-metre field goal but he got a bad pass that bounced on the ground, so he was forced to run the ball. He put Craig Wing into space and Brett Kimmorley tagged on before passing to Locky, who put Luke Ricketson over for a try. We won the series three–nil, the first time that had been done since the 1986 Kangaroo tour.

Wayne Bennett took over from Chris Anderson as Australian coach in 2004. Having Wayne as my Test coach was interesting in that he had such an aura about him; and a bit of mystery surrounding him, which I'm sure he intentionally created with the media. To finally meet him was awesome; and it coincided with my only Test played in Newcastle, against New Zealand in 2004. His knowledge about not just footy but life was great for me and he was the person who brought the reference to the Anzacs at Gallipoli into our preparation, which was special for all of us. Wayne developed an even greater sense of respect into the team, respect for the occasion and each other. He didn't want a drinking culture, although he was happy for the players to have a quiet beer, or a loose social culture. Being on time, showing discipline and respecting each other were of utmost importance to him. Typical of his own discipline, he would go for a run every morning before breakfast and no one was game to try to go with him and keep up with him.

Later that year we had the first Tri Nations series played mostly in England and our seating on the plane was done in alphabetical order; so I sat next to Craig Bellamy and Wayne was across the aisle. That long flight to England is always an opportunity to get to know someone and that was the case with me and the two coaches. When it came to Wayne, I found there was a big difference between the man and the myth. He loves a laugh more than anyone; his demeanour is more relaxed than I had expected, but he's a man whose respect you have to earn and obviously some of the media didn't do that over the years. He is a family man and has a lot of stories to tell about life. Wayne was interested in my background and my family and the Newcastle club and came across as a really genuine person.

23

'NEWCASTLE . . .
NEWCASTLE . . .'

I WAS 14 when our junior coach took our team to Marathon Stadium in Newcastle to watch the Knights play Manly. It was a Sunday afternoon and there were nearly 25,000 in the ground; we sat on the grassed hill and I was just spinning out with excitement watching the players and the crowd I'd only ever seen on television.

It was 1992 and it was the first time I'd attended an ARL match. I left for the bus trip back to Taree thinking, 'How good would it be to play in front of that crowd!' The people around us were so loud, so passionate and seemed to have such familiarity with the Knights players. While a few of my mates were checking out all the young girls around us, most of the time before kick-off (and after in some cases) the power of the crowd was what made the biggest impression on me.

Sixteen years later, when I waved farewell to that crowd – unfortunately while I had my arm strapped up inside my tracksuit top instead of after playing a match – that impression was still the same: 'How good is it to run out in front of this crowd!' The ground had changed a fair bit, with the new eastern grandstand standing there as the dominant structure where we had sat on the grass in 1992, but the loyalty and passion of the supporters hadn't.

The following year, when I was 15, I went down to stay at my cousin's at Merewether during the school holidays. I borrowed a bike and went for a ride; I asked him if we could go all the way to the stadium so I could get another glimpse of it. I rode inside the gates and just stood there looking around; it still seemed awesome to me, even though it was empty. I wanted to know more about the history of the club and the fans and what it all meant to them. I'd grown up a mad St George fan, but Newcastle was the closest team to Taree and I was just so taken by the whole set-up.

A couple of years later I played there with the Knights SG Ball team, and we had quite a few of the die-hard supporters come down to watch us go through our paces. When I got to play President's Cup at the end of that season, it was just a massive buzz for a teenager to run onto the field when there would be at least 10,000 spectators – and sometimes more than 20,000 by the end of the game as the fans flooded in to grab a spot on the hills.

That was one of the great things about Knights supporters – so many watched the players come through from either the junior rep teams or the President's Cup/Jersey Flegg when there used to be three games played on the main match days. I had so many people come up to me after I finished in 2008, telling me they'd watched my development since SG Ball or President's Cup and how much they had enjoyed my career. That was pretty special, but typical of Newcastle. I think they get a lot of satisfaction from being there through the hard times with players – when you get injured or are doing it tough as a team – as much as when you play for your state, or Australia, or in a grand final. It makes them feel really proud that they have seen the ups and downs of your career.

I don't think there are any more loyal supporters in rugby league than Newcastle Knights supporters. That was proved in 2005 when we lost 13 games straight and, despite a great rally in the last third of the season, finished with the wooden spoon. Our crowds for the season averaged 18,469, still fourth in the NRL that year – only 300 a game fewer than Wests Tigers, who won the competition. Being such an educated rugby league crowd, they knew the effort we were putting in with so many players out injured – and that's high in the expectations of the Knights' faithful: that their team has 'a dig'. We were still playing physically and working hard for each other. The fans' support and loyalty was a big motivation in the team sticking at it. When we came good and won eight of our last 11 games, we genuinely felt it was a reward not just for the team and the club, but our supporters too. We spoke about that so many times, saying things like, 'Look at this crowd. We have lost 13 games in a row, and there are 18,000 here. This is pretty special.' It was just sensational that we got the chance to repay them late in the season, and then made the finals the following year in 2006.

One thing I have noticed is the Knights crowd is getting older. A large proportion of them have been watching the team since the first season of 1988, and kept their season ticket seats. The club has worked hard to introduce younger fans as well, which is great; it's wonderful to see a real generational culture in the supporter base – parents taking their kids or grand-kids, and I can see that coming through now.

The new stand on the eastern side changed the impact of the crowd quite a bit. It's just awesome to run out straight towards it; it feels like the spectators are right over the top of you.

Every time I ran out into the unbelievable roar of a big crowd at the Newcastle stadium it was always a massive buzz and it just became automatic that I'd run towards the hill (and later the eastern stand) and salute our supporters and recognise their support; it was like a signal within me that it was 'game on'. When I ran out first as captain it was a bigger privilege. Those sorts of moments are something any player misses when he retires. It was also a tradition for most of the crowd to stay behind and clap you after full-time and we'd always applaud them and thank them for their support.

We were reminded about the link between the team, the town and the supporters every time we walked out of the dressing room with the drawing above the door of the hand grabbing another and helping it out of the rubble after the 1989 earthquake that hit the city. Unlike some earlier players, I didn't tap it and salute it when I ran out, but I was conscious it was always there and I usually had a glimpse of it as I went out the dressing room door . . . I certainly never under-estimated what that drawing stood for. It sums up the whole of Newcastle's ethic: you help a mate out.

Newcastle, and the whole Hunter region, is a parochial place that some people can find a bit stifling; I know Andrew Johns did in the end, because he was so widely recognised and couldn't go anywhere without people, intentionally or unin-tentionally, being in his face a bit. I never found that; I loved living there and found it a privilege to be recognised and have people supporting me and wanting to talk footy with me. It's not hard to be nice to people and talk about the game for a few seconds – especially after we'd won.

But you just took it for granted the questions you'd get were always different after a loss than a victory; everyone wanted to know what went wrong. Mark Hughes discovered the perfect solution to address that. We'd do the shopping at Coles at 5 pm during the week after a good win; if we lost we'd wait until Sunday morning when no one was awake! There was a lady who used to stack the shelves who would always say hello and want to have a chat. If we didn't see her, we'd invariably hear, 'Hmm . . . hmm,' with a cough as if to say, 'Excuse me, how dare you walk past without having a chat?'

Newcastle is the kind of town, and the Knights the type of club, where the people regard it as a community club, as if they have a sort of ownership of it. That was very evident in 2007, when many of them felt the club was getting derailed a bit with all the drastic changes in the playing personnel. They didn't appreciate that; they could sense it was not right and that the Knights were becoming like just another 'franchise' and they didn't want that to happen. But it appears a lot of that has settled down now.

The other major feature of a one-team town is the media coverage, and the people of the Hunter are very loyal to their local media – the *Newcastle Herald* newspaper, NBN (the Channel 9 affiliate) and the radio stations. There is so much local coverage that everyone seems to have an opinion or knows what's going on. The media interest certainly puts pressure on the team in a way, although naturally regional media is pretty supportive and parochial. We used to have a media conference every Tuesday to announce the team for the upcoming game. It was a way of funnelling a lot of the media inquiries into the one formatted conference rather than have a mountain of ad-hoc requests. But local media would still be at most training sessions getting vision for TV or mingling with the players, and you knew the local guys so well that the relationships were usually very good.

We all talk about the thousands that were at Newcastle Workers Club after the 1997 grand final, then the 15,000 that turned up at the stadium when we returned in the early hours of the morning after winning the 2001 grand final – both incredible examples of the extraordinary support we enjoyed. But another memory that sticks out for me was the finals game we played against the Roosters at the Sydney Football Stadium in 2000. We ran out to warm up on the field about 20 minutes before the match, and the sea of red and blue just erupted and the chant of 'Newcastle . . . Newcastle . . .' went up. The players were just stoked, and so proud of their community for turning up like that.

And it wasn't just the support from Newcastle people that I appreciated. The people of my home town of Taree were great too, and Forster, where my parents moved in 2002. It was always a buzz for me when the Taree Panthers junior players would come down for a Knights game (I'm an ambassador for the club) and I would show them around. The Knights would always try to accommodate kids in the dressing room and I loved seeing the starry-eyed looks on their faces; I know what a dream it would have been for me to see the inner sanctum of an NRL team when I was a kid.

That was one of the great features of the Knights – the club always made family, friends and fans welcome, and that was evident in the dressing room. Matt Parsons used to sit in his corner and have a beer and his family would come in and sit with him – usually his brother and son. Many of the families used to come in. Geoff Gidley was a regular; he's passionate about footy and seeing his sons do well. Jack Newton was also a regular; I found it really good to see proud parents welcomed in the rooms.

I strongly believe that you have to return the support to the community and I'd try to support Ronald McDonald House at the John Hunter Hospital whenever they needed me. Adam Woolnough and Kurt Reynoldson would go to the children's ward at John Hunter every couple of weeks off their own bat and visit the kids, often on a Friday afternoon, but did it without the media around so it didn't look like anyone was trying to get special recognition. That goes on a lot in rugby league, and it's not always heard about.

When Mark Hughes and I lived together, we'd always be available to do promotions for the club or attend functions. I think we were a pretty easy 'get' for the club if they wanted volunteers, because we liked going out and seeing the supporters and sponsors and Mark was such a devoted club man; he won the club man of the year award three times – they should rename it the Mark Hughes Trophy. Plus we also saw the benefit of 'networking' with people; it's good to have contact with people outside of rugby league when it is an all-consuming existence. As well, we need to find careers after football days are finished, so making contacts in the community and business world can be beneficial. I always tried to impress that on young players who might have been reluctant to attend events or do their promotions.

I look at the 'goldfish syndrome' that interrupts the lives of a lot of high-profile people and am thankful that I never reached that status. The Knights players had a 'haven' in the Burwood Inn at Merewether, where Barry 'Baz' Bradley and his family were fantastic publicans. From the late 1990s, a large percentage of the Knights players had moved to Merewether; there's probably nowhere else in Australia where so many NRL players are such a short walking distance from each other. Over the years Merewether residents have included Matthew and Andrew Johns, Ben Kennedy, Mark Hughes, Matthew and Kurt Gidley, Robbie O'Davis, Clinton O'Brien, Russell Richardson, Chris Bailey, Josh Perry, me, and a few others. Often one of the players would buy a four-bedroom home and a couple of others would move in with them before getting their own place. That's how Mark Hughes and I set up; Josh Perry had Adam Woolnough and Kurt Gidley living with him and when 'Woolly' moved out Anthony Quinn moved in.

The Burwood became a bit of a home away from home; it was the type of pub that created its atmosphere from the characters who drank there and their chit chat, rather than music and noise. It was a good central meeting point; there was the beach up the road, and a couple of different options if you wanted to kick on or have a meal. We might have a quiet Sunday afternoon drink there and a few players used to have a 'Monday Club', which was pretty much instigated by Evan Cochrane in the late 90s.

We even did a team review in there one time; we had a pig on a spit out the back and went through the previous game. All the punters were there and one of them went home and got his guitar and amplifier and we all threw in $5 each and he entertained us for the afternoon. They are the things that can happen at the Burwood and that's what we appreciated about the place. But as we became older and 'more responsible' and had kids, the 'Monday Club' died off a bit and our get-togethers were just as often over a coffee somewhere.

I always felt comfortable around Newcastle, where people generally gave us space and support; I couldn't think of a better club, place or supporters to have been aligned with during my footy career.

24

MY MATE JOEY

HOW MANY adjectives can I use to describe Andrew Johns? So many come to mind – inspirational, complex, larger-than-life, brilliant, freakish, determined, incessantly competitive, genuine, generous, temperamental, unpredictable. And the one that he revealed in 2007 – bipolar. I also refer to him as rugby league's closest thing to a rock star; he certainly lived the life of a rock star in Newcastle.

While he was all of those things – but not all of them anymore – mostly he's just rock-solid as a great mate. It's fascinating when I think of my relationship with Joey, or Nugget as I more regularly call him. It started with me being a starry-eyed teenage fan; the next stage saw him become (with his brother Matthew) my mentor. We were first grade team-mates from 1998 and then really good mates who played for New South Wales and Australia together. Even now he's retired and we live further apart, seeing he's in Sydney (and I'm in England for a while), we still keep in close contact.

Joey and I had an interesting introduction. I first met him when he agreed to a request from the Newcastle Knights to attend a dinner in Taree to raise money to fund my trip to

England with the Australian Schoolboys side in 1995. I was 17 and playing in the Knights' SG Ball side and he was the first grade halfback who'd just played his first State of Origin series. I can still remember telephoning him to arrange details for the trip, and calling him 'Mr Johns'. He told me, 'Enough of this Mr Johns bit, call me Joey.' I had a beat-up old car and was nervous as hell driving to Marathon Stadium to pick him up, thinking, 'What am I going to do for conversation for two hours in the car?' He had a couple of long-neck beers for the trip and we talked the whole way; he made me feel really comfortable. He was only 21 but he rattled off story after story; something he is legendary for still.

I took him to my parents' place when we got to Taree and Dad asked him if he wanted a beer, which he naturally accepted. We insisted he stayed at our place for the night but Knights football manager Dave Morley came up from Newcastle too and Joey stayed at a hotel with him. Joey actually had a few too many beers by the end of the night and didn't get on stage to speak, but people kept coming up to him all night for a chat and he was very receptive, so he proved good value anyway.

From there we struck up what developed into a close relationship. When I broke my leg a few weeks later playing President's Cup, he was one of the first in the dressing room to console me and encourage me to keep my head up and after that he would always come over and have a yarn if he saw me at the after-match function or out having a quiet drink.

It's interesting to think about why we hit it off so well. To start with, we respected each other's work ethic and passion for footy. I loved his humour and I think I understood him at an early age; Joey is a complex character. I really believe that trip to Taree was invaluable for me; he was never one to make much eye contact and couldn't sit still for more than 10 minutes in those days, but he had to stay in the car for two hours and make conversation. That was a good stepping stone in our relationship as friends.

Around the start of the next season, Joey asked all the players around to his place for a few beers one night; he was living with Billy Peden and Andrew Tanga-ta-toa then and was the Australian halfback, after going to the World Cup. A few boys from the under 21s thought we should go, but we weren't sure of our place with all the first graders and we sat out the front of his place for ages, trying to work up the courage to knock on his door. Here we were, sitting in the dark, thinking, 'Will we or won't we; or should we ring first to make sure it is okay?' Finally, I knocked on the door and he said he was glad we had turned up and we had a great night – which ended up at the Jolly Roger pub in Newcastle. I'd just turned 18 a month or so earlier and it was the first time I observed how being with Joey opens doors; they were so accepting of us and there were seafood platters being brought around and free beers.

Bit by bit I became more comfortable around him and he could see how serious I was about working hard to make it as a footballer. Later in the season I asked him about some plays and could we do some training, and he and Matty would invite a few of the younger players to work a bit on footwork and passing down at a local park.

As a footballer, he was the best I've seen – a freakish talent, as I have touched on elsewhere in this book. He was the team's safety blanket. His greatest asset was that he was ultra-competitive; he hated to lose at anything, and that's part of the make-up of any champion. Second, he understands the history of the game and is respectful of people who had gone before him. And three, he had an extraordinary will to succeed, plus the passion for rugby league that made him a perfect model for others to emulate.

An incredible confidence and ruthless competitive streak came out of him when he laced his boots and I can't quantify how he helped my football career. He left me and dozens of other Knights players something to aspire to – his mental toughness and ability to shake off whatever else was in his life every time he crossed the white line; his loyalty; and his work ethic (he was a real 'closet' trainer, doing a lot of fitness by himself, as much to run energy out as to improve his condition). Even though he was demanding, because he set high standards for everyone around him, he made footy fun.

The energy and banter he brought to dressing sheds was amazing. There was always a sense of enjoyment in the sheds; he'd bring music with him and play it loud before a game. But he was always stringent in his preparation: he'd have to get the same parts of his body rubbed, he'd get the *Big League* program and sit on the toilet and read it, he'd wear the same Speedos, sit in the same spot. After a match, his mood would flatten out; he was never comfortable doing the captain's media conferences but as soon as that was over and the dressing room emptied out a bit, he'd go on a high again, ready to party.

He always wanted to reach for the highest level, be it at training, on the field, or when he was out enjoying himself; which, as it turned out, often meant escaping the demons that surrounded him as he battled being such a public figure.

But I also saw the down times, the dark moods. His mates knew it was part of his make-up, but we didn't know why. I just thought it must have been because he was going through a tough time personally with his break-up from his first wife Renae and their son Samuel going to live with her. But also he was frustrated that he couldn't escape the fame. Joey seemed a magnet for so many people who just wanted to be around him, rub shoulders with him. He had to deal with a lot of pressure from fans, many of whom were over the top.

People would be screaming in his face or calling out his name, sometimes with a smart comment; others just wanted to talk to him, but would invade his space when he was out at night. I'd watch him put up with it for the first half-hour but then he'd tire of it and I could see it unfold inside of him; he'd get a bit short and rude to people sometimes. I could see what he had to put up with and it wasn't easy; it was just so constant. At times we'd be out and people would just lock in on him; their night was going to revolve around being with him, or staring at him. Sometimes I would feel embarrassed for them.

The real Andrew Johns, the person, is a shy country boy from Cessnock, who is a loyal mate – thoughtful, highly intelligent and genuine; for example, he never misses making a fuss of your birthday and is always excited about your successes. Yet he would go from being the humble bloke I was sitting down having a coffee with one day, to another person altogether that night – a hyperactive showman who wanted to be the life of every party.

I sometimes saw the depressive bloke who couldn't open the blinds in the morning or get out of the house. When I did, I just wanted to help him through it, because I knew he'd do the same for me.

I was never one to judge him, although I didn't always agree with the reckless way he lived his life at times. Hughesy and I just had to be there for him, to look out for him when he was on a manic high; as were a lot of his close mates and his brother Matt. It was tough sometimes, that's for sure; you'd try to pull him back and talk sense to him but he'd tell you he could do what he liked and to 'piss off'. When he was drunk, he said some awful things, but I knew that wasn't Joey. I also knew he was going through tough times personally, so I let it slide. The next day, if I brought it up, he'd say he couldn't remember it.

There were times when we'd get a call in the middle of the night, asking for help in finding or helping rescue Joey. I recall one day when Mark Hughes was out and I was home by myself and one of the staff at the Burwood Inn rang and asked could one of us get straight down to the Burwood; that Joey was in a real bad state and needed our help. They also rang his good mate Matt Hoy. We rocked up and there was Joey sitting at the bar drowning himself in hysterics of emotion. I'd never seen him like that. It might have been the last straw with his marriage; he was emotionally wrecked, crying uncontrollably. He refused to move and we tried for an hour to get him to go home but he wouldn't budge. I stayed a while, then 'Hoyo' stayed on; it was like a shift rotation to make sure he was all right.

His lifestyle was crazy and, as we found out later, much of that is explained by his bipolar disorder. If I'd tried to straighten out his lifestyle, he wouldn't have listened anyway; only his brother Matthew would have any chance of slowing down the train and avoiding the inevitable crash, and often even Matty couldn't get through to him. Joey was a magnet when he was out; all sorts gravitated to him and wanted to party with him. Most often I would slink back to the corner of the room when there was a crowd.

It was his rock-star mentality in force. He was in his prime, and at his loosest, after winning the 1997 grand final. The published images of him express this – from the look in his eyes at the stadium in a shot that shows him portraying the devil sign; to one of him crowd-surfing during the civic reception; to what I still reckon is the best shot I've seen of him on and off the field, on a skateboard, with shirt off, top hat and make-up on, beer in hand, still wearing his game-day slacks and celebrating a couple of days after the match. He read autobiographies of hard-living creative people and his mentality was also to push things as far as he could, on and off the field. He was larger than life to be around and his behaviour certainly had an influence on the culture of the Newcastle Knights during that period: play hard, train hard and party hard; although no one could even attempt to keep up with him. As part of his illness, he'd just keep going beyond anyone else's capabilities; then privately he'd crash. He loved getting back to the Burwood Inn with his mates; it was our refuge and I loved kicking back there with hardly anyone else around.

Being out in the surf on his board has become a real haven for him too. I love to get out and surf too and often there'd be six or eight of the players out there together – Billy Peden, Robbie O'Davis, me, and later Kurt Gidley, while Matt Hoy was almost always out there too putting us all to shame, being a professional surfer. Joey would sometimes surf for an hour before going to the gym at seven in the morning; often he'd call and want me to go surfing; I'd be absolutely stuffed and he'd say, 'Come on, let's go, it'll make you feel better.' And I'd feel great afterwards; you'd bond out there, talking about different things. That was when he was at his happiest, plodding around in that water; he'd paddle for wave after wave – his surfing fitness was a replica of his rugby league energy. We'd be happy to catch one and go back and have a chat, but he'd be paddling after every wave while we sat there watching in awe.

Back on land, it was hard for him to be himself. The media wanted their bit of him; kids idolised him; mums and dads just wanted to talk to him. He was uneasy about it; he didn't like the fuss and attention. But get him out that night and get a few beers into him and he was the opposite; the rock star emerged and he welcomed all the attention of being the party animal who had no limits.

There were random, but regular, times he'd blow out a few cobwebs and find someone to have a few more beers with; he'd be playing Uno or other card games with the bar flies in a pub, or betting on the horses in the pub TAB; he couldn't sit still. To show how he could so easily mix with any demographic, when we went away for Newcastle Knights games he'd grab our doctor, Peter McGeogh, and go to an art exhibition or a museum. He loves art, and when any art show came to Newcastle, he'd go.

Then you'd see him on the training paddock, gym or playing field and he was neither of those characters. That was his work; he was a perfectionist with a ruthless serious streak who was almost obsessive with his demands; he'd push himself and others around him to an almost unachievable level.

We both started to grow up a lot from about 2003. That's when Cathrine came into Joey's life and the next year Kris and I started to get serious about our relationship. Seeing his son Samuel grow up was great for him too; he put a lot of focus on being a good father, and he is. He is very protective of keeping Samuel out of the public glare.

I still remember the day I learnt about his bipolar disorder. Joey and I had kicked on after a party at Clint Newton's. The next day I went around to his place and he was on a real low and I couldn't coax him out of bed. That night Cathrine came around to speak to Kris and me and confided in us that he suffered from bipolar disorder. I had an inkling, obviously, that something was wrong with him; he used to call himself different names when he was pissed, like 'Head Case'. Cath just said, 'Listen, there is a website called Black Dog; can you please have a look at it; this is what you are dealing with.' I looked right into it and it explained a lot of things. Joey and I never talked about it in any depth, though; I wasn't going to bring it up as a subject of conversation but he knew I was there for him and understood what he was going through. He found it hard to talk about it and was embarrassed by it, so it was good the way he used his book to reveal his life to everyone all in the one hit.

I know Joey has confessed to drug taking when he was out on the town on a manic high, and that has raised some questions about who knew about it, and who should have done what to stop it. I'll be honest, it's not a subject I want to drag up again. As he has said himself, it was no revelation around the nightclubs of Newcastle; nor is the fact that social drugs are freely available at plenty of night spots around the country. Joey was probably an easy target for those who peddle them. But I think he – and most others who see him now living such a contented, positive life – have moved on from that. Did I know or suspect Joey took drugs sometimes? Yes. Could I have stopped that if I wanted to? Unfortunately not.

It's good to see he's a happy person now, and a lot of that is due to a loving and supporting family, and his wife Cathrine, who was prepared to confront his condition head-on. Someone asked me recently if I missed Andrew Johns the party animal. I don't. We have some great memories of some incredible crazy and funny times that we can laugh about; but I'm happy that they are just memories now. I don't miss the bloke who would go out for two or three days without stopping, only to crash hard afterwards. The ramifications were too great. I'd marvel when he'd come back from his 'stress leave' and blow the opposing team off the park that weekend. I'd think what I'd be like if I'd put my body through what he had.

He's still a great character to be around and he knows how to enjoy himself – but within limits. Having Cath has been a godsend, and so is having Samuel and now their new son, Louis; he wants to be the very best father he can be.

The rugby league community has embraced him and he is making such a remarkable life for himself now with his coaching and his commentary. He's definitely more at ease with his bipolar disorder and you can tell he's got nothing to hide anymore; he looks people in the eye now when he speaks to them; he's not jittery; rarely are there benders. He is still up for a few beers and a laugh . . . and his legendary stories that seem to grow every year; to his mates this is as much a part of his character as his famous banana-kicks.

I feel very fortunate to be one of his best mates. Joey has enriched my life, beyond just making a lot of us at Newcastle better footballers. I look forward to a close friendship for a lot more years yet.

25

AUSSIES ABROAD

AFTER ARRIVING at Leeds in late 2008 it didn't take me long to realise why so many NRL players move to England and stay longer than they first planned. And it's not all about the money. There is so much appeal about the less intense rugby league environment and a more attacking style of play – and everyone here agrees the professionalism and standard of the competition have improved over the past three years or so.

Mind you, I admit I had a tough first few months at the Leeds Rhinos and I started to question whether I had made the right career move. That was caused by the frustration of injuries that saw me play only one of the first 10 matches after I arrived. I also had to get used to coming off the bench and playing only about half a match, which was new for me.

I missed the team's 'friendly' (trial match) and the first Super League game before making my debut at home in the home local derby clash with Wakefield Wildcats (we won 18–4). Then my knee played up and I went in for arthroscopic surgery and didn't play for seven weeks, meaning I also missed the World Club Challenge game against Manly. My comeback game was against St Helens in the Challenge Cup fourth round (again off the bench), which we lost 22–18 at home – which meant one dream I had when I decided to play in England, to play at Wembley in a Cup final, was put on hold for 12 months. We then lost three of our next four games – and were booed off the field by our fans after each of those losses.

Leeds have a good hooker called Matt Diskin, who is a popular local lad and was used to playing 80 minutes, or close to, every game, just as I was at Newcastle. It must have been tough for him to see the club bring in someone from Australia, just as it was for me to learn to come off the bench in matches and play no more than 40 minutes. But Matt and I get on well and are working together on adapting to sharing the hooking role – which is common with quite a few English sides, including St Helens, who have two internationals in Keiron Cunningham and James Roby splitting duties at number nine.

It was tough coming from a background of being a one-club man in Australia, where I was familiar with the environment and team-mates and had been the number one hooker for ten seasons. I was really excited about meeting new players but I thought it best to bide my time and find out how it all worked and do what was best for the team. It's a skill starting the game from the bench and coming on late in the first half, playing just a few minutes before the half-time break then getting momentum again; but I worked hard to get my head around it. I was still using some Knights calls for a while; it is habitual. But I'm a real Rhinos man now; I've been moulded into a 'short-spell hooker' and had to change my preparation and approach to games. I'm 31, so it will be good for me in the long run.

It can be tough to break into the player group when you join a new club; and it was for me, even though the Leeds players were tremendous in making me feel welcomed. I was in rehab for a fair bit at first; I came into a premiership-winning team, which is a real tight-knit group (which is a credit to them) and I knew 'Disco' was a good player and very popular with the fans.

I know plenty of Rhinos fans wondered why the club bought another hooker, and when I played little football in the first couple of months, they would have been questioning it even more. That's one thing NRL players have to face – we're expected to be match-winners when we're imported to take the place of local players; in fact, I think many Australians themselves expect to be match-winners too. Yet it can be difficult moving to the English Super League and adapting quickly; you are hard on yourself if you don't make an instant impression because you're aware of the expectations surrounding you. You naturally have confidence in what you have achieved in the NRL, but it is a different game and a different culture and you have new team-mates and team patterns you have to get used to.

There is no doubt the NRL is more intense, week in week out, than the English league, but the claims you get from back home that Super League is not as tough a league as the NRL are irrelevant in some ways – it's just different. It's a more open style of football; rule interpretations are slightly different; it is not as structured; there's a different emphasis in training. The main aspect is that the Australian and New Zealand players love the fact that rugby league is not in your face 24/7 like it is back home. In many ways there is a greater enjoyment playing the English game, which is much more focused on attack.

I know a lot of Aussie fans feel as though most players go to England only for the money, but that certainly wasn't the case with me. I would have received more money if I had taken up my option to play another season with the Knights. Every case is different; I know some blokes come for the money or to secure a contract after being squeezed out by the NRL salary cap; but many come for the change in lifestyle. It's a great break from the pressure and scrutiny that surrounds the NRL; when you get in the car after finishing training, the last thing you hear about is football; that's a big attraction.

A lot of players stay longer than they originally intended because they enjoy it so much. We have guys who came here well before they were 30 who could turn out to be long-time English players – like Phil Bailey, Brent Webb, Scott Donald, Chris Flannery, Jason Cayless, Matt Gidley, Pat Richards, Ben Jeffries, Jason Croker, Casey McGuire, and Chad Randall. There are also a lot of Kiwis who fall into the same category, who have all played at least three seasons in the UK. In the past two seasons, Mark Riddell, Amos Roberts, Clint Newton, Motu Tony, Shaun Berrigan, Dane Carlaw, Casey McGuire, Jason Ryles, Adam Mogg, Paul Whatuira, David Faiumu, Brent Sherwin, Michael Monaghan and Rangi Chase were playing very good NRL football when they elected to head to England or France and play in Super League.

If you're not playing well, the fans will let you know, as I found after arriving at Leeds surrounded by a lot of expectations. Matt King was a current Australian Test and Origin player when he joined Warrington in 2008 on a four-year deal and I think the fans, and probably his team-mates, thought he'd walk on water and he'd break the line every time he touched the ball. But he came into a side that was struggling badly and was being alternated between centre and wing and the style of play didn't suit him. He copped an awful time from the spectators, but after Tony Smith took over the coaching in 2009 and put more discipline and structure into their play, he hit some form. Off the field, 'Kingy' has really enjoyed it; he is a huge music fan and the owner of Warrington is rock promoter Simon Moran, so Matt is enjoying some opportunities there and enjoying life away from the game.

The big difference between the two leagues, Super League and the National Rugby League, is in the play the ball – the pivotal part of the game. And that large difference is the major reason why the Poms struggled so much in the 2008 World Cup and haven't been able to beat the Aussies in a series for so long.

In England, players are traditionally coached to have two defenders in a tackle, not three as is the norm in Australia, and they don't 'wrestle' nearly as much when the tackled player is on the ground. So they get quicker play the balls and more space to work in, particularly with a larger emphasis on 'using' the football.

While that's a great style to play, it means they always seem to be a step behind the Australians when they come up against each other, especially if Aussie referees control the games. I think Great Britain coach Tony Smith and his players had a fair point complaining about interpretations during the World Cup. After playing in the English Super League, I can see what a big difference it made to them. My Leeds team-mate and British captain Jamie Peacock reckons the Poms just couldn't see a way through the defence because it was always set and they couldn't get a quick play the ball and put the Aussies on the back foot. The English have a perception that interpretations in international games are too skewed towards the Australian way, because the Aussies and most of the Kiwis play in the NRL.

While the English competition hasn't had as big an emphasis on wrestling in the tackle as there is in the NRL, it's changing. Most clubs have just started a wrestling program, whereas in Australia teams like Melbourne have had a wrestling program for probably six years. All NRL clubs have specialist wrestling coaches – we had two at the Knights – while in England it is left to the coaching staff to do that training. We have a 'ruck room' at Headingley which has a padded floor and walls and we do our wrestling technique there. Until recently, players have been coached to get the man to the ground as quickly as possible with two men in the tackle but now more intricate manoeuvres are being employed.

The ruck started to really change in 2009, with Australian coaches in Super League having a big influence. Nathan Brown joined Huddersfield in 2009 and was accused by other coaches early in his stint of teaching his team to 'grapple', but what he was doing was just introducing wrestling techniques. Tony Smith, who hadn't coached at club level for a couple of seasons after taking on the Great Britain job, is at Warrington and if you add Kevin Walters (Les Catalans), Terry Matterson (Castleford), Justin Morgan (Hull KR), Mick Potter (St Helens), Sean McRae (Salford), John Dixon (Celtic Crusaders), plus Brian McLennan (Leeds), that's nine of the 14 Super League clubs coached by overseas men (eight Aussies). The English coaches were very critical of the wrestling trend; it was seen as an unwanted 'Australianism'. With that change, though, came another one – ball carriers 'surrendering' (diving at the defenders' feet). But after a while it seemed like the local coaches started to think, 'Well, if it (the Australian game) is good enough for them, it's good enough for us.'

The English players and coaches, however, still retain a more positive, less structured, attacking philosophy which I love – even though it's a bit of a catch-22 situation. If they can include the wrestle in the rucks and three men in a tackle, it will give them a better chance of winning (at club level and eventually at Test level), but it might make the local games less spectacular – it is a dilemma the game in England has to confront. What certainly has to happen is for someone to educate the referees about the development; they are not schooled on the skills like Aussie refs are and weren't talking to the players about surrender and dominant tackles.

The English referees are a level behind their Australian counterparts but it has actually added a bit more fun to playing rather than making me frustrated. The English refs have a bit of a joke on the field and laugh at themselves sometimes and generally get on well with the players. And that's obviously one benefit of a system where they don't get every questionable decision churned up in the media and coaches referring to them in every press conference, as is the case in the NRL. There is a much bigger acceptance that you'll get some good calls and bad calls and it will even out over a game and a season. The fact there are no Sports Ears over here and the television coverage rarely taps into what the refs say encourages more banter and conversation between players and refs; and captains don't come up and question every second penalty just to give their team a few extra seconds break.

In one game, I was running downfield in a kick-chase and about to get in the line to defend and the ref put his arm up to signal 'play on' and accidentally slapped me around the head. We both looked at each other and burst out laughing; it is far more relaxed with an attitude of, 'What will be will be; let's just get on with it.' The senior Leeds players really get annoyed if their team-mates bark at the referee; that sets a really good example at our club.

There are certainly some very good players in the English game, good enough to compete with Australia in Test football. I think there are a couple of fundamental reasons why the Great Britain team hasn't been as successful as the Kiwis have. First, they play too many games and their season is too long. At Leeds, for example, we have nine players who were involved in the World Cup in Australia (seven in the England squad; an eighth but Gareth Ellis has since moved to Wests Tigers; two in the Samoan side) who didn't return until late November 2008. I think they only had four weeks' break before getting back into training just after Christmas.

They were only back a couple of weeks before they left for a training camp in Orlando in the USA (on 8 January) before returning for a testimonial game for Jamie Jones-Buchanan on 26 January. The Super League competition began on 6 February and ends with the grand final on 15 October. The disappointment of losing the first Challenge Cup clash at least meant we didn't have to fit in potentially four more Cup games before the 26 competition rounds were over. Great Britain played a Test against France in June; there is the four-week final series starting on 18 September. With the World Club Challenge game played early March against Manly, that's a minimum of 30 club games and up to 34; it could have been 39 if the Rhinos had made it to the Challenge Cup final. They'll likely then have six to eight players in the Great Britain squad that will play the Four Nations tournament that will run to late November. That will be over 10 months of playing matches, 11 months of training solidly, and they'll get less than a month off again before starting the 2010 campaign. And we complain about too much demand on NRL players!

I think they need more quality and less quantity of matches in their season. I think they also need an English equivalent to Australia's State of Origin series. They have had their War of the Roses – Lancashire v Yorkshire – which began in rugby league's first year of 1895 but, after 20 years of an ad-hoc history, it was abandoned after the 2003 match. The English boys tell me it never really grabbed the public's or the players' imagination and that Yorkshiremen are more passionate than their Lancashire equivalents. But that was the same with Queenslanders and New South Welshmen when Origin started in the 1980s.

If it became a three-match series and was marketed well, it could be a real hit. I think the English game would be better off with that as a focal point in progressing to the Test team, as State of Origin is in Australia, and cutting the number of club games cut back to 22, which I know alters the schedule of two full rounds now they have 14 clubs in Super League (up from 12 in previous seasons). I just think they could start the season at least two or three weeks later and squeeze the inter-county games into the schedule – even if it meant players missing a club round as is the case in Australia. It would give their best players three games higher in standard than club football. I'd even look at picking a Great Britain side at the end of the War of the Roses to play Other Nationalities, a team made up of the best non-British players from Super League. That game was apparently a popular part of the English scene until the 1960s. The money generated from potential large crowds and good sponsorship could go back to the 14 clubs to compensate for the loss of a couple of home gates each. Anyway, it's an idea; I obviously don't know the history of previous War of the Roses clashes (mostly they were just one match per year), but I know if it was able to gather some momentum it could be a massive plus for the players as State of Origin is for the Aussies.

The English players were devastated about the team's poor performance in 2008 World Cup because it didn't reflect their ability or how far the English competition has progressed. From what I hear, St Helens and Leeds providing 16 of the 24-man English squad caused a bit of a clash of club cultures. The players were allowed to pick their own room-mates, which is something that would never have happened in the Australian team. That just leads to natural segregation. Rooming with players you didn't know so well previously is a major way to break down the barriers in a touring team.

There are quite a few established players in the English competition who I believe could be successful in the NRL, and Gareth Ellis's form with Wests Tigers in 2009 has backed that argument. There are also some exciting young prospects who have caught my eye during my first few months with Leeds, and I reckon they could make it in Australia, and would really benefit from a season or two in the NRL. There's a centre at Leeds, Kallum Watkins, who was just 17 when he played first grade early in 2009; he looks an exceptional talent. There is another great prospect who has caught my eye: a halfback from Salford called Richie Myler, who played for England at age 18 in 2008; watch out for him in the future. Leeds winger Ryan Hall, who made his debut for England in 2009, is another stand-out. Sam Burgess, a second-rower from Bradford, and Sam Tomkins, a half/backline utility at Wigan, have also impressed me. Mark down those five players as likely household names in the English game for years to come.

I can't speak highly enough of Great Britain captain Jamie Peacock as a leader; he's one of the best I have seen in either country. As a front-rower he just keeps bashing that ball up; he is very knowledgeable on the game and off the field he's really interested in the welfare of the juniors; he coaches the under-16s Rhinos with Robbie Burrow and Jamie Jones-Buchanan. He's tremendous with the younger players in the first grade squad and is concerned about life outside of football for those guys and takes a real interest in them all. He has left a massive imprint wherever he's played and is one of the few players to receive a testimonial year for services to the game, despite not having the 10 years at one club (he played seven seasons with Bradford before joining Leeds in 2006). While 'JP' captains the Test team, Kevin Sinfield has been the long-term Leeds captain and he is also a great leader, a local Leeds boy who is an outstanding, consistent, skilful all-round player who has made a major contribution to Leeds's success in the past decade. The Rhinos are fortunate to have them both in the side, along with Keith Senior – senior players who are classic examples of professionalism for the younger lads. Senior, who just chalked up his 500th club game, is an amazing competitor and that is an incredible achievement.

The weather obviously has an impact on rugby league training in the UK. Most clubs head off to Spain and Portugal or the USA for 'warm weather' pre-season training camps to get some decent preparation. When late spring and summer come around, suddenly I noticed the players at Leeds outside doing extra training by themselves before and after each session, but that lasts only about four months, compared to Australia where you can do it year-around. Leeds have a set-up comparable with any NRL club; we have two full-time physiotherapists, good access to massage and strappers, a good gymnasium and rehab facilities. In 2009 the Rhinos even introduced 'sat navs', which was a step forward, and have detailed feedback of performance and fitness.

There are fewer easy games in the English Super League now and the absolute dominance of the 'big four' – St Helens, Leeds, Wigan and Bradford – has ended, with Bradford and Wigan struggling in 2009 and Huddersfield and Hull Kingston Rovers in the top four as I write this. Every team has proved to be competitive; the Celtic Crusaders have struggled a bit in their first season of Super League, but they have some good players and will definitely improve with experience.

There is quite a good connection that exists between the Aussies and Kiwis playing in England. We get around to see each other regularly and once a month we have a big get-together where 20 to 30 players turn up for a meal, a few drinks and maybe a movie. Ali Laui'ititi and Kylie Leuluai, who both play at Leeds, are the prime organisers and the Kiwis are particularly close. The nights are usually held in Yorkshire – often at a place called 'Escape' at Castleford, which is a huge complex that has cinemas, restaurants and bars. It's a bit far to come for some of the Lancashire-based players (it would be a couple of hours drive along the M62 motorway for most of them) but a lot of players make a point of getting there. Players like Mitchell Sargent, Clint Newton, Dave Solomona, Steve Menzies, Glenn Morrison, Brent Webb, Scott Donald, Rangi Chase, Matt Petersen and Motu Tony are regulars.

The partners of the expats also have a regular night out together, which I think is great. There's a good social network, which is important when we are all so far away from home.

A really good part of the English game is that after a match most clubs provide a buffet meal for both teams which players and their families attend. It's great how players from both sides can mingle after competing so hard against each other and it's another opportunity for expats to catch up. After we played St Helens at Knowsley Road one week (I was out injured, un-fortunately), Keiron Cunningham – who played a few Tests against me when he was the Great Britain hooker and is a player I have a lot of respect for – came up to me at the post-match function, put his arm around me and wished me the best and welcomed me to England and said it was great to have me playing in Super League. It was a really nice moment that I appreciated.

Another thing I have taken to is the locker-room atmos-phere (everyone has their own locker); you spend a lot of time there, so there's a bit of skulduggery going on. There are a lot more old characters around the clubs. Billy Watts looks after our equipment and everything around the dressing room, does the mail, acts as our timekeeper on game days and keeps us in check – and he loves it. Our chairman Harry Jepson is 89 and he has a photographic memory of certain Leeds (and Hunslet) games and players going back half a century or more. They have a 'Gold Club' for those who have supported the Rhinos for 50 years or more, and there are plenty of members.

Super League is a good standard of football with good players and good facilities and we have a really strong following at Leeds (our home crowd averages something like 17,000), but it's more sport than business, if I can put it that way. There's more passion than pressure; it's less stressful; there's the opportunity to get away from it all and have a good time together with the boys off the field in a much more relaxed way, without having to look over your shoulder wondering where the next off-field scandal or drama is going to come from.

The weather is obviously a bit hard to get used to. Kris, Ella and I arrived in December in the depths of the English winter, when it would only be light between about 8 am and 4 pm and it was wet and freezing. You gradually come out of that, through spring to summer, when it's light well before 5 am and doesn't get dark until after 9 at night. It was a bit weird getting used to the fact that we'd kick off at 8 pm in broad daylight!

Mind you, one game I played – against Castleford at their old ground which is called 'The Jungle' (the traditional name is Wheldon Road) – was like the English games of old when they played in the winter months. After showers earlier in the day, the sun was blazing as we warmed up. Shortly after kick-off it bucketed down and there were sheets of water over the field and when the ball was kicked downfield, it would hit a puddle and stop dead. We were behind our goal-line getting ready for a line drop-out and our captain Kevin Sinfield came over to me and said, 'Welcome to England, lud.' I was wondering if adidas made gumboots to play in!

POSTSCRIPT:

I knew straight away I'd broken my leg, and the irony was that I was only passed fit to play in the game – against Wigan at JJB Sports Stadium on 24 July 2009 – half an hour before kick-off, when my troublesome back loosened up enough for me to run freely.

That was the end of what was a pretty frustrating first season playing for Leeds. The club couldn't have made me more welcome and I was just feeling as though I'd reached the standard I was happy with after playing in 15 of 16 matches, being the starting hooker and playing 80 minutes in a couple of games while Matt Diskin was out injured, which helped me get consistent, quality game time.

I had a good physio session at our training venue before we left for Wigan, and the physio said to see how I felt after the bus trip. It felt okay after I had another hour of physio after we arrived at the ground, so I went out onto the field to give it a test. The funny thing was I had to warm up on the field by myself, five minutes before the rest of the team, to determine whether I could run flat-out or not. The Leeds fans all started cheering, thinking we were all coming out, only to be disappointed it was just me. After that brief fitness test I was declared a starter, and I was keen to rip in; you want to play the big games, and there were over 23,000 people in for the clash between two traditional clubs. Also I was up against a lot of ex-NRL players, which I was looking forward to.

We were ahead 10–0 when I finished my first stint after 30 minutes; it was probably my best half-hour of the season. When I came back on around the halfway mark of the second half, I chased a loose ball and kicked out at it just as the Wigan front-rower got there and threw his body on the ball. I was keen to give the team a lift as we'd fallen behind 14–10, but it proved not the cleverest thing I've done in footy. I only had eyes for the ball and didn't see the Wigan player come across; I collected his elbow with my ankle and, bang, broke the tibia. The next morning I was given the diagnosis: six weeks in a cast and, with the grand final 11 weeks away if we made it, a very, very slim chance of playing again in 2009. I thought I had to hold onto that hope, but two weeks later I had to have a plate inserted because the fracture had moved slightly.

To say I'm feeling pretty down as I write this, just as this book is near the end of editing stage, is an understatement. I felt as though I'd finally let go of my old club, the Knights, and had put some good consistent form together, and could really make a contribution at the important part of the season as we neared the finals (we were second on the ladder behind St Helens). Kris's family were staying with us when it happened, but left the next day. We'd enjoyed their company, and not only did we have to wave them goodbye, but I had to adapt to being laid-up, so it was an eventful weekend all round. Kris suddenly had to baby-sit two of us – and she reckons I whined more than our daughter.

It's too early to think too deeply about the future: I've got another year to run on my contract at Leeds and I'd love to have a big season to prove myself and reward the Rhinos. But all sorts of things go through your mind when you get a setback like this. By the time you read this, all will have been settled and decided. This is not the note I want to finish on, though – I went out with the Newcastle Knights injured just under a year earlier, and I don't want to end things with Leeds the same way. Although I've had 12 months of bad injuries, each has been an impact injury, so I feel it hasn't been a case of my body being worn out. I've got no doubt I can come back fresher and fitter next year – that's the intention, anyway.

26

MY BEST OF THE BEST

I HAVE been fortunate to have played with some wonderful players at club, interstate and international level. I've already stated that I agree with probably hundreds of other players in declaring Andrew Johns as the best.

When picking 'best ever' lists it has to be about more than individual talent. Judging someone's true ability as a footballer has to also be weighted towards his consistency over a long period of time; his ability to perform at the highest level when the going gets tough; and the respect he gets from team-mates – that quality that I was brought up on when I was trying to make my mark with the Newcastle Knights: 'be the player others want to play with'.

I started the process of coming up with the ten best players I've played with or against, but I found it too difficult to leave some out. So instead I'd like to finish this book with my special tribute to the players who have left the biggest impression on me during my career – eleven players who I regard as the best in their categories. Between them they have won seven Golden Boot Awards (for the world's best player).

Best overall player: Andrew Johns What more can be said about him? Whatever 'gear' the opposing team came out using, he'd quickly determine it, match it, then exceed it to take the whole game to another level; and he'd invariably take his team-mates with him. That's the biggest compliment I can give him. He'd just assess the feel of a game, the tactics of the opposition, and decide how he was going to assert his control. I've never come across any other player who could do that to the extent and with such effect as he could.

Best strike forward: Ben Kennedy He's the best example of the all-round package of the perfect modern-day footballer. He was aggressive, fast, highly skilled and as emotional a player as anyone could hope to play with. He was tough, he could play injured and he was all for the team. Inspirational best sums him up. The fact he has made both the Newcastle and Manly 'best ever' line-ups (he only played two seasons with Manly) shows what an impact he made on the teams he played with.

Best strike back: Anthony Minichiello There was no better sight in rugby league than 'The Mountain Cat' in his prime, running the ball back after putting himself in a miraculous position to take an under-pressure bomb or deep kick, then bouncing off people like a pin-ball as they failed to put him down. He could do some amazing things on the football field, especially in 2005, when he won the Golden Boot. It's one of the real tragedies of rugby league that he has rarely been fit since a back injury cut him down just after he received that recognition, at age 25, but I pray we haven't seen the last of his rare talent.

Best leader as a player: Brad Fittler Freddy was an incredible captain and taught me a lot about leadership. He was an unbelievable trainer, very disciplined; he was at the top for so long – not just because of his awesome talent, but his attitude and passion. He was one of those guys who made others feel so much more assured just having him around – and he showed that when he returned to State of Origin in 2004 when he was 32. Freddy could cruise through some club games and he copped a bit of criticism for that, but often still came up with the big plays when his team needed it. At rep level, I never saw him play a poor game; the bigger the match, the more he wanted to dominate. I'll never forget when the Knights played the Roosters in the 2000 finals and we were up 16–2 at half-time before Freddy sussed out what we were doing and completely changed the Roosters plan of attack, deciding he'd go over and around us with long passes to his outside men on the fly. He led them to a 26–20 victory.

Best international performer – Australia: Darren Lockyer
Locky is the ultimate big occasion player; whether for Brisbane, Queensland or Australia he has the ability to come up with the special play or take control of a match when his team most needs him. So many Tests or Origin games have been won on the back of this little bloke. I know it is a cliché, but the stand-out players seem to have time to do things that others don't have, and that is one of Locky's greatest assets – he can make time for himself and seems to do things with such ease. And he's tough; while people point to him missing tackles, he had to adapt quickly to defending in the front line when he moved from fullback to five-eighth and he puts his slight body on the line, takes some knocks, but just shakes it off and puts himself back into the firing line.

Best international performer – New Zealand: Ruben Wiki To play 55 Tests for New Zealand, a record for all nations, says it all about the man they called 'The Muss' (after Jake the Muss from the movie *Once Were Warriors*). Even though he played for a fanatical rugby union nation, everyone in New Zealand knew and respected what he stood for. He was tough but always clean; and had the intimidation factor that few players have in the modern game. He was the heart and soul of the Kiwi team; like a father figure others knew would lead and protect them. He got better as he got older and was still a great Test competitor at age 33 in 2006. He's played more NRL/ARL games than any Kiwi, with 287 appearances, from age 20 to 35. He's a very humble person too; a man of great respect.

Best international performer – Britain: Jamie Peacock I had a big rap on this bloke before I joined Leeds and what I have seen of him since has only vindicated my opinion. He's a wonderful leader; after every game I played against him I always used to wish he was on our team. He puts his hand up no matter how tough his team is doing it, is always willing to throw himself into the teeth of the defence and he's consistent and passionate; the model tough, relentless team man. He's also a deep thinker on what makes a man what he is.

Most inspirational Test team-mate: Shane Webcke Every young front-rower wanted to be Shane Webcke. I've never seen a player who better typified the saying 'Train the way you play'. In England on Kangaroo tours he'd wear just shorts and a T-shirt or training singlet and slide around in the mud, sleet and cold and put 110 per cent into it. He played a semi-final five days after having knee surgery and despite his knee 'locking' the morning of the match. That shows how tough he is; few people could have that strength of mind. He never gave an inch on the field. One game I'll never forget him dominating was the Australia–Great Britain Test in July 2002 when we won

64–10 – with 'Webby' ripping into an English pack that had some very good players in Terry O'Connor, Keiron Cunningham, Barrie McDermott, Jamie Peacock, Stuart Fielden and Andy Farrell.

Most inspirational club performer – Australia: Nathan Hindmarsh I can't believe the 'motor' that 'Hindy' has in that body of his; his ability to do so much quality work on the football field week after week since becoming a permanent first grader since 1998 is mind-boggling, really. I think he should never have been dropped from the New South Wales Origin side (he's been overlooked since 2008) because he typifies the reliable, high-standard player who does all the 'dirty work' that is essential to winning the big games. His consistency for Parramatta (where he'll end up with the record for appearances) has been phenomenal – you couldn't count how many games he has won, or saved, with his quality workrate. He's tough, resilient, tops the tackle count most weeks, but can still break a tackle and offload when he puts himself into the play. And he's a top, unassuming bloke who is a pleasure to play with.

Most inspirational club performer – New Zealand: Stacey Jones While Ruben Wiki is regarded as the greatest Kiwi forward of all time (although he began his career in the centres), the 'Little General' is undoubtedly their greatest back. His career coincided with Andrew Johns's and he was the Kiwi and the Warriors' equivalent, playing 46 Tests, 261 club games and winning the 2002 Golden Boot. He could stamp his mark on a game with his brilliant speed, or a pass, or a smart chip and chase. Who will ever forget his 35-metre individual try for the Warriors in the 2002 grand final – one of the best in 'GF' history. As an opponent, you knew you could never take your eyes off Stacey for the whole 80 minutes.

Most inspirational club performer – England: Keiron Cunningham He pioneered the running game of the modern-day hooker in England and is the best British hooker I have seen. I regard it with regret that we only played three Tests against each other because of his battle with injuries. He's very big (107 kg), powerful and has speed and awareness. When the tide is turning against St Helens, he's the man who seems to be able to turn that momentum with a run from dummy-half or some aggressive defence; he's almost unstoppable close to the line and has scored over 160 tries for the Saints.

They are my individual 'awards'. When it comes to the brilliant combinations I've played with, what Matthew Gidley and Timana Tahu did on Newcastle's right-hand edge from 2000 to 2003 took my breath away at times. T scored 59 tries in three seasons when he and Gids were at their best and I haven't seen a better centre–winger combination than them in the NRL.

Compiling this book is the first time I've had a reason to so thoroughly take stock of my time in rugby league. As I have mentioned, I've never been one to look back while my career is still active. But I've enjoyed this exercise. It has made me appreciate even more than I already did just how fortunate I am to have had the experiences I've had; to have played with such a great club as the Knights in such a great rugby league region as Newcastle and the Hunter Valley and with and against so many great players – and people – as those I've mentioned throughout the book. I'm not at the end of the road yet; I'm very determined to leave some sort of legacy at the Leeds Rhinos and help them win some silverware.

When that final day does come . . . I'll have very few regrets.

I've seen a lot of players with a whole lot more talent than me and plenty like me who have had to work hard with the abilities they have. Talent is never enough to ensure success; it's what you do with it that will count most. I'm satisfied I've done my absolute best.

ACKNOWLEDGEMENTS

Danny Buderus

Special thanks go to Neil Cadigan, who I put in a tough position when I asked him to write this with me; I could not have done it without him. Thanks, mate, for all the early morning and late night chats, and for going above and beyond to make the process as easy as possible. Thanks to my special girls, Kris and Ella, for your encouragement and patience while I was doing this on the other side of the world. To the mates I have called on to help out with photos – Booze, Nugg and Kurt, Mum and Dad – a big thanks, as well as to Col Whelan at Action Photographics, Darren Pateman at the *Newcastle Herald* and the photographers at Fairfax, Getty Images and News Limited for capturing significant events in my footy career so well. Thanks also to Dave Williams at rlphotos.com in the UK, who provided the cover shot and was very helpful.

To my family, for allowing me to follow my dream and being there every step of the way – I will always be grateful, and I would not have had the opportunity to have a story to convert to a book without you. Thanks also to Random House for being so supportive, and believing in the book. Last, but certainly not least, I am indebted to the team-mates, coaches, support staff and fans that have made my footy career so memorable, and have shared experiences I'll be forever grateful for.

Neil Cadigan

It has been a pleasure to help write the story of a player – and a bloke – I have admired so much, not just for how he plays the game, but for how he carries himself on and off the field. Thanks for the opportunity, 'Bedsy', and for being so committed, even though it meant being up at midnight or six in the morning talking over the phone when you were sometimes doing it a bit tough on the other side of the world; it's typical of your character. Thanks also to Kris, who has been a brilliant proofreader, photo researcher and all-round springboard for the editorial considerations, and a great support all the way.

Again David Middleton's *Rugby League Annuals* has been an essential reference tool – thanks, Middo. Thanks to champion transcriber Janette Doolan for again converting taped conversations into word form so quickly for me. To Random House – Alison Urquhart and Elizabeth Cowell – and freelance editors Tricia Dearborn and Mark Evans, thanks for your great work in the publishing process, and for being so supportive and sympathetic to my heavy workload while knocking out this book.